Treasury of

RELIGIOUS QUOTATIONS

Compiled and edited by
Gerald Tomlinson

PRENTICE HALL
Englewood Cliffs, New Jersey 07632

Prentice-Hall International (UK) Limited, *London*
Prentice-Hall of Australia Pty. Limited, *Sydney*
Prentice-Hall Canada, Inc., *Toronto*
Prentice-Hall Hispanoamericana, S.A., *Mexico*
Prentice-Hall of India Private Limited, *New Delhi*
Prentice-Hall of Japan, Inc., *Tokyo*
Simon & Schuster Asia Pte. Ltd., *Singapore*
Editora Prentice-Hall do Brasil, Ltda., *Rio de Janeiro*

© 1991 by

Gerald Tomlinson

Englewood Cliffs, NJ

10 9 8 7 6 5 4 3 2 1

Library of Congress Cataloging-in-Publication Data

Encyclopedia of religious quotations / compiled and edited by Gerald
Tomlinson.
    p.   cm.

Includes bibliographical references and index.
    ISBN 0–13–276429-6.—ISBN 0-13-276411-3 (PBK)
    1. Religion—Quotations, maxims, etc.   I. Tomlinson, Gerald,
1933-   .
PN6084.R3E53   1991
291—dc20   91–18940
                                                                           CIP

ISBN 0-13-276429-6

ISBN 0-13-276411-3 (PBK)

PRENTICE HALL
Business Information Publ~~~~~ ~~~~
Englewood Cliffs, NJ 076

Simon & Schuster, A Paramount Co

PRINTED IN THE UNITED STATES OF

INTRODUCTION

The art of quotation is well worth mastering. If you can acquire the technique of finding and using "jewels five-words-long" that "sparkle forever" (in the words of Alfred, Lord Tennyson), you can add force, substance, and zest to whatever you say or write. (Make that ten words, though, or twenty—or even half a dozen lines.)

"By necessity, by proclivity, and by delight," says Ralph Waldo Emerson, "we all quote." In his essay "Quotation and Originality" (from which *that* quote is taken) Emerson, a Unitarian minister for a time, underscores his point by quoting the words of Plato, Edmund Burke, Robert Southey, the Duke of Wellington, King Louis XVI, Lady Mary Wortley Montague, Rabelais (whose dying words were, "I am going to see the great Perhaps"), Goethe, an old Scottish ballad, Thomas Moore, the Comte de Crillon, Pindar, and others.

Yes, we all quote—and for the reasons Emerson states. First, we cannot avoid it. A writer or speaker who tries to be wholly original in every sentence is well on the road to madness. So much has been written and said that we quote without realizing it. A great deal of unconscious and uncredited quotation occurs all the time. There is no art in it, nor any plagiarism, only ignorance.

Emerson's second reason, quoting "by proclivity," is another matter. The clergy quote Scripture by proclivity. That is, they intend to quote Scripture. It is their basic text. And they want to quote it as appropriately and effectively as possible. This book should help them achieve that goal. Wherever possible, one or more quotes from the Jewish Scriptures (Old Testament) and the Christian Scriptures (New Testament) appear under each of the 149 subject-matter headings.

To illustrate: If a quotation is needed to introduce or illustrate Salvation, two such can be found on pages 216–217 under Christianity/Judaism (Psalms 25:5 and Jeremiah 8:20) plus two more under Christianity (Matthew 7:14 and John 11:25-26). You may find other possibilities in a good concordance, but the *Treasury* offers two distinct advantages: (a) careful screening and selection of the choices and (b) entries based on ideas rather than simply on key words. Admittedly, not all the famous phrases in the Bible are included here. They would make a book in themselves.

Emerson's third reason for quoting is "delight." And who can argue? A well-chosen quotation *is* a delight. It has the energy to transform a commonplace assertion into a passage that sings. It can make the expression of a familiar idea exciting to the writer and inspiring to the audience.

A number of good general collections of quotations exist: Bartlett's, Stevenson's, Evans's, Seldes's. They contain excerpted religious thoughts along with literary, political, and other kinds of quotations. Some of them, like Bartlett's, are organized by authors. Others, like Stevenson's, are organized by subject matter. None of the general collections, for obvious reasons, classifies either the quotations or the people quoted according to their religion.

This book does. Generally speaking, it matches the writers with their faiths. In that respect it is unique, even among collections limited to religious quotations. Every subject-matter heading in the book is followed by two or more subheadings, alphabetically arranged, that specify the religion either of the persons quoted, or of the content of the quotes, or typically of both. A few representative subject-matter headings are Ambition, Brevity, Character, Destiny. Some of the principal religion subheadings—there are 30 altogether—are Buddhism, Christianity/Judaism, Christianity, Hinduism, Islam, and Judaism. (The religions and philosophies cited in the book are explained briefly on pages 297–305.)

So far, so good. But this organizational scheme raises a number of questions not faced by compilers of other books of quotations. The answers to these questions are important to an understanding of the *Treasury*. Perhaps the most practical way to deal with them is simply to list them and respond to them one by one.

1. How do you draw the line between religious quotations and general quotations?

It isn't easy. Many ministers use literary quotations to make religious points. But since these quotations are not in themselves religious, they are not included in the *Treasury*. This means leaving out some of the world's most familiar and memorable lines about love, politics, war, and so on. So be it. The boundary must be drawn. Only quotes from religious sources and sermons or quotes about religious faith and concerns are included. That still lets in, one way or another, most of the world's great writers.

2. How significant to religious quotations is the skill of the translator?

In a word, paramount. Remember that all the sacred texts of all the major religions of the world first saw the light of day in a language other than English. First-rate translation is indispensable—and it can be unforgettable. Consider the lasting impact of the King James version of the Bible, a brilliant translation if ever there was one. Note, by contrast, the lament of a modern Muslim scholar: "It is generally agreed that the Qur'an . . . is impossible to translate because of the multiplicity and subtlety of shades of meaning in the original Arabic text." The "musical and emotional impact" of the Koran is lost, he believes, even with the most skillful and poetic translation into English.

3. Do the subject-matter headings reflect the everyday English language of today?

Yes, and this is quite important. The word *charity*, for example, has meanings in historical Judeo-Christianity that come closer to "love" than to "kindly liberality." Since today's customary meaning of *charity* is "kindly liberality," that is the operative definition. This hardly solves all the semantic problems, however. Meanings shift, similes become clichés, metaphors die—and misunderstandings abound. As Paul Tillich notes, "A hopeless situation arises when a speaker uses a word in its original symbolic sense but the listener understands the word in a contemporary scientific sense."

Translation into English rears its head here, too. Versions of the same text can vary astonishingly. One translator from Arabic, for instance, may transmit a word into English as *knowledge* while another presents it as *wisdom*. The interpretation of the chosen translator is the one that prevails. The ideal compiler-editor would no doubt boast multilingual talents rivaling those of Pope John Paul II, but . . .

4. Are there any other quirks involving subject-matter headings?

Yes. There are a couple of additional points to keep in mind: Sometimes a quotation appears under a heading that may be its polar opposite. This reduces the number of subject-matter headings (which are somewhat arbitrary divisions at best) and tends to simplify the search for the right quotation. Nevertheless, there are a few headings in the book that are antonyms. Pride and Humility are two of them. One stanza of Rudyard Kipling's "Recessional" appears under Pride, another under Humility. The second point: The subject-matter headings are nearly all high-level abstractions, and most of them have complex meanings. Some are defined literally, by quotation. Others are defined operationally, by example. Others are not defined at all, strictly speaking. Whatever entries seem to fit comfortably under a heading have been put there. A heading such as Humor is regarded as all-encompassing, with no distinction being made among definitions, commentary, and selected examples. Many quotations could fit easily under more than one subject-matter heading.

5. What problems arise with the various religion subheadings?

Labeling poses challenges. Teilhard de Chardin is usually listed under Christianity, but on page 207 he is shown under Pantheism, because in that particular quotation his topic is Pantheism. Carl Jung, a psychologist, appears under Nonsectarian but also under Christianity. The explanation of these apparent inconsistencies lies in the nature of each quotation. The judgment is subjective. The religion labels are endlessly arguable—and not just in the case of dual labeling. Even so, they are informative and should prove useful.

Whether a given label is accurate is sometimes open to discussion. How does one categorize the Greek philosopher Heraclitus, for example? What exactly *was* he? Or the ancient Greeks generally? Even so notable and relatively recent a writer as William Shakespeare presents problems. As Henry Sebastian Bowden writes in

The Religion of Shakespeare, "He [Shakespeare] constantly speaks of God; does he mean a personal and intelligent, omniscient, omnipotent, and all-perfect Creator, or a mere *anima mundi*, coincident with the phenomena of the universe and bound by its laws?" If Bowden remains in doubt after writing a book on the subject, how is a harried compiler-editor to cope? I have come down on the side of Christianity, not only with Shakespeare but with a few other authors whose backgrounds are Christian but whose true religious commitments, or noncommitments perhaps, remain elusive.

6. Do the quotations accurately reflect the beliefs of the religion under which they appear?

Not always. Indeed, some quotations under the same subheading are flatly contradictory. Compare George A. Buttrick's remark about the historicity of the Bible with Hans Küng's (page 18). Or contrast Mencius's view of human nature with that of Confucius (page 103). There is nothing bothersome about this diversity of opinion. The *Treasury* is a collection of viewpoints, not a philosophical system.

Sometimes the writers' viewpoints are at odds with one another or with the Church itself. Many Christians have questioned certain aspects of the thought of Pierre Teilhard de Chardin or Hans Küng or Karl Barth. Similarly, many Jews have wondered about some of the ideas put forward by Martin Buber or Franz Rozenzweig. The writings of these influential thinkers represent personal explorations—significant ones, to be sure—but they should not be mistaken for Scripture.

It is especially important to consider the historical context and the intended audience for a quotation. Thomas a Kempis's advice in *The Imitation of Christ*, for example, was aimed at his fellow 15th-century monks. You will do well to take this fact into account in assessing its relevance to the average person of the 20th century. And in literature you should keep in mind that the thought being expressed may come from someone other than the writer. Which is to say, don't necessarily credit Robert Browning with the airy optimism of Pippa's song in "Pippa Passes."

By their very nature, books of quotations lack any explanatory verbal context. Interpretation is often required. That is a task for you, the user, who will naturally want to know whom you are quoting—which means putting each quotation into an understandable context in your own mind before putting it into a speech or sermon. Fine, you say. Now, how? Broad general knowledge is the best resource, of course. But the 170 Thumbnail Biographies on pages 277–293 should help.

7. Have any kinds of religious quotations been excluded from the Treasury?

Yes: principally two kinds. Just as the user has to consider historical context, so has the compiler-editor. Not all religious quotations wear well. In his introductory remarks in *The Nature and Destiny of Man*, Reinhold Niebuhr promises, "We will say nothing about the insights which have been refuted and cast into the dustpan of history." All right. But a book of quotations inevitably contains some such abandoned "insights." They are a part of the world's religious heritage. Still, a great many now-discarded views of earlier religious leaders have been left out of the book; for example, the sometimes inflammatory statements (by today's standards) of Pope Leo XIII [1810–1903]. No useful purpose would be served by including them. By the same token, antireligious sentiments, which have proliferated throughout history, have not been entirely banned from the *Treasury* but are severely limited in number. You will not find many quotations from Karl Marx, Friedrich Nietzsche, Sigmund Freud, or H.L. Mencken (to name a few), even though these worthies commented extensively on religion.

8. Are the quotations in any sense controversial?
Absolutely. They could hardly be otherwise. Religion is both a quiet haven and a powder keg. There can be undoubted comfort in one's own sacred texts. But ecumenism is not everyone's favorite -ism. Religious controversies have raged since the time of Osiris and probably before. They rage today. Few readers, however liberal-minded, will find every quotation in this book to their liking. Feminists will be doubly troubled, because religion has been sturdily sexist for a very long time. The sacred texts are as they are. God the Father is immutable. Abraham, Moses, Jesus, Muhammad, Confucius, Buddha—all were men. The theologians, religious writers, and others who are cited in this book are predominately male. Reassessment will not change facts. A book of quotations is a record; it cannot be politically correct text.

Now, to take refuge in a quotation myself, let me record how Frederick Franck, a translator, explains his position on the sexist-language issue in *The Buddhist Eye*: "I can only hope that the female reader will be forgiving," he writes. ". . . trying to replace *man* in the original by *person* wrought intolerable confusion; to complicate sentences by *his or her* would have compounded the trouble. To cure what is essentially a deficiency disease of the English language will require more than this one editor's despair."

Quite so, Mr. Franck—my sentiments exactly.

Gerald Tomlinson

ACKNOWLEDGMENTS

Any compiler of a book of religious quotations owes an obvious and enormous debt to the various sacred texts, the theologians and saints, priests, preachers, and rabbis, evangelists, psychologists, and, yes, even agnostics and other unbelievers throughout history, not to mention some of the leading literary figures of every age. In addition, since the compiler builds in an already developed area, he or she is greatly obliged to those like-minded toilers who have gone before—not just to the Bartletts and Stevensons and Evanses and Seldeses, but, more specifically, to such previous compliers of religious quotations as Ralph L. Woods, Margaret Pepper, Geoffrey Parrinder, Frank S. Mead, and Jill Haak Adels.

I also owe debts of gratitude closer to home. My personal thanks go mainly and deeply to my wife Alexis and to the members of the Unitarian Universalist Fellowship of Sussex County, New Jersey, including but not limited to Rhoda Bell, Robert and Verena Brennan, Paul and Clare Callender, Brian and Jerilyn Doherty, Norton and Joan Karp, and Paul and Florence Lighty. Their example and encouragement over the years have been invaluable.

TABLE OF CONTENTS

A

ACHIEVEMENT

Christianity/Judaism

What hath God wrought!

Holy Bible, Numbers 23:23

[Note: Samuel F.B. Morse used this quotation on May 24, 1844, as the first message on his newly invented telegraph.]

Christianity

A city that is set on a hill cannot be hid.
Neither do men light a candle and put it under a bushel.

Holy Bible, Matthew 5:14-15

Human affairs have never gone so well that the best pleases the majority. Hence some express it like this: "Refuse the king's highway and take the byroads." This piece of advice agrees with the teaching of the Gospel, which recommends us to avoid the broad road where most people walk, and take the narrow way, trodden by few but leading to immortality.

Erasmus, *Adages*

And now the matchless deed's achieved,
Determined, dared, and done.

Christopher Smart, *A Song to David*

Every act leaves the world with a deeper or a fainter impress of God.

Alfred North Whitehead, *Religion in the Making*

It is a truly Christian duty to grow, even in the eyes of men, and to make one's talents bear fruit.

Pierre Teilhard de Chardin, *The Divine Milieu*

Hinduism

The brilliant steeds, bay coursers of the sun-god,
Refulgent, dappled, meet for joyful praises,
Wafting our worship, heaven's ridge have mounted,
And in one day round earth and sky they travel.

Rig-Veda

Judaism

A king devised a plan for a palace. He summoned skillful builders, who erected it for him. When it was erected, it was known as the king's palace. What had he given to it? He had contributed the idea.

Talmud, Zohar ii, 161a

ACTION

Christianity/Judaism

I heard the voice of the Lord saying, Whom shall I send, and who will go for us? Then said I, Here am I; send me.

Holy Bible, Isaiah 6:8

Christianity

What man of you, having a hundred sheep, if he lose one of them, doth not leave the ninety and nine in the wilderness, and go after that which is lost, until he find it?

Holy Bible, Luke 15:4

[God's] essence is all act: He did that He
    All act might always be.
    His nature burns like fire;
His goodness infinitely doth desire
    To be by all possessed;
    His love makes others blest
It is the glory of His high estate
And that which I forever more admire,
He is an act that doth communicate.

Thomas Traherne, "The Anticipation"

We were made for action, and for right action—for thought, and for true thought.

> John Henry Newman, *Essays and Sketches*

Onward, Christian soldiers,
   Marching as to war,
With the cross of Jesus
   Going on before.

> Sabine Baring-Gould, "Onward, Christian Soldiers"

When we act, as it seems, with the greatest spontaneity and vigor, we are to some extent led by the things we imagine we are controlling.

> Pierre Teilhard de Chardin, *The Divine Milieu*

Action springs not from thought, but from a readiness for responsibility.

> Dietrich Bonhoeffer, *Letters from Prison*

Do you want my hands, Lord, to spend the day helping the sick and the poor who need them? Lord, today I give you my hands.

> Mother Teresa of Calcutta, *Life in the Spirit*

Confucianism

Chi Wen Tzu always thought three times before taking action. Twice would have been quite enough.

> Confucius, *Analects*

People today distinguish between knowledge and action and pursue them separately, believing that one must know before he can act. Consequently, to the last day of life, they will never act and also will never know.

> Wang Yang-ming, *Instructions for Practical Living*

Existentialism

Formerly it was agreed that a man stood or fell by his actions; nowadays, on the contrary, everyone idles about and comes off brilliantly.

> Søren Kierkegaard, *The Present Age*

Hinduism

Verily, one becomes good by action, bad by inaction.

> *Upanishads*, Brihadaranyaka

On action alone be thy interest, never on its fruits.

Bhagavad Gita, 2:47

Perform thy allotted work, for action is superior to inaction; even the maintenance of thy body cannot be accomplished without action.

Bhagavad Gita, 3:8

Judaism

What is required is a deed that a man does with his whole being.

Martin Buber, *I and Thou*

The fabulous fact of man's ability to act, *the wonder of doing*, is no less amazing than the marvel of being.

Abraham Joshua Heschel, *God in Search of Man*

Nonsectarian

All of life, every little and every important action, is devoted to the knowledge of God, but a knowledge not in right thought, but in right action.

Erich Fromm, *The Art of Loving*

Zoroastrianism

They truly shall be Saviours of the lands, who follow knowledge of Thy teaching Mazda, with good purpose, with acts inspired by truth. They indeed have been appointed opponents of Fury.

Avesta, Yasna

ADVICE

Christianity/Judaism

A word spoken in due season, how good it is!

Holy Bible, Proverbs 15:23

Christianity

Always take counsel of a wise man, and desire to be instructed and governed by others rather than to follow your own ingenuity.

Thomas à Kempis, *The Imitation of Christ*

We ask advice, but we mean approbation.

Charles Caleb Colton, *Lacon*

Ever since I served as an infantryman in the First World War I have had a great dislike of people who, themselves in ease and safety, issue exhortations to men in the front line.

C.S. Lewis, *Mere Christianity*

My advice to an ordinary religious man ... would be to avoid all arguments about religion, and especially about the existence of God.

Thomas Merton, *The Seven Storey Mountain*

Islam

O my heart!
How long, O how long,
Will you heed not to good advice?
Why not give up your frivolous life?

Al-Murtaza ibn al-Shahrozuri

Judaism

Beware of him who gives thee advice according to his own interests.

Talmud, Sanhedrin 76a

AMBITION

Christianity/Judaism

Seekest thou great things for thyself? Seekest them not.

Holy Bible, Jeremiah 45:5

Christianity

What shall it profit a man, if he shall gain the whole world, and lose his own soul?

Holy Bible, Mark 8:36

To know your ruling passion, examine your castles in the air.

Richard Whately, Archbishop of Dublin

The ambition of man to be something is always partly prompted by the fear of meaninglessness which threatens him by reason of the contingent character of his existence.

Reinhold Niebuhr, *The Nature and Destiny of Man*

Hinduism

Whenever bright ones, growing strong,
You have decided on your course,
The mountains bend and bow themselves.

Rig-Veda

ANGELS

Christianity/Judaism

What is man? For thou hast made him a little lower than the angels.

Holy Bible, Psalms 8:4-5

Christianity

We should pray to the angels, for they are given to us as guardians.

St. Ambrose, *On Bereavement*

An angel is a spiritual creature created by God without a body, for the service of Christendom and of the Church.

Martin Luther, *Table Talk*

Then if angels fight,
Weak men must fall: for heaven still guards the right.

William Shakespeare, *Richard II*, Act 3, Sc. 2

Angels are bright still, though the brightest fell.

William Shakespeare, *Macbeth*, Act 4, Sc. 3

Make yourself familiar with the angels, and behold them frequently in spirit. Without being seen, they are present with you.

St. Francis de Sales, *Introduction to the Devout Life*

Hark! the herald angels sing
Glory to the newborn king.

Charles Wesley, "Hark! the Herald Angels Sing"

I looked over Jordan and what did I see,
Coming for to carry me home?
A band of angels coming after me,
Coming for to carry me home.

American spiritual, author unknown, "Swing Low, Sweet Chariot"

While mortals sleep, the angels keep
Their watch of wondr'ing love.

> Phillips Brooks, "O Little Town of Bethlehem"

Angels can fly because they take themselves lightly.

> G.K. Chesterton, *Orthodoxy*

Angels are not all-knowing, but they do know more than we do.

> Corrie ten Boom, *Not I, But Christ*

Deism

It is not known precisely where angels dwell—whether in the air, the void, or the planets. It has not been God's pleasure that we should be informed of their abode.

> Voltaire, *Philosophical Dictionary*

Islam

Many are the angels in the heavens; yet their intercession will avail nothing until Allah gives leave to whom He chooses and accepts.

> *Koran*, 53:26

Judaism

Only man is capable of creative interpretation [of the Torah], something which is beyond the power of angels, for since the Holy One, blessed be He, created them in a state of perfection, they need not and, therefore, cannot develop and progress.

> Hayyim Volozhin, *Ruah hayyim*

Swedenborgianism

Since angels are men, and live together in society like men on earth, therefore they have garments, houses, and other things familiar to those which exist on earth, but of course infinitely more beautiful and perfect.

> Emanuel Swedenborg, *Arcana Coelestia*

ANGER

Christianity/Judaism

A soft answer turneth away wrath: but grievous words stir up anger.

> *Holy Bible*, Proverbs 15:1

Christianity

Be ye angry, and sin not: let not the sun go down upon your wrath.

Holy Bible, Ephesians 4:26

Stir not the fire with a sword; that is, do not provoke a man who is already in a rage. It is wiser to give way, and soothe the fuming spirit with gentle words.

Erasmus, *Adages*

The Greek word for wrath means unrighteous fits of rage, passionate outbursts of anger and hostile feelings. . . . Man's wrath can be righteous or unrighteous. . . . There is a righteous wrath, but it is not a fit of anger. . . . Someone has well said, "Righteous indignation is usually one part righteous and nine parts indignation."

Billy Graham, *The Holy Spirit*

Confucianism

When one is angry, if one can directly forget his anger and examine the right and wrong according to principle, then right and wrong will be clearly seen and desires will naturally be unable to persist.

Chu Hsi, *Complete Works of . . .*

Islam

Anger is the foundation of every evil.

Hasan Askari

Judaism

We can sympathize fully with the little fellow whose angry outburst brought him swift punishment. "Dear God," he was later heard praying, "please take away my temper, and while you're at it, take away my father's temper too."

Sidney Greenberg, *Say Yes to Life*

Stoicism

Reckon the days in which you have not been angry. I used to be angry every day; now every other day; then every third and fourth day; and if you miss it so long as thirty days, offer a sacrifice of thanksgiving to God.

Epictetus, *How the Semblances of Things Are to Be Combated*

APATHY

Christianity

We seek repose, fighting against obstacles, and when we have conquered these, repose becomes unbearable through the ennui which it begets.

Blaise Pascal, *Pensées*

The forces of good in the world are immobilized less by their adversaries than by their sleep.

E.M. Poteat, *These Shared His Passion*

Science may have found a cure for most evils, but it has found no remedy for the worst of them all—the apathy of human beings.

Helen Keller, *My Religion*

The nonstriving person who elects to avoid problems actually creates new ones.

Robert H. Schuller, *Tough Times Never Last, But Tough People Do!*

Navajo

Clear my feet of indolence,
Keeper of the paths of men.

Prayer to the Mountain Spirit

ASSISTANCE

Christianity/Judaism

The Lord is my shepherd; I shall not want.

Holy Bible, Psalms 23:1

Our soul waiteth for the Lord: he is our help and our shield.

Holy Bible, Psalms 33:20

Christianity

Lord, help me.

Holy Bible, Matthew 15:25

God helps those who help themselves.

Algernon Sidney, *Discourse Concerning Government*

O God, our help in ages past,
    Our hope in years to come,
Our shelter from the stormy blast,
    And our eternal home.

Isaac Watts, "O God, Our Help in Ages Past"

It is religion's peculiar secret that it brings to the individual a solemn assurance unlike anything else in life, a tranquility, an ever-present help in trouble, that makes the next steps easier no matter what mesh of circumstances may entangle the life.

Gordon W. Allport, The Individual and His Religion

I must not keep looking over my shoulder at God when I turn to my fellowman, nor indulge in pious talk when I am supposed to be helping somebody. The Samaritan helps without dragging in religious reasons.

Hans Küng, On Being a Christian

Hinduism

Aided by thee no man is slain or vanquished;
To him from near or far no trouble reaches.

Rig-Veda

Islam

He who helps another for the sake of God, he has made a house for himself in Paradise.

Muhammad Taqi

ATHEISM

Atheism

RELIGION. A daughter of Hope and Fear, explaining to Ignorance the nature of the Unknowable.

Ambrose Bierce, The Devil's Dictionary

Religion is comparable to a childhood neurosis.

Sigmund Freud, The Future of an Illusion

My atheism, like that of Spinoza, is true piety towards the universe and denies only gods fashioned by men in their own image, to be servants of their human interests.

George Santayana, "On My Friendly Critics"

Christianity/Judaism

The fool hath said in his heart, There is no God.

Holy Bible, Psalms 14:1

Christianity

How did the atheist get his idea of that God whom he denies?

Samuel Taylor Coleridge

Atheism in art, as well as in life, has only to be pressed to its last consequences in order to become ridiculous.

Coventry Patmore, "Emotional Art"

An atheist is a man who believes himself an accident.

Francis Thompson, *Paganism Old and New*

An atheist is a man with no invisible means of support.

Harry Emerson Fosdick

Absolute atheism starts in an act of faith in reverse gear and is a full-blown religious commitment.

Jacques Maritain, *The Range of Reason*

An atheist is a guy who watches a Notre Dame-SMU football game and doesn't care who wins.

Dwight D. Eisenhower

There are no atheists in foxholes.

William T. Cummings, Sermons on Bataan, March 1942

Atheism can only mean the attempt to remove any ultimate concern—to remain unconcerned about the meaning of one's existence.

Paul Tillich, *Dynamics of Faith*

An atheist had a sign on the wall of his office that read, "God is Nowhere." A little girl saw it and exclaimed, "Look! It says, 'God is Now Here!'"

Vance Havner, *The Vance Havner Quotebook*

One thing must be conceded to atheism from the very beginning: it is *possible to deny God*. Atheism cannot be eliminated rationally. It is unproved, but it is also irrefutable.

Hans Küng, *The Christian Challenge*

Deism

The philosopher who recognizes a God has with him a crowd of probabilities equivalent to certainty, while the atheist has nothing but doubts.

Voltaire

Islam

They say: "There is this life and no other. We live and we die; and nothing but time destroys us." Of this, however, they have no knowledge. They can only guess.

Koran, 45:24

Judaism

A disciple comes to his rabbi, inquiring whether it is not the case that everything in the world has a purpose. The rabbi agrees. "Then what," the disciple demands, "is the purpose of atheism?" The rabbi answers: "When a poor person comes to you asking for help, then be an atheist! Don't tell that person that God will help! Act as though no one existed to help except you!"

Emil L. Fackenheim, *What Is Judaism?*

Platonism

No one who in early life had adopted this doctrine of the nonexistence of gods has ever persisted to old age constant to that conviction.

Plato, *Laws*

BEAUTY

Buddhism

In the twilight rain
These brilliant-hued hibiscus—
A lovely sunset.

Basho

Christianity/Judaism

Worship the Lord in the beauty of holiness.

Holy Bible, 1 Chronicles 16:29

Christianity

Beauty bears repeating twice and thrice.

Erasmus, *Adages*

God passes through the thicket of the world, and wherever his glance
falls he turns all things to beauty.

St. John of the Cross, *The Spiritual Canticle*

The world is a mirror of infinite beauty. . . . It is a temple of majesty. . . . It
is a region of light and peace. . . . It is more to man since he has fallen than
it was before. It is the place of angels and the gate of heaven.

Thomas Traherne, *Centuries of Meditations*

The love of beauty is super-personal and disinterested, like all the spiritual values; it promotes common enjoyment and social sympathy. Unquestionably it is one of the three ultimate values, ranking with Goodness and Truth.

William Ralph Inge, *Wit and Wisdom of Dean Inge*

All that talk about the divinity and dignity of the human body is stolen from theology, and is quite meaningless without theology. It dates from the Garden of Eden, and the idea (which I happen to hold firmly) that God created Man in His own image. But, if you remove the religious idea, there is no more sense in saying that every human being is lovely than in saying that every hippopotamus is lovely. It is a matter of taste; and many of us, after watching a sufficient number of human beings at Brighton, might prefer the hippopotamus.

G.K. Chesterton, "On Dress and Decorum"

Beauty is the supreme mystery of this world. It is a gleam which attracts the attention and yet does nothing to sustain it. . . . It feeds only the part of the soul that gazes.

Simone Weil, "Human Personality"

Hinduism

A bud is lovelier on the bough than in a golden vase.

Rabindranath Tagore, "The Auspicious Vision"

Unitarianism

Things are pretty, graceful, rich, elegant, handsome, but, until they speak to the imagination, not yet beautiful.

Ralph Waldo Emerson, *The Conduct of Life*

BELIEF

Agnosticism

I think an agnostic would be the . . . correct description of my state of mind. The whole subject (that of God and immortality) is beyond the scope of man's intellect.

Charles Darwin

Buddhism

In Buddha
I believe
wheat-ears' green
truth.

Ogiwara Seisensui

Christianity/Judaism

And the Lord said unto Moses, How long will this people provoke me? and how long will it be ere they believe me, for all the signs which I have shewed among them?

Holy Bible, Numbers 14:11

Christianity

Jesus said unto him, If thou canst believe, all things are possible to him that believeth.

And straightway the father of the child cried out, and said with tears, Lord, I believe.

Holy Bible, Mark 9:23-24

Jesus said unto her, I am the resurrection and the life: he that believeth in me, though he were dead, yet shall he live.

Holy Bible, John 11:25

There are three means of believing: by inspiration, by reason, and by habit.

Blaise Pascal

Orthodoxy is my doxy; heterodoxy is another man's doxy.

William Warburton, Bishop of Gloucester

There are some men who are capable of believing everything but the Bible.

Napoleon Bonaparte

Belief in God is acceptance of the basic principle that the universe makes sense, that there is behind it an ultimate purpose.

Carl Wallace Miller, *A Scientist's Approach to Religion*

Hinduism

The knot of the heart is loosened,
All doubts are cut off,
And one's karma ceases
When the imperishable Brahma is seen.

Upanishads, Mundaka

Islam

We believe in God, and in the revelation given to us, and to Abraham, Ishmael, Isaac, Jacob and the Tribes. We believe in the revelation that was sent to Moses, Jesus and all other Prophets from their Lord. We make no distinction between them, and unto Him we surrender.

Koran, 3:83

Those who read the Book of Allah and attend to their prayers and give alms both secretly and openly may look forward to imperishable gain.

Koran, 35:29

Judaism

One can be a rationalist, a freethinker, or an atheist in a religious sense, but one cannot, in a religious sense, be a collector of "experiences," a boaster of moods, or a prattler about God.

Martin Buber, *On Judaism*

Nonsectarian

Believe that life is worth living, and your belief will help create the fact.

William James, *The Will to Believe*

Religious experience is absolute. It is indisputable. You can only say that you have never had such an experience, and your opponent will say: "Sorry, I have." And there your discussion will come to an end. No matter what the world thinks about religious experience, the one who has it possesses the great treasure of a thing that has provided him with a source of life, meaning and beauty and that has given a new splendor to the world and to mankind.

Carl Jung, *Psychology and Religion*

BIBLE

Buddhism

There is no such thing as a Buddhist "Bible," in the sense of an authoritative statement of the teachings of Buddhism. . . . The Buddhist Scriptures . . . are a vast collection of writings in a dozen languages having this in common, that they stem from the Buddha's Enlightenment as expressed through the medium of his own or lesser minds.

Christmas Humphreys, *The Wisdom of Buddhism*

Christianity

Search the scriptures.

Holy Bible, John 5:39

All scripture is given by inspiration of God, and is profitable for doctrine, for reproof, for correction, for instruction in righteousness.

Holy Bible, 2 Timothy 3:16

Let sleep find you holding your Bible, and when your head nods let it be resting on the sacred page.

St. Jerome

Each man marvels to find in the divine Scriptures truths which he himself thought out.

St. Thomas Aquinas, *De Potentia*

The Spirit breathes upon the Word,
    And brings the truth to sight;
Precepts and promises afford
    A sanctifiying light.
A glory gilds the sacred page
    Majestic like the sun;
It gives a light to every age—
    It gives, but borrows none.

William Cowper, "The Spirit's Light"

Both read the Bible day and night,
But thou read'st black where I read white.

William Blake, "The Everlasting Gospel"

The English Bible, a book which, if everything else in our language should perish, would alone suffice to show the whole extent of its beauty and power.

Thomas Babington Macauley, *Essays and Biographies*

The man of one book is always formidable; but when that one book is the Bible he is irresistible.

William Mackergo Taylor

Those who talk of the Bible as "a monument of English prose" are merely admiring it as a monument over the grave of Christianity.

T.S. Eliot, *Religion and Literature*

There is obviously interpretation in the Gospels. They are indeed a faith-proclamation, necessarily written in the language and thought-forms of their time; and they involve mythic elements. But their core is history, not myth. . . . The Bible at base is history.

George A. Buttrick, *Christ and History*

Apart from the Fundamentalists . . . most people who take the Bible seriously are endorsive of those texts which strike them as wholesome and good and ignore the rest.

James A. Pike, *If This Be Heresy*

We honor God precisely by honoring Scripture as his written Word.

James I. Packer, "Contemporary Views of Revelation"

What is true of the Gospels as a whole is particularly true of the Easter stories: they are *not unbiased reports* by disinterested observers but depositions in favor of Jesus submitted in faith by supremely interested and committed persons. They are therefore not so much historical as theological documents: not records of proceedings or chronicles, but testimonies of faith.

Hans Küng, *The Christian Challenge*

The Bible is the inerrant, inspired Word of the living God. It is absolutely infallible, without error in all matters pertaining to faith and practice, as well as in such areas as geography, science, history, etc.

Jerry Falwell, *Finding Inner Peace and Strength*

Islam

To any student of the Koran the presence in it of Jewish and Christian elements is evident almost at the first glance.

Richard Bell, *The Origin of Islam in Its Christian Environment*

The Koran is supposed to have been kept in heaven, dictated sentence by sentence as God's direct word for man, and therefore to be infallibly true in every sentence. It is thus regarded in every respect (linguistically, stylistically, logically, historically) as a perfect, holy book which has to be literally believed and may not even be interpreted or provided with a commentary.

Hans Küng, *On Being a Christian*

Judaism

The Song of Songs is Wisdom; the Book of Ecclesiastes is Understanding; and the Book of Proverbs is Knowledge.

Talmud, Zohar iii, 64b

It is not entirely by accident that the Bible is the most widely translated of all books. (It is probably the first book of consequence to have been translated.) The word of God implies the certainty that it will become the word of all.

Franz Rosenzweig, *Understanding the Sick and the Healthy*

To believe, we need God, a soul, and the Word. Having rejected the Bible as a paper pope, many are left with the Bible as a collection of ill-composed records on a mass of paper.

Abraham Joshua Heschel, *The Insecurity of Freedom*

The writers of the Bible were . . . not cool historians but passionate prophets. They did not select, organize, and judge facts the way a modern university professor does.

Herman Wouk, *This Is My God*

Mormonism

And because my words shall hiss forth—many of the Gentiles [non-Mormons] shall say: A Bible! A Bible! We have got a Bible, and there cannot be any more Bible.

Book of Mormon, 2 Nephi 29:3

Secularism

The gospel narratives in the main give you a biography which is quite credible and accountable on purely secular grounds when you have trimmed off everything that . . . any modern bishop would reject as fanciful.

George Bernard Shaw, *Androcles and the Lion*, Preface

Unitarianism

The current notions respecting the infallible inspiration of the Bible have no foundation in the Bible itself. Which Evangelist, which Apostle of the New Testament, what Prophet or Psalmist of the Old Testament, ever claims infallible authority for himself or for others? . . . Would not these modest writers themselves be confounded at the idolatry we pay them?

Theodore Parker, "A Discourse on the Transient and Permanent in Christianity"

BREVITY

Christianity/Judaism

He that hath knowledge spareth his words.

Holy Bible, Proverbs 17:27

Christianity

Speaking much and speaking well are not the same thing. . . . One is almost bound to fall into error if one tries to say a great deal.

Erasmus, *Adages*

Brevity flatters and does better business; it gains by courtesy what it loses by curtness. Good things, when short, are twice as good.

Baltasar Gracian, *The Art of Worldly Wisdom*

Few sinners are saved after the first twenty minutes of a sermon.

Mark Twain

Judaism

Many centuries ago, a heathen asked a great sage for a definition of Torah, brief enough not to extend beyond the time the questioner could balance himself "on one foot." The achievement of the sage has remained unique since his time. And, even at that, the teacher concluded his concise statement with the adminition, "Go, study."

Morris Adler, *The World of the Talmud*

BROTHERHOOD

Christianity/Judaism

Behold, how good and how pleasant it is for brethren to dwell together in unity!

Holy Bible, Psalms 133:1

Christianity

If a man says, I love God, and hateth his brother, he is a liar: for he that loveth not his brother whom he hath seen, how can he love God whom he hath not seen?

Holy Bible, 1 John 4:20

Your brother needs your help, but you meanwhile mumble your little prayers to God, pretending not to see your brother's need.

Erasmus, *Enchiridion militis christiani*

America! America!
God shed His grace on thee,
And crown thy good with brotherhood
From sea to shining sea!

Katharine Lee Bates, "America the Beautiful"

It is impossible to love Christ without loving others (in proportion as these others are moving towards Christ). And it is impossible to love others (in a spirit of broad human communion) without moving nearer to Christ.

Pierre Teilhard de Chardin, *The Divine Milieu*

Islam

Wear the Kafan which consists of plain white material. You will be dressed like everyone else. See the uniformity appear! Be a particle and join the mass; as a drop, enter the ocean.

Ali Shariati, *Hajj*

Judaism

Not only every member of our family, our tribe, and our people, but every man is our brother.

Leo Baeck, *The Essence of Judaism*

Stoicism

The universe is but one great city, full of beloved ones, divine and human by nature, endeared to each other.

Epictetus

BUSINESS

Christianity/Judaism

Seest thou a man diligent in his business? He shall stand before kings.

Holy Bible, Proverbs 22:29

Christianity

Avoid, as you would the plague, a clergyman who is also a man of business.

St. Jerome

Dispatch business quickly, and keep out of long debates . . . be swift to hear, and slow to speak, and let it be in the grace, which seasons all words.

George Fox, *Epistles*

Businesses are, in reality, quasi-religious sects. When you go to work in one you embrace *a new faith*. And if they are really big businesses, you progress from faith to a kind of mystique. . . . Why not face it? Advertising treats all products with the reverence and the seriousness due to sacraments.

Thomas Merton, *Conjectures of a Guilty Bystander*

Judaism

When a sage engages in many business undertakings, they interfere with his wisdom.

Talmud, Shemot Rahhah 6,2

Rava said that on Judgment Day the first question God asks a man is: "Were you reliable in your business dealings?"

Louis Jacobs, *What Does Judaism Say About . . . ?*

CHANGE

Buddhism

Even if heaven and earth turn upside down, it does not mean that they are not at rest, and even if floods overflow heaven, it does not mean that they are in motion.

Seng-chao, *Treatises*

When Buddhist philosophy changes it becomes Zen; when Zen grows worse it turns devilish; when the devil is allowed to prosper, there is perversity of nature.

Daisetz Teitaro Suzuki, *Essays in Zen Buddhism*

Christianity/Judaism

Can the Ethiopian change his skin, or the leopard his spots?

Holy Bible, Jeremiah 13:23

I am the Lord, I change not.

Holy Bible, Malachi 3:6

Christianity

We shall all be changed.
 In a moment, in the twinkling of an eye, at the last trump: for the trumpet shall sound, and the dead shall be raised incorruptible, and we shall all be changed.

Holy Bible, 1 Corinthians 15:51-52

Satan himself is transformed into an angel of light.

Holy Bible, 2 Corinthians 11:14

Religion will not regain its old power until it can face change in the same spirit as does science.

Alfred North Whitehead, *Science and the Modern World*

Though we ought always to imitate the procedure of Christ and His saints, this pattern has to be adapted to the changing conditions of history. We are not to preach in Aramaic because [John] the Baptist did so nor to recline at table because the Lord reclined.

C.S. Lewis, *Present Concerns*

All mortals tend to turn into the thing they are pretending to be.

C.S. Lewis, *The Screwtape Letters*

There is no sense in getting into a dither just because we have split the atom and are photographing Mars. The Bible is still God's Word and Jesus Christ is the same yesterday, today, and forever. Nothing important has changed.

Vance Havner, *The Vance Havner Quotebook*

Confucianism

The Master said, "It is only the very wisest and the very stupidest who cannot change."

Confucius, *Analects*

Judaism

"God," a Hasidic master remarked, "does not say that 'it was good' after creating man; this indicates that while the cattle and everything else were finished after being created, man was not finished."

Erich Fromm, *You Shall Be As Gods*

Unitarianism

The religion of one age is the literary entertainment of the next.

Ralph Waldo Emerson

CHARACTER

Christianity/Judaism

Shall mortal man be more just than God? shall a man be more pure than his maker?

Holy Bible, Job 4:17

Eat thou not the bread of him that hath an evil eye, neither desire thou his dainty meats.
    For as he thinketh in his heart, so is he.

Holy Bible, Proverbs 23:6-7

Christianity

By their fruits ye shall know them.

Holy Bible, Matthew 7:20

What manner of man is this, that even the wind and the sea obey him?

Holy Bible, Mark 4:41

Men go abroad to wonder at the height of mountains, at the huge waves of the sea, at the long courses of the rivers, at the vast compass of the ocean, at the circular motion of the stars, and they pass by themselves without wondering.

St. Augustine

I thought King Henry had resembled thee
In courage, courtship, and proportion:
But all his mind is bent to holiness,
To number Ave Maries on his beads;
His champions are the prophets and apostles;
His weapons holy saws of sacred writ;
His study is his tilt-yard, and his loves
Are brazen images of canonized saints.

William Shakespeare, *Henry VI*, Part 1, Act 1, Sc. 3

He whose own worth doth speak, need not speak his own worth.

Thomas Fuller, *The Holy State and the Profane State*

Character is what you are in the dark.

Dwight L. Moody, *Sermons*

Confucianism

The Master said, "A gentleman takes as much trouble to discover what is right as lesser men take to discover what will pay."

Confucius, *Analects*

Existentialism

To be witty without possessing the riches of inwardness is like squandering money upon luxuries and dispensing with necessities, or, as the proverb says, like selling one's trousers to buy a wig.

Søren Kierkegaard, *The Present Age*

Hinduism

A man is exactly what he has made himself and what he therefore deserves to be.

Franklin Edgerton, *The Bhagavad Gita*

Hinduism/Islam

The man who is kind and who practices righteousness, who
    remains passive against the affairs of the world, who
    considers all creatures on earth as his own self,
He attains the Immortal Being; the true God is ever with him.

Kabir, *Songs of Kabir*

Islam

A man worthy of applause is oftentimes despised during his lifetime. But when he is removed by death, his loss comes to be severely felt.

Al-Din Razi, *A Rosary of Islamic Readings*

Judaism

If a peasant becomes a king, he will not take his basket off his shoulders.

Talmud, Megillah 7b

The one great requisite is character.

Talmud, Sotah 27a

One's own character is such a puzzle. Here I am, a comfortable middle-aged rabbi, blessed with central heating, and a food processor, and aspiring to a microwave, devouring books on suffering, affliction and asceticism as I go to work in the morning.

Lionel Blue, *Kitchen Blues*

Stoicism

If you see a man who is unterrified in the midst of dangers, untouched by desires, happy in adversity, peaceful amid the storm, who looks down on men from a higher plane, and views the gods on a footing of equality, will not a feeling of reverence for him steal over you?

Seneca, *Epistolae Morales*

CHARITY

Christianity

And now abideth faith, hope, charity, these three; but the greatest of these is charity.

Holy Bible, 1 Corinthians 13:13

If something uncharitable is said in your presence, either speak in favor of the absent, or withdraw, or, if possible, stop the conversation.

St. John Vianney

Charity is above all a hymn of love.

Pope Pius XII

I rather think there is an immense shortage of Christian charity among so-called Christians.

Harry S Truman

Let us, like [Mary], touch the dying, the poor, the lonely and the unwanted according to the graces we have received and let us not be ashamed or slow to do the humble work.

Mother Teresa of Calcutta, *Life in the Spirit*

Hinduism

The wealthier man should give unto the needy,
Considering the course of life hereafter;
For riches are like chariot wheels revolving:
Now to one man they come, now to another.

Rig-Veda

Islam

The best of alms is that which the right hand giveth, and the left hand knoweth it not.

Muhammad

Judaism

Better is he who gives little to charity from money honestly earned, than he who gives much from dishonestly gained wealth.

Talmud, Kohelet Rabbah 4

We are obligated to be more scrupulous in fulfilling the commandment of charity than any other positive commandment because charity is the sign of the righteous man.

Maimonides, *Mishneh Torah*

Don't use the impudence of a beggar as an excuse for not helping him.

Rabbi Shmelke of Nicolsburg

One's obligation is not discharged when one offers sustenance to the impoverished. One must not offend the sensibilities and self-respect of the recipient. One should consider the suppliant's rights as well as his need. The effects of the charitable act should not be vitiated by the inconsiderate spirit in which it might be administered.

Morris Adler, *The World of the Talmud*

Mormonism

You will not suffer that the beggar putteth up his petition to you in vain, and turn him out to perish. . . .

For behold, are we not all beggars? Do we not all depend upon the same Being, even God, for all the substance which we have?

Book of Mormon, Mosiah 4:16,19

CHILDREN

Christianity/Judaism

He that spareth his rod hateth his son: but he that loveth him chasteneth him betimes.

Holy Bible, Proverbs 13:24

Train up a child in the way that he should go: and when he is old, he will not depart from it.

Holy Bible, Proverbs 22:6

Christianity

Suffer the little children to come unto me, and forbid them not: for such is the kingdom of God.

Holy Bible, Mark 10:14

Men see a great way with telescopes; eagles and vultures see a vast distance: but I take it that there is no eye so unerring and that sees so far and so sure as a parent's eye looking for a lost child.

Henry Ward Beecher, "The Prodigal Son"

Just as the children's crusade may be said to typify the Middle Ages, precocious children are typical of the present age.

Søren Kierkegaard, *The Present Age*

The modern child is brought up in a decent
    cultured
       comfortable
          but thoroughly irreligious home.

Peter Marshall, *Mr. Jones, Meet the Master*

There is always one moment in childhood when the door opens and lets the future in.

Graham Greene, *The Power and the Glory*

Concern for the child, even before birth, from the very moment of conception and then throughout the years of infancy and youth, is the primary and fundamental test of the relationship of one human being to another.

Pope John Paul II, Speech at the United Nations, October 2, 1979

Hinduism

The months of impious men shall pass by sonless;
May those on worship bent increase their homestead.

Rig-Veda

Islam

The wish of a mother is sacred for a dutiful son.

Asma bin Zaid, *A Rosary of Islamic Readings*

Judaism

There is great sadness in a Jewish home which has no child. Stories are still told, and songs are sung, but there is no one to pass this inheritance to, and a great commandment cannot be fulfilled.

Lionel Blue, *To Heaven, with Scribes and Pharisees*

The firstborn very often seem to be losers in Genesis by the very condition of their birth—the epithet "firstborn," hardly needed as identification, is asserted twice here [in Genesis 38:6-7] almost as though it explained why Er [Judah's son] displeased God.

Robert Alter, The Art of Biblical Narrative

CHRIST

Christianity

Now when Jesus was born in Bethlehem of Judea in the days of Herod the king, behold, there came wise men from the east to Jerusalem.

Saying, Where is he that is born King of the Jews? for we have seen his star in the east, and are come to worship him.

Holy Bible, Matthew 2:1-2

I am the way, the truth, and the life.

Holy Bible, John 14:6

In his life, Christ is an example, showing us how to live; in his death, he is a sacrifice, satisfying for our sins; in his resurrection, a conqueror; in his ascension, a king; in his intercession, a high priest.

Martin Luther

All hail the power of Jesus' name;
    Let angels prostrate fall;
Bring forth the royal diadem
    To crown him Lord of all.

Edward Perronet, "All Hail the Power of Jesus' Name"

How sweet the name of Jesus sounds
    In a believer's ear;
It soothes his sorrows, heals his wounds,
    And drives away his fear.

John Newton, "How Sweet the Name of Jesus Sounds"

Christ is ascended!
Bliss hath invested him—
Woes that molested him,
Trials that tested him,
Gloriously ended!

Goethe, *Faust*, Easter Chorus

A young village girl told me, "When I am about to talk to anyone, I picture to myself Jesus Christ and how gracious and friendly he was to everyone."

St. John Vianney

O morning stars together
    Proclaim the holy birth,
And praises sing to God the King
    And peace to men on earth.

Phillips Brooks, "O Little Town of Bethlehem"

Christ is the universal man, the ideal of humanity; and it is right that He should be "crowned with many crowns," as each nation and each century invests Him with its own ideal attributes.

William Ralph Inge, *Wit and Wisdom of Dean Inge*

If we have not died with Christ, we cannot possibly live with him.

Karl Barth, *Credo*

The foundation of Christian belief is the biblical picture of Christ, not the historical Jesus.

Paul Tillich, *On the Boundary*

Take Jesus out of the perfumed cloisters of pious sentiment, and let him walk the streets of the city.

Peter Marshall, "Gallery Christians"

Jesus had no organization, no headed notepaper, no funds, no registered premises, no distinguished patrons or officers, except only a treasurer—the ill-famed Judas Iscariot.

Malcolm Muggeridge, *Jesus, the Man Who Loves*

The Son of God became man in weakness, to help us to be fully human, giving us the power to become children of God.

Pope John Paul II, *The Word Made Flesh*

A great deal would have been achieved if it were remembered today . . . that Christianity is obviously not some sort of world view nor a kind of idealist philosophy, but has something to do with a person called Christ.

Hans Kung, *The Christian Challenge*

Islam

There are those who say, "The Most Gracious has begotten a son." They utter a monstrous falsehood, at which the skies could crack, the earth split asunder, and the mountains fall in ruin.

Koran, 19:88-90

Judaism

If a man tell thee, "I am God," he lies. If he tell thee, "I am the Son of Man," he will end by regretting it. If he says, "I shall ascend into Heaven," he merely makes this utterance, but he cannot fulfill it.

Talmud, Y. Taanit 2,1

Mormonism

[The people of Nephi] saw a Man descending out of heaven; and he was clothed in a white robe; and he came down and stood in the midst of them. . . .

And . . . he stretched forth his hand and spake unto the people, saying:

Behold, I am Jesus Christ, whom the prophets testified shall come into the world. And behold, I am the light and the life of the world. I have drunk out of that bitter cup which the Father hath given me.

Book of Mormon, 3 Nephi 11:8-11

Secularism

If Jesus had been indicted by a modern court, he would have been examined by two doctors; found to be obsessed by a delusion; declared incapable of pleading; and sent to an asylum.

George Bernard Shaw, *Androcles and the Lion*, Preface

Unitarianism

It cannot be emphasized too often that Jesus was not a theologian. He interpreted religion as something not primarily to be believed but to be lived.

John Haynes Holmes, *The Sensible Man's View of Religion*

CHURCH

Christianity

And Jesus answered and said unto him . . .
    Thou art Peter, and upon this rock I will build my church.

Holy Bible, Matthew 16:17-18

He cannot have God to be his Father who owns not the Church as his mother.

St. Cyprian of Carthage

He who comes not willingly to church shall one day go unwillingly to hell.

The Venerable Bede

Clearly the person who accepts the Church as an infallible guide will believe whatever the Church teaches.

St. Thomas Aquinas, *Summa Theologica*

We ourselves are God's true temples.

John Calvin, *Institutes of the Christian Religion*

The Church consists principally of two parts, the one called the Church triumphant, and the other the Church militant.

Council of Trent, 1563

Wherever God erects a house of prayer,
The Devil always builds a chapel there;
And 'twill be found, upon examination,
The latter has the largest congregation.

Daniel Defoe, *The True-Born Englishman*

The poorer the church, the purer the church.

W.C. Hazlitt, *English Proverbs*

May erring minds that worship here
    Be taught the better way;
And they who mourn, and they who fear,
    Be strengthened as they pray.

William Cullen Bryant, "Dedication"

The Church, if it is to hold men, and keep its influence in the march of life, must be nothing less than a revealing place for God. It is *prophetic* ministry that serious people want—prophetic in the deepest sense. I mean by that a ministry that reveals God and interprets life in its nobler and diviner possibilities.

Rufus M. Jones, *The Faith and Practice of the Quakers*

People, who commonly call themselves progressive, . . . see in front of them a solid block of brick called a church. They accept that; they cannot conceive a real revolt against that; they are even ready to throw themselves into all sorts of schemes for making this mere brick building fashionable, so that people shall "flock" to it.

C.K. Chesterton, "On Flocking"

The Church is a symbol of eternity in the midst of the self-sufficient world.

Rudolf Bultmann, *This World and the Beyond*

In the Church, man is neither a vessel of supernatural authority, insight, and power, as Roman Catholicism teaches, nor is he the free religious personality of modernistic Protestantism. . . . Rather, the constitution and preservation of the Church rests in this, that man hears God.

Karl Barth, *God in Action*

The Church is nothing but a section of humanity in which Christ has really taken form. The Church is the man in Christ, incarnate, sentenced and awakened to new life.

Dietrich Bonhoeffer, *Ethics*

Her Christianity [his mother's] belonged in a social context: good works, regular church attendance, and a visiting card framed in brass at the end of the pew.

Patrick White, *Flaws in the Glass*

Deism

Lighthouses are more helpful than churches.

Benjamin Franklin

Islam

Islam has . . . liberated man's *'ibadah* [worship] from . . . confinement to specific places. Islam regards every place—whether it is one's dwelling place, the back of an animal, the board of a vessel on the surface of the sea, or a mosque specifically built for worship—as pure enough for the performance of worship. Wherever a man might be, he can turn towards his Lord and enter into communion with Him.

Mustafa Ahmad al-Zarqa, "The Islamic Concept of Worship"

Judaism

He who does not enter a synagogue in this world will not enter a synagogue in the World to Come.

Talmud, Y. Berakot 5,1

The first thing you must understand is that a synagogue is not a church, not a good one, not a defective one either. . . . The piety is not in the place, but in the people.

Lionel Blue, *To Heaven, with Scribes and Pharisees*

COMPARISON

Buddhism

An excellent man, like precious metal,
    Is in every way invariable;
A villain, like the beams of a balance,
    Is always varying, upwards and downwards.

She-rab Dong-Bu

Christianity/Judaism

The words of his mouth were smoother than butter, but war was in his heart: his words were softer than oil, yet were they drawn swords.

Holy Bible, Psalms 55:21

Christianity

And [Jesus] said, Whereunto shall we liken the kingdom of God? or with what comparison shall we compare it?

It is like a grain of mustard seed, which, when it is sown in the earth, is less than all the seeds that be in the earth:

But when it is sown, it groweth up, and becometh greater than all herbs, and shooteth out great branches; so that the fowls of the air may lodge under the shadow of it.

Holy Bible, Mark 4:30-32

Two criminals were crucified with Christ. One was saved; do not despair. One was not; do not presume.

St. Augustine

Some are born to sweet delight.
Some are born to endless night.

William Blake, "Auguries of Innocence"

The Catholic who has turned his back on the church usually develops a secret or manifest inclination toward atheism, whereas the Protestant follows, if possible, a sectarian movement. The absolutism of the Catholic church seems to demand an equally absolute negation, while Protestant relativism permits variations.

Carl Jung, Psychology and Religion

St. Paul proposes to . . . set aside the apparent wisdom of the Greeks, which is really folly, so as to make way for the apparent folly of Christianity, which is really wisdom.

Etienne Gilson, The Spirit of Medieval Philosophy

Although the truth in other religions can be recognized, it cannot be disputed that there are substantial differences between the fearsome grimacing gods of Bali . . . and a wall with icons of Orthodox saints in Zagorsk; between sacred temple prostitution and Christian consecration of virgins; between . . . a religion proclaiming a holy war against the enemy and a religion which makes love of enemies an essential part of its program.

Hans Küng, On Being a Christian

Confucianism

Lung Tzu said, "If a man makes shoes without knowing the size of people's feet, I know that he will at least not make them to be like baskets." Shoes are alike because people's feet are alike.

Mencius, The Book of Mencius

Deism

When we see a beautiful machine, we say that there is a good engineer, and that this engineer has excellent judgment. The world is assuredly an admirable machine; therefore there is in the world an admirable intelligence, wherever it may be. This argument is old, and none the worse for that.

Voltaire, Philosophical Dictionary

Hinduism

Heaven and Earth
Which of the two is earlier, which the later?
How were they born, ye sages, who discerns it?
They by themselves support all things existing.
As with a wheel the day and night roll onward.

Rig-Veda

Islam

Can the blind and the deaf be compared to those who can see and hear?
Such are the unbelievers compared to the faithful. Will you not then take
heed?

Koran, 11:24

The likeness of those who choose patrons other than Allah is as the likeness
of a spider when she takes unto herself a house; and Lo! The frailest of
all houses is the spider's house, if but they knew.

Koran, 29:41

An infidel before his idol with wakeful heart
Is better than the religious man asleep in his mosque.

Muhammad Iqbal, *Javid Namah*

Judaism

Why is it easier to appease a male than a female? Because the first male
was created out of soft dust, but the first female out of hard bone.

Talmud, Niddah 31

In biblical days prophets were astir while the world was asleep; today
the world is astir while church and synagogue are busy with trivialities.

Abraham Joshua Heschel, *The Insecurity of Freedom*

Unitarianism

Priests are no more necessary to religion than politicians to patriotism.

John Haynes Holmes, *The Sensible Man's View of Religion*

COMPASSION

Buddhism

Compassion is no attribute. It is the Law of Laws . . . a shoreless universal essence, the light of everlasting right and fitness of all things, the law of love eternal.

"The Seven Portals"

Christianity/Judaism

He delighteth in mercy. He will turn again, he will have compassion upon us; he will subdue our iniquities.

Holy Bible, Micah 7:18-19

Christianity

When [Jesus] saw the multitudes, he was moved with compassion on them, because they . . . were . . . as sheep having no shepherd.

Holy Bible, Matthew 9:36

By compassion we make others' misery our own, and so, by relieving them, we relieve ourselves also.

Sir Thomas Browne, *Religio Medici*

Compassion is the chief law of human existence.

Fyodor Dostoyevsky, *The Idiot*

The compassion of the so-called godless is precisely not godless.

George A. Buttrick, *God, Pain, and Evil*

Judaism

He who hath compassion upon others receives compassion from Heaven.

Talmud, Shabbat 151

COMPETITION

Christianity/Judaism

The race is not to the swift, nor the battle to the strong . . . but time and chance happeneth to them all.

Holy Bible, Ecclesiastes 9:11

Christianity

I have fought a good fight, I have finished my course, I have kept the faith.

Holy Bible, 2 Timothy 4:7

Islam

Lo! Allah loves those who fight for His cause in battle array, as if they were a mighty edifice.

Koran, 61:4

CONFIDENCE

Christianity/Judaism

It is better to trust in the Lord than to put confidence in princes.

Holy Bible, Psalms 118:9

Christianity

We are made partakers of Christ, if we hold the beginning of our confidence steadfast unto the end.

Holy Bible, Hebrews 3:14

A little boy playing on the deck of a ship in a mighty storm was asked by a passenger if he wasn't afraid. "No, I'm not afraid. My father is the captain of the ship."

Rufus M. Jones, *The Radiant Life*

The weaker and less confident you feel in yourself, the more you need to strengthen in yourself the vision of the omnipotent Being to whom you have vowed your effort.

Pierre Teilhard de Chardin, *Letters to Leontine Zanta*

A father asked one of his three little girls who had just gone to bed if she had said her prayers. She said that she had not. He asked her if she were not afraid to go to sleep without having prayed. She answered, "Not tonight, for it is my turn to sleep in the middle."

Donald Grey Barnhouse, *Words Fitly Spoken*

Islam

Are you confident that He who is in Heaven will not cause the earth to swallow you up should it shake to pieces?

Koran, 67:16

CONFLICT

Christianity/Judaism

I will put a division between my people and thy people.

Holy Bible, Exodus 8:23

Christianity

If a house be divided against itself, that house cannot stand.

Holy Bible, Mark 3:25

Avoid foolish questions, and genealogies, and contentions, and strivings about the law; for they are unprofitable and vain.

Holy Bible, Titus 3:9

We think we love not God except we hate our brother; and we have not the virtue of religion unless we persecute all religions but our own.

Jeremy Taylor, *The Liberty of Prophesying*

When the consensus of scholarship says one thing and the Word of God another, the consensus of scholarship can go plumb to hell for all I care.

Billy Sunday

The easy subservience of reason to prejudice and passion, and the consequent persistence of irrational egotism, particularly in group behavior, make social conflict an inevitability in human history, probably to its very end.

Reinhold Niebuhr, *Moral Man and Immoral Society*

Such civilized, sensible, and rational institutions as the League of Nations, the United Nations, or even the Olympic Games have been far too fragile to cope with the furies of national, racial, and ethnic diversities. Indeed, it seems that technological progress in communication and transportation have made such primal conflicts more serious and more of a threat to the central cosmos than ever before.

Andrew M. Greeley, *The New Agenda*

Islam

Until Karl Marx and the rise of communism, the Prophet [Muhammad] had organized and launched the only serious challenge to Western civilization that it has faced in the whole course of its history. . . . The attack was direct, both military and ideological. And it was very powerful.

William Cantwell Smith, *Islam in Modern History*

Judaism

There is a creative power embedded within antithesis; conflict enriches experience, the negation is constructive, and contradiction deepens and expands the ultimate destiny of both man and the world.

Joseph B. Soloveitchik, *Halakhic Man*

CONSCIENCE

Christianity

The wrath of God is revealed from heaven against all ungodliness and unrighteousness of men. . . .

Because that which may be known of God is manifest in them; for God hath shewed it unto them.

Holy Bible, Romans 1:18-19

I cannot revoke anything, nor do I wish to; since to go against one's conscience is neither safe nor right: here I stand, I cannot do otherwise. God help me. Amen.

Martin Luther, Reply at the Diet of Worms, April 18, 1521

The doctrine of persecution for cause of conscience is most evidently and lamentably contrary to the doctrine of Jesus Christ, the Prince of Peace.

Roger Williams, *The Bloody Tenet of Persecution*

God never ordained you to have a conscience for others. Your conscience is for you, and for you alone.

Henry Ward Beecher, "The Courtesy of Conscience"

Conscience is . . . the surest moral authority within our reach—a voice to be implicitly obeyed in the crisis of an action. It is our highest guide. No command on earth can take precedence over it.

Rufus M. Jones, *The Nature and Authority of Conscience*

More potent than all the brass-buttoned policemen in the land is the restraining power of conscience.

John A. O'Brien, *Truths Men Live By*

Conscience is the perfect interpreter of life.

Karl Barth, *The Word of God and the Word of Man*

Deism

Conscience never deceives us; she is the true guide of man; it is to the soul what instinct is to the body; he who obeys his conscience is following nature and need not fear that he will go astray.

Jean Jacques Rousseau, *Emile*

Judaism

A bullet has no conscience; neither does a malignant tumor or an automobile gone out of control. That is why good people get sick and get hurt as much as anyone.

Harold S. Kushner, *When Bad Things Happen to Good People*

Swedenborgianism

Conscience is God's presence in man.

Emanuel Swedenborg, *Arcana Coelestia*

CONTENTMENT

Buddhism

There is a Buddha beside me, sitting upon his lotus of stone just as he sat in the days of Kato Kiyomasa. His meditative gaze slants down between his half-closed eyelids upon the Government College and its tumultuous life; and he smiles the smile of one who has received an injury not to be resented.

Lafcadio Hearn, "The Stone Buddha"

Christianity

I have learned, in whatsoever state I am, therewith to be content.

Holy Bible, Philippians 4:11

Contentment is a sleepy thing!

Thomas Traherne, *Christian Ethics*

Drop Thy still dews of quietness,
    Till all our strivings cease;
Take from our souls the strain and stress,
And let our ordered lives confess
    The beauty of Thy peace.

> John Greenleaf Whittier, "Dear Lord and Father of Mankind"

God's in his heaven—
All's right with the world.

> Robert Browning, "Pippa Passes"

Serenity is the basis of powerful activity. There is no art, no creativeness, no release of moral power . . . without it. If a man is going to help lift the world he must have some solidity within him to lean his lever on.

> Harry Emerson Fosdick, *Riverside Sermons*

Judaism

Who is truly rich? He who is happy in his portion.

> *Talmud*, Aboth 4,1

COURAGE

Christianity/Judaism

Be strong and of good courage, fear not, nor be afraid.

> *Holy Bible*, Deuteronomy 31:6

David said to Saul, Let no man's heart fail because of [Goliath]; thy servant will go and fight with this Philistine.

> *Holy Bible*, 1 Samuel 17:32

Christianity

The chief activity of courage is not so much attacking as enduring, or standing one's ground against dangers.

> St. Thomas Aquinas, *Summa Theologica*

Out of the night that covers me,
    Black as the pit from pole to pole,
I thank whatever gods may be,
    For my unconquerable soul.

> William Ernest Henley, "Invictus"

Courage is almost a contradiction in terms. It means a strong desire to live taking the form of a readiness to die.

G.K. Chesterton, *Orthodoxy*

Life is essentially a series of events to be lived through rather than intellectual riddles to be played with and solved. Courage is worth ten times more than any answers that claim to be total.

George A. Buttrick

Confucianism

The Master said, "To see what is right and not to do it is want of courage."

Confucius, *Analects*

The Master said, "Meng Chi-fan is no boaster. When his people were routed he was the last to flee; but when they neared the city gates, he whipped up his horses, saying, 'It was not courage that kept me behind. My horses were slow.'"
[Note: A superior man was expected to belittle his own deeds.]

Confucius, *Analects*

Judaism

It requires religious courage to belong to a minority such as Judaism always has been and always will be.

Leo Baeck, *The Essence of Judaism*

Navajo

Hear a prayer for courage.
Lord of the peaks,
Reared amid the thunders;
Keeper of the headlands
Holding up the harvest,
Keeper of the strong rocks.

Prayer to the Mountain Spirit

Unitarianism

It requires little courage to kill; but it takes much to resist evil with good, holding obstinately out, active or passive, till you overcome it.

Theodore Parker, "A Sermon of War"

CREATION

Buddhism

The event of creation did not take place so many kalpas or aeons ago, astronomically or biologically speaking. Creation is taking place every moment of our lives.

Daisetz Teitaro Suzuki, "The Buddhist Conception of Reality"

Christianity/Judaism

In the beginning God created the heaven and the earth.

And the earth was without form, and void; and darkness was upon the face of the deep. And the spirit of God moved upon the face of the waters.

And God said, Let there be light: and there was light.

Holy Bible, Genesis 1:1-3

Christianity

By him were all things created, that are in heaven, and that are in earth, visible and invisible, whether they be thrones, or dominions, or principalities, or powers.

Holy Bible, Colossians 1:16

The created world is but a small parenthesis in eternity.

Sir Thomas Browne, *Christian Morals*

The whole character of the creation was determined by the fact that God was to become man and dwell in the midst of His own creation.

Thomas Merton, *The New Man*

Confucianism

From the beginning of the universe to this day, it has not yet been ten thousand years. I do not know how things looked before then.

Chu Hsi, *Complete Works of . . .*

Hinduism

Who verily knows and who can here declare it, whence it was
    born and whence comes this creation?
  . . .
Whose eye controls this world in highest heaven, he verily
    knows it, or perhaps he knows not.

Rig-Veda

In the beginning the world was merely nonbeing. It was existent. It developed. It turned into an egg. It lay for the period of a year. It was split asunder. One of the two eggshell-parts became silver, one gold. That which was of silver is this earth. That which was of gold is the sky.

Upanishads, Chandogya

Brahman, the Supreme Being, having desired to create the world of beings, by a mere act of will first created water into which he cast his seed; this turned into an egg of golden color, resplendent like the light of the sun. In this egg was born Brahma, the earliest progenitor of all creatures. This Brahman having dwelt in the egg for one celestial year, split it into two parts by his meditations and made the heaven out of one part, the earth out of the other, and placed the sky between them.

Radhagovinda Basak, "The Hindu Concept of the Natural World"

Humanism

My father taught me that the question, "Who made me?" cannot be answered, since it immediately suggests the further question, "Who made God?"

John Stuart Mill

Islam

Are ye more difficult to create, or the heaven?
    He built it,
Lifted up its vault and poised it,
Made dark its night and brought forth its dawn;
The earth thereafter he spread out,
Brought forth from it its water and its pasture;
The mountains he set firm,
A provision for you and your flocks.

Koran, 79:27-33

We witness a superb, flawless plan in the universe—can it be without a Planner? We see great enchanting beauty in its working—can it be without a Creator? We observe wonderful design in nature—can it be without a designer?

Khurshid Ahmad, "Islam: Basic Principles and Characteristics"

Judaism

Because every man is unique, another first man enters the world whenever a child is born. By being alive, everyone groping like a child back to the origin of his own self, we may experience the fact that there is an origin, that there is creation.

Martin Buber, "The Man of Today and the Jewish Bible"

Leni-Lenape

At first, forever, lost in space,
    the great Manito was.
He made the extended land and the sky.
He made the sun, the moon, the stars.
    . . .
But an evil Manito made evil beings
    only, monsters.
He made the flies, he made the gnats.

Walam Olum

D

DEATH

Buddhism

For fifty-six years I lived as best I could,
Making my way in this world.
Now the rain has ended, the clouds are clearing,
The blue sky has a full moon.

Shoun

The venerable Ananda said to the venerable Anuruddha: "O my Lord
. . . , the Blessed one is dead!"

"Nay, brother Ananda, the Blessed One is not dead. He has entered into
that state in which both sensations and ideas have ceased to be!"

T.W. Rhys Davids, Buddhist Suttas

You are facing the Primary Clear Light. Be alert and attentive to all that
happens. You can now see and hear ultimate reality.

The Tibetan Book of the Dead

Christianity/Judaism

Yea, though I walk through the valley of the shadow of death, I will fear
no evil: for thou art with me; thy rod and thy staff they comfort me.

Holy Bible, Psalms 23:4

Christianity

O death, where is thy sting? O grave, where is thy victory?

Holy Bible, 1 Corinthinians 15:55

Behold a pale horse: and his name that sat on him was Death, and Hell followed with him.

Holy Bible, Revelation 6:8

The hour of death will shortly come, and therefore take care how you conduct yourself, for the common proverb is true: Today a man; tomorrow none.

Thomas à Kempis, *The Imitation of Christ*

The fate of the dead is known to God alone.

Huldrych Zwingli, "Sixty-seven Theses" (No. 58)

Death be not proud, though some have called thee
Mighty and dreadful, for thou art not so,
        . . .
One short sleep past, we wake eternally,
And death shall be no more; death, thou shalt die.

John Donne, "Holy Sonnets"

Any man's death diminishes me, because I am involved in mankind; and therefore never send to know for whom the bell tolls; it tolls for thee.

John Donne, *Devotions upon Emergent Occasions*

Teach me to live, that I may dread
The grave as little as my bed.

Thomas Ken, "Morning and Evening Hymn"

Now I lay me down to sleep;
I pray the Lord my soul to keep.
If I should die before I wake,
I pray the Lord my soul to take.

New England Primer

Death is the liberator of him whom freedom cannot release, the physician of him whom medicine cannot cure, and the comforter of him whom time cannot console.

Charles Caleb Colton, *Lacon*

Nearer, my God, to Thee,
    Nearer to Thee.

Sarah Flower Adams, "Nearer, My God, to Thee"

Sunset and evening star,
    And one clear call for me!
And may there be no moaning of the bar,
    When I put out to sea,
  . . .
I hope to see my pilot face to face
    When I have crossed the bar.

                        Alfred, Lord Tennyson, "Crossing the Bar"

Fear death?—to feel the fog in my throat,
    The mist in my face,
  . . .
I was ever a fighter, so—one fight more,
    The best and the last!

                              Robert Browning, "Prospice"

Because I could not stop for Death,
He kindly stopped for me—
The carriage held but just Ourselves,
And Immortality.

               Emily Dickinson, "Because I Could Not Stop for Death"

"You should not be discouraged; one does not die of a cold," the priest said to the bishop.

    The old man smiled. "I shall not die of a cold, my son. I shall die of having lived."

                 Willa Cather, *Death Comes for the Archbishop*

We must, in the shadow of death, have forced ourselves not to look back to the past, but to seek in utter darkness the dawn of God.

          Pierre Teilhard de Chardin, *Writings in Time of War*

We certainly know nothing of the fact that the passing of man in death is curse, punishment and ordeal. We know it only as one of the riddles of our existence.

                                  Karl Barth, *Credo*

Death is the supreme festival on the road to freedom.

              Dietrich Bonhoeffer, *Letters and Papers from Prison*

Death. An instantaneous state, without past or future. Indispensable for entering eternity.

> Simone Weil, *Gravity and Grace*

The Christian...believes that death is an illusion—a painful, terrifying, mysterious illusion, but an illusion nonetheless.

> Andrew M. Greeley, *Life for a Wanderer*

Someone who now talks bravely about death can be reduced to silence by fear of its actual onset.

> Hans Küng, *Eternal Life?*

Confucianism

Confucius said, "If we do not yet know about life, how can we know about death?"

> Confucius, *Analects*

Hinduism

Depart, depart, along those ancient pathways,
On which have passed away our fathers' fathers.

> *Rig-Veda*

I am death that carries off all,
    And the origin of things that are to be.

> *Bhagavad Gita*, 10:34

Humanism

Men are convinced of your arguments, your sincerity, and the seriousness of your efforts only by your death.

> Albert Camus, *The Fall*

Islam

When the soul is taken from the body, the eyes follow it and look toward it. On this account the eyes remain open.

> Muhammad, *Speeches and Table Talk*

Time sets its vicissitudes before us,
That they become a lesson for us.
But man, in his arrogance,

Turns his face and heeds them not.
He forgets that the day of death
Must come inescapably.

Al-Salib ibn Ruzziq

Judaism

A man cannot say to the Angel of Death: I wish to arrange my affairs before I die.

Talmud, Debarim Rabbah 9,3

Only the singular can die, and everything mortal is solitary.

Franz Rosenzweig, *The Star of Redemption*

Stoicism

Think not disdainfully of death, but look on it with favor; for even death is one of the things that Nature wills.

Marcus Aurelius, *Meditations*

Taoism

Dying is life's only certainty.

Deng Ming-Dao, *Seven Bamboo Tablets of the Cloudy Satchel*

DEMOCRACY

Christianity

The real democratic idea is, not that every man shall be on a level with every other, but that every one shall have liberty, without hindrance, to be what God made him.

Henry Ward Beecher, *The Dishonest Politician*

Democracy is a form of government which may be rationally defended, not as being good, but as being less bad than any other.

William Ralph Inge, "Our Present Discontents"

You can never have a revolution in order to establish a democracy. You must have a democracy in order to have a revolution.

G.K. Chesterton, *Tremendous Trifles*

Democracy is not simply a political system; it is a moral movement and it springs from adventurous faith in human possibilities.

Harry Emerson Fosdick, *Adventurous Religion*

Man's capacity for justice makes democracy possible, but man's inclination to injustice makes democracy necessary.

Reinhold Niebuhr, *The Children of Light and the Children of Darkness*

Islam

Keep away from Democracy; follow the Perfect Man,
For the intellect of two hundred asses cannot bring forth a single man's thought.

Muhammad Iqbal

Democracy without education is hypocrisy without limitation.

Iskander Mirza, President of Pakistan, on abolishing Pakistani parliament, 1958

[In] the so-called Western secular democracy . . . a divorce has been effected between politics and religion, and as a result of this secularization, the society and particularly its politically active elements have ceased to attach much or any importance to morality and ethics.

Abu'l A'la Mawdudi, *Islamic Law and Constitution*

Unitarianism

The instinct of the people is right.

Ralph Waldo Emerson, *The Conduct of Life*

We [in the United States] will not be commanded, at least only by such as we choose to obey. Does someone say, "Thou shalt," or "Thou shalt not," we ask, "Who are you?"

Theodore Parker, "The Political Destination of America
and the Signs of the Times"

DESPAIR

Christianity/Judaism

My God, my God, why hast thou forsaken me?

Holy Bible, Psalms 22:1

Christianity

And about the ninth hour Jesus cried with a loud voice, saying, *Eli, Eli, lama sabachthani?* that is to say, My God, my God, why hast thou forsaken me?

Holy Bible, Matthew 27:46

Lord, make me an instrument of Your peace. Where there is hatred let me sow love; . . . where there is despair, hope.

St. Francis of Assisi

In time of desolation one should never make a change, but stand firm in the resolutions and decisions that guided him the day before the desolation.

St. Ignatius of Loyola

Snails, snakes, and scorpions cannot despair; neither can cabbages, camels, or centipedes. Only man, with the infinite and eternal in him, can despair. The greater the expectation, the more keen can be the disappointment. The more there is to hope, the greater is the grief at not realizing it.

Fulton J. Sheen, *On Being Human*

Despair . . . is at root a form of infidelity and self-destruction. It is the refusal to have faith, it is the refusal to believe in the world and in one's self, it is the refusal to attempt to love.

Andrew M. Greeley, *Life for a Wanderer*

Judaism

Even Hamlet persists in his despair only as long as he remains in soliloquy. As soon as the requirements of the moment take hold of him, once the solitude of his soliloquy is destroyed, he does the correct thing unhesitatingly.

Franz Rosenzweig, *Understanding the Sick and the Healthy*

DESTINY

Christianity

If thou follow thy star, thou canst not fail of glorious heaven.

Dante, *Divine Comedy: Purgatory*

There is no such thing as fortune or chance. . . . God's children . . . are governed by God's secret plan in such a way that nothing happens except what is knowingly and willingly decreed by him.

John Calvin, *Institutes of the Christian Religion*

Our Lord has created persons for all states in life, and in all of them we see people who have achieved sanctity by fulfilling their obligations well.

St. Anthony Mary Claret

Destiny waits in the hand of God.

T.S. Eliot, *Murder in the Cathedral*

Confucianism

Mencius said, "Everything is destiny. A man should accept obediently what is correct . . . he who knows destiny does not stand beneath a precipitous wall.

Mencius, *The Book of Mencius*

Hinduism

Is not karma just another name for fate? . . . [No.] The doctrine of karma teaches that man himself is the architect of his life. What he did in the past life is entirely responsible for what he is in the present life. This is the very opposite of fatalism.

R.N. Dandekar, "The Role of Man in Hinduism"

Islam

There will nothing befall us but what God hath written down for us.

Koran, 9:51

Judaism

A man does not hurt his finger unless it is decreed from above.

Talmud, Hullin 7

Pantheism

All things have been predestined by God, not indeed, . . . from an absolutely arbitrary decree, but from the absolute nature or infinite power of God.

Spinoza, *Ethics*

Stoicism

Whatever befalls thee was preordained for thee from eternity.

Marcus Aurelius, Meditations

DEVIL

Christianity

Get thee behind me, Satan.

Holy Bible, Luke 4:8

Resist the devil, and he will flee from you.

Holy Bible, James 4:7

Be sober, be vigilant; because your adversary the devil, as a roaring lion, walketh about, seeking whom he may devour.

Holy Bible, 1 Peter 5:8

Heed not the demons even if they awaken you for prayer.

St. Anthony of Egypt

Satan transforms himself as it were into an angel of light, and often sets a snare for the faithful by means of the divine Scriptures themselves. Thus does he make heretics, thus weaken faith, thus attack the requirements of piety.

St. Ambrose

Who is the most diligent bishop and prelate in England? . . . I will tell you. It is the devil. . . . He is never out of his diocese. . . . The devil is diligent at his plow.

Hugh Latimer, "Sermon of the Plow"

The devil can cite Scripture for his purpose.

William Shakespeare, The Merchant of Venice, Act 1, Sc. 2

Speak boldly, and speak truly,
Shame the devil.

John Fletcher, Wit Without Money

The heart of man is the place the devils dwell in: I feel sometimes a hell within myself.

Sir Thomas Browne, *Religio Medici*

The devil is the hero of all good literature.

William Blake

An apology for the Devil: It must be remembered that we have heard only one side of the case. God has written all the books.

Samuel Butler, *Notebooks*

If the lower animals, as we call them, were able to formulate a religion, they might differ greatly as to the shape of the beneficent Creator, but they would nearly all agree that the devil must be very like a big white man.

William Ralph Inge, "Patriotism"

The long, dull, monotonous years of middle-aged prosperity or middle-aged adversity are excellent campaigning weather [for the Devil].

C.S. Lewis, *The Screwtape Letters*

Satan was created by God, banished by God, and holds his influence by God's sufferance.

Jill Haak Adels, *The Wisdom of the Saints*

Hinduism

God seeks comrades and claims love, the Devil seeks slaves and claims obedience.

Rabindranath Tagore, *Fireflies*

Islam

Understand that for every rule which I have mentioned from the Koran, the Devil has one to match it, which he puts beside the proper rule in order to cause error.

Al-Ghazali, *The Just Balance*

Judaism

The sounding of the ram's horn on the New Year confounds Satan.

Mishnah, Rosh Hashanah 16

DISSENT

Christianity

There arose a dissension between the Pharisees and the Sadducees: and the multitude was divided.

For the Sadducees say that there is no resurrection, neither angel, nor spirit: but the Pharisees confess both.

Holy Bible, Acts 23:7-8

Genuine dissent must always keep a human measure. It must be free and spontaneous. The slighter gestures are often the more significant, because they are unpremeditated and they cannot be doctored beforehand by the propagandist.

Thomas Merton, *Conjectures of a Guilty Bystander*

Hinduism

Those who, murmuring against it, do not follow my doctrine, deluded in all knowledge, you must know that they are lost, the fools.

Bhagavad Gita, 3:32

Islam

A maimed nature and a deficient intelligence are far worse than simplicity. . . . One must use the sword and lances to prevent these people from using dialectic as 'Umar (the second Caliph) did with a man who asked him about ambiguous verses of the Koran. He hit him with a whip.

Al-Ghazali, *The Just Balance*

DOMINANCE

Christianity/Judaism

Thou shalt have no other gods before me.

Holy Bible, Exodus 20:3

It is he that sitteth upon the circle of the earth, and the inhabitants thereof are as grasshoppers.

Holy Bible, Isaiah 40:22

Christianity

If God be for us, who can be against us?

Holy Bible, Romans 8:31

I am Alpha and Omega, the beginning and the end.

Holy Bible, Revelation 21:6

Man proposes, but God disposes.

Thomas à Kempis, *The Imitation of Christ*

Jesus shall reign where'er the sun
Doth his successive journeys run;
His kingdom stretches from shore to shore,
Till moons shall wax and wane no more.

Isaac Watts, "Jesus Shall Reign Where'er the Sun"

All the kings of earth, before God, are as grasshoppers; they are nothing,
and less than nothing.

Jonathan Edwards, "Sinners in the Hands of an Angry God"

Holy, Holy Holy! Lord God Almighty!
    All thy works shall praise thy name, in earth and sky and sea:
Holy, Holy, Holy! Merciful and Mighty!
God in three persons, blessed Trinity!

Reginald Heber, "Holy, Holy, Holy!"

However great an individual may be, his total influence depends upon
his focusing strong social trends and drives precedent to him and now
concentrate in him.

Harry Emerson Fosdick, *Great Voices of the Reformation*

There is something both sublime and ridiculous in expecting either the
meek or the weak to inherit the earth.

Reinhold Niebuhr, *Moral Man and Immoral Society*

Confucianism

The Master said, "He who rules by moral force is like the pole star, which
remains in its place while all the lesser stars do homage to it."

Confucius, *Analects*

Hinduism

No other thing whatsoever exists higher than Me; all this universe is
strung on Me like heaps of pearls on a string.

Bhagavad Gita, 7:7

Islam

All that is in heaven and on earth declares the glory of Allah, the Sovereign, the Holy One, the Almighty, the Wise.

Koran, 62:1

DOUBT

Christianity/Judaism

If thou wilt not hearken unto the voice of the Lord thy God . . .

Thou [shalt] find no ease, neither shall the sole of thy foot have rest: but the Lord shall give thee . . . a trembling heart, and failing of eyes, and sorrow of mind:

And thy life shall hang in doubt before thee.

Holy Bible, Deuteronomy 28:15,65-66

Christianity

O thou of little faith, wherefore didst thou doubt?

Holy Bible, Matthew 14:31

A castle, called Doubting Castle, the owner whereof was Giant Despair.

John Bunyan, *The Pilgrim's Progress*

Doubt is the vestibule which all must pass before they can enter into the temple of truth.

Charles Caleb Colton, *Lacon*

There lives more faith in honest doubt,
Believe me, than in half the creeds.

Alfred, Lord Tennyson, "In Memoriam"

"Do you believe in God, yourself?" "I believe in Russia . . . I believe in her orthodoxy . . . I believe in the body of Christ . . . I believe that the new advent will take place in Russia . . . I believe . . . ," Shatov muttered frantically.

Fyodor Dostoyevsky, *The Possessed*

If you pray for bread and bring no basket to carry it, you prove the doubting spirit which may be the only hindrance to the boon you ask.

Dwight L. Moody

Doubt is nothing but a trivial agitation on the surface of the soul, while deep down there is a calm certainty.

Francois Mauriac, *God and Mammon*

Jesus blames no man for wanting to be sure. Jesus did not blame [St.] Thomas for his doubts; Jesus knew that once Thomas had fought his way through the wilderness of his doubts he would be the surest man in Christendom.

William Barclay, *The Master's Men*

Islam

There is no conviction in my heart which the thorns of doubt have failed to pierce: there is no faith in my soul which has not been subjected to all the conspiracies of disbelief.

Mawlana Azad, *Tarjuman al-Qur'an*

Judaism

Doubt is good for the human soul, its humility, and consequently its greater potential ultimately to discover its Creator.

Emanuel Rackman, *One Man's Judaism*

Secularism

God be with you if you can find him! He is not with me.

George Bernard Shaw, *The Black Girl in Search of God
and Some Lesser Tales*

DREAM

Buddhism

One should not discuss a dream
In front of a simpleton.

Mu-mon, *The Gateless Gate*

Christianity/Judaism

Your old men shall dream dreams, your young men shall see visions.

Holy Bible, Joel 2:28

Christianity

To die: to sleep.
To sleep? perchance to dream. Ay there's the rub;
For in that sleep of death what dreams may come,
When we have shuffled off this mortal coil,
Must give us pause.

William Shakespeare, *Hamlet*, Act 3, Sc. 1

They are not long, the days of wine and roses:
    Out of a misty dream
Our path emerges for a while, then closes
    Within a dream.

Ernest Dowson, "Vitae Summa Brevis Spem Nos Vetat Incohare Longam"

Dreams can be a strategic point for the Enemy since we cannot control them. Before I go to sleep, I often pray, "Lord, will you fill my subconscious with Your peace and love, by Your Holy Spirit?"

Corrie ten Boom, *Not I, But Christ*

I have a dream today.
    I have a dream that one day every valley shall be exalted, every hill and mountain shall be made low, the rough places will be made plain, and the crooked places will be made straight, and the glory of the Lord shall be revealed, and all flesh shall see it together.

Martin Luther King, Jr., Speech at the Lincoln Memorial, August 28, 1963

Hinduism

When he goes to sleep . . . he becomes a great king, as it were. Then he becomes a great Brahman, as it were. He enters the high and the low, as it were.

Upanishads, Brihadaranyaka

DUTY

Buddhism

Let no one forget his own duty for the sake of another's, however great; let a man, after he has discerned his own duty, be always attentive to his duty.

Dhammapada

Christianity/Judaism

Fear God and keep his commandments: for this is the whole duty of man.

Holy Bible, Ecclesiastes 12:13

Christianity

Yea, so much must I live for others that I am almost a stranger to myself.

Pope Innocent III

Each state of life has its special duties; by their accomplishments one may find happiness.

St. Nicholas of Flue

If the plowmen of the country were as negligent in their offices as prelates are, we should not long live, for the lack of sustenance.

Hugh Latimer, "Sermon of the Plow"

A sense of duty pursues us ever. It is omnipresent, like the Deity.

Daniel Webster, Oral argument in a murder case, April 6, 1830

The man of duty will end by having to fulfill his obligation even to the devil.

Dietrich Bonhoeffer, *Ethics*

Confucianism

Confucius said, "Filial duty nowadays means to be able to support one's parents. But we support even dogs and horses. If there is no feeling of reverence, wherein lies the difference?"

Confucius, *Analects*

Hinduism

The Gita attempts no concrete defintion of duty, but contents itself with saying that man should do his duty simply because it *is* his duty, and with perfect indifference to the results—reminding us of Kant's categorical imperative.

Franklin Edgerton, *The Bhagavad Gita*

Judaism

As men are in duty bound to win the approval of God, so are they in duty bound to win the approval of their fellows.

Talmud, Shekalim 3,2, Mishnah

Duty cannot exist without faith.

Benjamin Disraeli, Tancred

Kantianism

There is . . . only a single categorical imperative, and it is this: Act only on that principle which you could wish to become a universal law.

Immanuel Kant, The Metaphysic of Morals

Unitarianism

So nigh is grandeur to our dust,
    So near is God to man,
When duty whispers low, "Thou must,"
    The youth replies, "I can."

Ralph Waldo Emerson, "Voluntaries"

EDUCATION

Christianity/Judaism

Poverty and shame shall be to him that refuseth instruction.

Holy Bible, Proverbs 13:18

Train up a child in the way he should go: and when he is old, he will not depart from it.

Holy Bible, Proverbs 22:6

Christianity

Much learning doth make thee mad.

Holy Bible, Acts 26:24

Never be hard with children. Many a fine character has been ruined by the stupid brutality of pedagogues.

Martin Luther

More is often taught by a jest than by the most serious teaching.

Baltasar Gracian, *The Art of Worldly Wisdom*

The Lord opened unto me that being bred at Oxford or Cambridge was not enough to fit and qualify men to be ministers of Christ.

George Fox, *Journal*

I would rather be in heaven learning my ABCs than sitting in hell reading Greek. We have been clamoring for forty years for a learned ministry, and we have got it today. . . . Half of the literary preachers in this town are ABs, PhDs, LLDs, and ASSs.

Sam Jones

In a Christian society education must be religious, not in the sense that it will be administered by ecclesiastics, still less in the sense that it will exercise pressure, or attempt to instruct everyone in theology, but in the sense that its aims will be directed by a Christian philosophy of life.

T.S. Eliot, *The Idea of a Christian Society*

A nation of dunces can be safe only in a world of dunces.

C.S. Lewis, *Present Concerns*

A university, like a monastery . . . , is at once a microcosm and a paradise.

Thomas Merton, *Love and Living*

It should . . . be clear that the Religion Department is not a source of pervasive Christian influence at Yale, that its impact on the vast majority of students is negligible, and that the University does not recognize religion as an indispensable field of study for an educated man.

William F. Buckley, Jr., *God and Man at Yale*

Confucianism

The Master said, "I have transmitted what was taught to me without making up anything of my own. . . . I have listened in silence and noticed what was said; I have never grown tired of learning nor wearied of teaching others what I have learned."

Confucius, *Analects*

Hinduism

The knowledge that has been learned from a teacher best helps one to attain his end.

Upanishads, Chandogya

Islam

I say most unambiguously that on the Day of Judgment God will say, "You were the educated. Why did you not stop the ignorant ones from straying into sin?" Thus on Judgment Day the educated will be held responsible.

Sayyid Sultan

Judaism

Rabbi Nehorai said: "Move to a place where there is learning, because you cannot expect learning to move to you."

Pirke Aboth

One coin in a bottle rattles, but a bottle full of coins makes no sound. Similarly, the scholar who is the son of a scholar is modest; but the scholar who is the son of a yokel trumpets his knowledge all around.

Talmud, Baba Metzia 85b

Just as a person is commanded to honor and revere his father, so is he under an obligation to honor and revere his teacher, even to a greater extent than his father; for his father gave him life in this world, while his teacher who instructs him in wisdom secures for him life in the world to come.

Maimonides, *Mishneh Torah*

The Talmud scoffs at those who are "laden with books," people who have acquired much knowledge but little comprehension; who know the conclusions but not the principles which underlie them or the processes of thought which led to them.

Morris Adler, *The World of the Talmud*

It is wrong to define education as *preparation* for life. Learning *is* life, a supreme experience of living, a climax of existence.

Abraham Joshua Heschel, *The Insecurity of Freedom*

Stoicism

Only the educated are free.

Epictetus, *Discourses*

Unitarianism

There should be no economy in education. Money should never be weighed against the soul of a child.

William Ellery Channing

The things taught in colleges and schools are not an education, but the means of education.

Ralph Waldo Emerson, *Journals*

ENEMY

Christianity/Judaism

My desire is . . . that mine adversary had written a book.

Holy Bible, Job 31:35

If thine enemy be hungry, give him bread to eat; and if he be thirsty, give him water to drink.

Holy Bible, Proverbs 25:21

Christianity

Love your enemies, bless them that curse you, do good to them that hate you, and pray for them which despitefully use you, and persecute you.

Holy Bible, Matthew 5:44

The last enemy that shall be destroyed is death.

Holy Bible, 1 Corinthians 15:26

We wrestle not against flesh and blood, but against principalities, against powers, against the rulers of the darkness of this world, against spiritual wickedness in high places.

Holy Bible, Ephesians 6:12

May I be no man's enemy, and may I be the friend of that which is eternal and abides.

Eusebius of Caesarea

A wise man gets more use from his enemies than a fool from his friends.

Baltasar Gracian, *The Art of Worldly Wisdom*

He who loves his enemies betrays his friends; this is surely not what Jesus meant.

William Blake, "The Everlasting Gospel"

Deism

I have never made but one prayer to God, a very short one: "O Lord, make my enemies ridiculous." And God granted it.

Voltaire, *Letter to M. Damiliville*

Hinduism

My enemies' assaults press me on every side.
Since ye [the god Indra] control the fortunes of friend and foe,
Do ye then favor me on war's decisive day.

Rig-Veda

Islam

We will never get rid of our cousins, the children of Cain who always
support each other. If you defeat one by seizing his arm, the second one
will try to buy you with his money; if this fails, the third one will cheat
you in the name of faith! If none of these methods succeed, they will try
to achieve their ends by using science, art, philosophy or ideology.

Ali Shariati, *Hajj*

Judaism

Do no wrong to any enemy—that is the beginning. From the definite
negative follows the definite positive act. Only on this basis does the love
of the enemy not evaporate into empty sentiment.

Leo Baeck, *The Essence of Judaism*

Taoism

There is no greater mistake than to make light of an enemy. By making
light of an enemy many a kingdom has been lost.

Lao-tzu, *Tao-te ching*

ENVY

Christianity/Judaism

Fret not thyself because of evildoers, neither be thou envious against the
workers of iniquity.
  For they shall soon be cut down like the grass, and wither as the green herb.

Holy Bible, Psalms 37:1-2

Christianity

Let us not be desirous of vain glory, provoking one another, envying one
another.

Holy Bible, Galatians 5:26

Envy's a coal comes hissing hot from hell.

Philip James Bailey, *Festus*

Envy does not so much want the things for itself; it merely wants to take them away from the other person. The Stoics defined it as "grief at someone else's good."

William Barclay

Islam

The Moon was asked:
"What is your strongest desire?"
It answered:
"That the Sun should vanish, and should remain veiled forever in clouds."

Attur of Nishapur

Judaism

A sage is jealous of another sage, but not of one unlearned in his subject.

Talmud, Abodah Zarakh 55

ERROR

Christianity/Judaism

O my people, they which lead thee cause thee to err, and destroy the way of thy paths.

Holy Bible, Isaiah 3:12

They err in vision, they stumble in judgment.

Holy Bible, Isaiah 28:7

Christianity

Jesus answered and said unto them, Ye do err, not knowing the scriptures, nor the power of God.

Holy Bible, Matthew 22:29

Let him know, that he which converteth the sinner from the error of his way shall save a soul from death.

Holy Bible, James 5:20

To err is human, to forgive divine.

Alexander Pope, *An Essay on Criticism*

Confucianism

To err and not reform, this may indeed be called error.

Confucius, *Analects*

Islam

How curious that a man who closes his hand upon air so often thinks that he has a ruby within his grasp.

Idries Shah, *Caravan of Dreams*

It was not acceptable in classical Islam to declare that a genuine prophet was mistaken about anything, and least of all that Muhammad was.

George F. Hourani, *Reason and Tradition in Islamic Ethics*

ETERNITY

Christianity/Judaism

One generation passeth away, and another generation cometh: but the earth abideth for ever.

Holy Bible, Ecclesiastes 1:4

Who can number the sand of the sea, and the drops of rain, and the days of eternity?

The Apocrypha, Ecclesiasticus 1:2

Christianity

There shall be no night there; and they need no candle, neither light of the sun; for the Lord giveth them light: and they shall reign for ever and ever.

Holy Bible, Revelation 22:5

The present's nothing: but eternity
Abides for those on whom all truth, all good,
Hath shone, in one entire and perfect light.

St. Paulinus of Nola

Glory be to the Father, and to the Son, and to the Holy Ghost;
  As it were in the beginning, is now, and ever shall be, world without end. Amen.

Book of Common Prayer

The created world is but a small parenthesis in eternity.

Sir Thomas Browne, *Christian Morals*

I saw Eternity the other night,
Like a great ring of pure and endless light.

Henry Vaughan, "The World"

To see a world in a grain of sand
And a heaven in a wild flower,
Hold infinity in the palm of your hand
And eternity in an hour.

William Blake, "Auguries of Innocence"

Eternal life is not continuation of life after death. Eternal life is beyond past, present, and future: we come from it, we live in its presence, we return to it. It is never absent—it is the divine life in which we are rooted.

Paul Tillich, *The Eternal Now*

The eternity which is part of the environment of man is . . . the changeless source of man's changing being. . . . A spirit who can set time, nature, the world and being *per se* into juxtaposition to himself and inquire after the meaning of these things, proves that in some sense he stands outside and beyond them.

Reinhold Niebuhr, *The Nature and Destiny of Man*

Judaism

We are eternal wanderers, but deeply rooted in our own body and blood. And it is this rooting in ourselves, and in nothing but ourselves, that vouchsafes eternity.

Franz Rosenzweig, *The Star of Redemption*

Taoism

Heaven is eternal and Earth everlasting.
They can be eternal and everlasting because they do not exist for
    themselves,
And for this reason can exist forever.

Lao-tzu, *Tao-te ching*

ETHICS

Christianity/Judaism

The path of the just is as the shining light, that shineth more and more unto the perfect day.

Holy Bible, Proverbs 4:18

Christianity

Whatsoever things are true, whatsoever things are honest, whatsoever things are just, whatsoever things are pure, whatsoever things are lovely . . . think on these things.

Holy Bible, Philippians 4:8

It is only an ethical moment which can rescue us from the slough of barbarism, and the ethical comes into existence only in individuals.

Albert Schweitzer, *The Decay and Restoration of Civilization*

According to Christian ethics, man as such, every man, has a legitimate claim to be seen, affirmed, and accepted. Christian ethics is not neutral. It is not interested in some mighty It, no matter how lofty. Rather, it is concerned wholly and solely with I and Thou.

Karl Barth, *God Here and Now*

Human beings, all over the earth, have this curious idea that they ought to behave in a certain way, and cannot really get rid of it.

C.S. Lewis, *Mere Christianity*

The basis of the Christian ethic is the basis of the being of God and of the life of Jesus Christ—it is concern.

William Barclay, *Ethics in a Permissive Society*

Life is full of choices for which there is not a verse of Scripture.

Jerry Falwell, *Finding Inner Peace and Strength*

Confucianism

Master Yu said,
"In your promises cleave to what is right,
And you will be able to fulfill your word."

Confucius, *Analects*

Deism

The only moral lesson which is suited for a child—the most important lesson for every time of life—is this: "Never hurt anybody."

Jean Jacques Rousseau, *Emile*

Islam

Islam is a complete way of life. It integrates man with God, awakens in him a new moral consciousness and invites him to deal with all the problems of life—individual and social, economic and political, national and international—in accordance with his commitment to God.

Salem Azzam, *Islam: Its Meaning and Message*

Judaism

When man appears before the Throne of Judgment, the first question he is asked is not, "Have you believed in God?" or, "Have you prayed or performed ritual acts?" but, "Have you dealt honorably, faithfully in all your dealings with your fellowman."

Talmud, Shabbat 31a

With this faith [of Judaism] in the commanding God there has come into the world the opposition to any sort of ethical opportunism, to any weakening or blurring of ethical standards, and to any despair about the reality of the absolute good.

Leo Baeck, *The Essence of Judaism*

Stoicism

Live among men as if God beheld you; speak to God as if men were listening.

Seneca, *Epistles*

Unitarianism

Share everything.
Play fair.
Don't hit people.

Robert Fulghum, *All I Really Need to Know I Learned in Kindergarten*

EVIL

Buddhism

And the Buddha said, "If a man foolishly does me wrong, I will return to him the protection of my ungrudging love; the more evil comes from him, the more good shall go from me."

The Sutra of Forty-two Sections

Christianity/Judaism

Yea, though I walk through the valley of the shadow of death, I will fear no evil: for thou art with me.

Holy Bible, Psalms 23:4

Christianity

Speak evil of no man.

Holy Bible, Titus 3:2

Men never do evil so completely and cheerfully as when they do it from religious conviction.

Blaise Pascal, *Pensées*

We shut our eyes to the beginnings of evil because they are small, and in this weakness is contained the germ of our defeat.

Samuel Taylor Coleridge, *Aids to Reflection*

Adam and Eve were guilty of disobedience and presumption, yet they did not create the snake.

George A. Buttrick, *God, Pain, and Evil*

We cannot contemplate without terror the extent of the evil which man can do and endure.

Simone Weil, *Gravity and Grace*

Evil is not guilt, as so many amateur psychiatrists pretend, but rather the effort to escape it. Evil is the human soul hiding from itself.

William Sloane Coffin, *Living the Truth in a World of Illusions*

Confucianism

People do evil simply because they do not know.

Ch'eng I, *I-shu*

Hinduism

Must I do all the evil I can before I learn to shun it? Is it not enough to know the evil to shun it? If not, we should be sincere enough to admit that we love evil too much to give it up.

Mohandas K. Gandhi, *Non-Violence in Peace and War*

Islam

Those who seek gain in evil, and are girt round by their sins—they are companions of the fire: Therein shall they abide forever.

Koran, 2:81

We deserve punishment for the moral evil that appears to proceed from us as its subject, by which we are guilty of rebellion against God, according to the decrees of His providence, which is justice and truth itself.

Ibn Hazm, *Fisal*

Judaism

Every ignoramus imagines that all that exists exists with a view to his individual sake; it is as if there were nothing that exists except him. And if something happens to him that is contrary to what he wishes, he makes the trenchant judgment that all that exists is an evil.

Maimonides, *Guide of the Perplexed*

The so-called evil is fully and as a primary element included in the power of God, who "forms the light and creates darkness" (Isa. 45:7). The divine sway is not answered by anything which is evil in itself, but by the individual human beings, through whom alone the so-called evil, the directionless power, can become real evil.

Martin Buber, *Israel and the World*

The new wicked ones [Nazis] were coldly sober, and their thirst for Jewish blood was unquenchable. They did not honor either Jewish martyrdom or Jewish heroism but did what they could to destroy the opportunity for both. . . . From the viewpoint of the wicked ones the ideal Jewish death was that of the *Muselmann* dropping dead from exhaustion, covered with filth and lice.

Emil L. Fackenheim, *What Is Judaism?*

Unitarianism

There are a thousand hacking at the branches of evil to one who is striking at the root.

Henry David Thoreau, *Walden*

EXPERIENCE

Buddhism

Facts of experience are valued in Zen more than representations, symbols, and concepts—that is to say, substance is everything in Zen and form nothing.

Daisetz Teitaro Suzuki, *Essays in Zen Buddhism*

Christianity/Judaism

I have learned by experience that the Lord hath blessed me.

Holy Bible, Genesis 30:27

God wishes to test you like gold in the furnace. The dross is consumed by the fire, but the pure gold remains and its value increases.

St. Jerome Emiliani

Christianity

I know for certain that God teaches me, for I know this by experience.

Huldrych Zwingli

There is . . . no substitute for first-hand experience in the spiritual life. We must believe the explorers of the high places of the unseen world when they tell us that they have been there, and found what they sought. But they cannot really tell us *what* they found; if we wish to see what they have seen, we must live as they have lived.

William Ralph Inge, *Wit and Wisdom of Dean Inge*

The older a man grows the more mysterious life becomes to him. We sometimes say to youth that when he grows up he will know more, but that is a half-truth. In general, an increasing experience of life only deepens the sense of its mystery.

Harry Emerson Fosdick, *Riverside Sermons*

The realities of faith are not felt with the same solidity as the reality of experience. . . . And so, inevitably, providentially, there must be terror and bewilderment when one has to pass from one to the other.

Pierre Teilhard de Chardin, *The Making of a Mind*

Confucianism

Fan Chi'ih asked the Master to teach him about farming. The Master said, "You had much better consult some old farmer."

Confucius, *Analects*

Cosmic

The cosmic religious experience is the strongest and noblest driving force behind scientific research.

Albert Einstein, *Cosmic Religion*

Judaism

Rabbi Johanan would rise before an aged Gentile and say: "How many events has he experienced!"

Talmud, Kiddushin 33

Pantheism

You cannot step twice into the same river; for other and ever other rivers flow on.

Heraclitus, *Cosmic Fragments*

FAILURE

Christianity/Judaism

How are the mighty fallen in the midst of the battle!

Holy Bible, 2 Samuel 1:25

They all shall fail together.

Holy Bible, Isaiah 31:3

Christianity

How many failures have there been for one success, how many days of misery for one hour's joy, how many sins for a solitary saint?

Pierre Teilhard de Chardin, *The Phenomenon of Man*

It is better to fail in a cause that will ultimately succeed than to succeed in a cause that will ultimately fail.

Peter Marshall

Failure is nothing but the kiss of Jesus.

Mother Teresa of Calcutta, *Life in the Spirit*

Failure doesn't mean God has abandoned you . . . it does mean God has a better idea!

Robert H. Schuller, *You Can Become the Person You Want to Be*

Liberal reformers and disappointed revolutionaries meet one another at the grave of their expectations.

Hans Küng, *On Being a Christian*

Hinduism

For one that has been esteemed, disgrace
  Is worse than death.

Bhagavad Gita, 2:34

Islam

Originally, with Allah's spirit in your heart, you were supposed to shoulder the responsibility of being Allah's trustee on earth. You were granted time as a means for fulfilling this task but you failed because the gift was used carelessly! . . . Oh trustee and viceregent of Allah on earth, you have turned to money, sex, greed, aggression, and dishonesty.

Ali Shariati, *Hajj*

Judaism

It is usually in the wake of frustration, in moments of crisis and self-disillusionment, and rarely out of astonishment at man's glorious achievements, that radical reflection comes to pass.

Abraham Joshua Heschel, *Who Is Man?*

FAITH

Buddhism

If a man's faith is unsteady, if he does not know the true law, if his only peace of mind is troubled, his knowledge will never be perfect.

Dhammapada

Christianity

Behold, there arose a great tempest in the sea, insomuch that the ship was covered with the waves; but [Christ] was asleep.

And his disciples came to him, and awoke him, saying, Lord, save us: we perish.

And he saith unto them, Why are ye fearful, O ye of little faith? Then he arose, and rebuked the winds and the sea; and there was a great calm.

Holy Bible, Matthew 8:24-26

Thy faith hath made thee whole.

Holy Bible, Luke 17:19

We walk by faith, not by sight.

Holy Bible, 2 Corinthians 5:7

How say some among you that there is no resurrection of the dead?
But if there be no resurrection of the dead, then is Christ not risen:
And if Christ be not risen, then is our preaching vain, and your faith is also vain.

Holy Bible, 1 Corinthians 15:12-14

Faith is the substance of things hoped for, the evidence of things not seen.

Holy Bible, Hebrews 11:1

Since gold and silver, which are only corruptible metals, are purified and tested by fire, it is but reasonable that our faith, which surpasses all the riches of the world, should be tried.

St. Peter

Faith is a living, well-founded confidence in the grace of God, so perfectly certain that it would die a thousand times rather than surrender its conviction.

Martin Luther, *Preface to St. Paul's Epistle to the Romans*

Faith is the union of God with the soul.

St. John of the Cross

Thou hast no faith left now, unless thou hadst two,
And that's far worse than none. Better have none
Than plural faith, which is too much by one.

William Shakespeare, *The Two Gentlemen of Verona*, Act 5, Sc. 4

To believe only possibilities is not faith, but mere philosophy.

Sir Thomas Browne, *Religio Medici*

Faith declares what the senses do not declare, but not the contrary of what they see. It is above them, not contrary to them.

Blaise Pascal, *Pensées*

To wish to have and hold a faith that is an echo proves that a man is incapable of religion; to demand it of others shows that there is no understanding of religion. You wish always to stand on your own feet and go your own way, and this worthy intent should not scare you from religion. Religion is no slavery, no captivity, least of all for your reason.

Friedrich Schleiermacher, *On Religion*

We have but faith: we cannot know;
    For knowledge is of things we see;
    And yet we trust it comes from thee,
A beam in darkness: let it grow.

> Alfred, Lord Tennyson, "In Memoriam"

I never talked with God,
    Nor visited in Heaven—
Yet certain am I of the spot
    As if the chart were given.

> Emily Dickinson, "I Never Saw a Moor"

Faith is a kind of climbing instinct, which draws us upward and onward.

> William Ralph Inge, *Wit and Wisdom of Dean Inge*

Faith is a prodigious power, to be used or misused; the fate of mankind depends largely on what is done with it. We can never solve the problem by eliminating faith. Of all mad faiths the maddest is the faith that we can get rid of faith.

> Harry Emerson Fosdick, *Riverside Sermons*

The seriousness and the power of faith are the seriousness and power of the truth, which is identical with God Himself.

> Karl Barth, *Credo*

The final test of religious faith . . . is whether it will enable men to endure insecurity without complacency or despair.

> Reinhold Niebuhr, "The Religious Traditions of Our Nation"

Faith is related not to self-assurance but to God; not to an event, but to truth.

> Fulton J. Sheen, *On Being Human*

Religious faith is not a storm cellar to which men and women can flee for refuge from the storms of life. It is, instead, an inner spiritual strength which enables them to face those storms with hope and serenity.

> Sam J. Ervin, Jr., *Humor of a Country Lawyer*

We take our faith for granted, and what we take for granted we never take seriously.

> Vance Havner, *The Vance Havner Quotebook*

The Christian faith is an interpretive scheme which copes with the ultimate questions man must ask himself, questions to which there are no demonstrable answers.

Andrew M. Greeley, *Life for a Wanderer*

Hinduism

When one has faith, then he thinks. One who lacks faith does not think.

Upanishads, Chandogya

The man unknowing and without faith,
    His soul full of doubt, perishes.

Bhagavad Gita, 4:40

Islam

Faith does not increase, nor does it decrease; because a diminution in it would be unbelief.

Abu Hanifa, *A Rosary of Islamic Readings*

Judaism

Rabbi Eliezer the Great said: "He who has a morsel of bread in his vessel and yet says, 'What shall I eat tomorrow?' is of those of little faith."

Talmud, Sotah 48b

Certainty of faith is not accessible to the Man of Today, nor can it be made accessible to him. . . . But he is not denied the possibility of holding himself open to faith. . . . He too may open himself to the book [Torah] and let its rays strike him where they will.

Martin Buber, "The Man of Today and the Jewish Bible"

Mormonism

Yea, there are many who do say: If thou wilt show unto us a sign from heaven, then we shall know of a surety; then we shall believe. Now I ask, is this faith? . . . Nay; for if a man knoweth a thing he hath no cause to believe, for he knoweth it.

Book of Mormon, Alma 32:17-18

Secularism

I admire the serene assurance of those who have religious faith. It is wonderful to observe the calm confidence of a Christian with four aces.

Mark Twain

Where there is the necessary technical skill to move mountains, there is no need for the faith that moves mountains.

Eric Hoffer

Unitarianism

Beautiful ideals, which are creeds, not deeds, are religious window dressing and are meaningless. The test of faith is life.

George N. Marshall, *Challenge of a Liberal Faith*

FAME

Christianity/Judaism

From a very far country thy servants are come because of the name of the Lord thy God: for we have heard the fame of him, and all that he did in Egypt.

Holy Bible, Joshua 9:9

Christianity

Jesus returned in the power of the spirit into Galilee: and there went out a fame of him through all the region round about.

Holy Bible, Luke 4:14

Fame sometimes hath created something of nothing.

Thomas Fuller, "Fame"

Hinduism

Mitra, whose fame is spread abroad,
In greatness who transcends the sky,
And in renown transcends the earth.

Rig-Veda

[Note: Mitra is a kindly solar deity.]

Stoicism

All is ephemeral—fame and the famous as well.

Marcus Aurelius, *Meditations*

FEAR

Christianity/Judaism

Though a host should encamp against me, my heart shall not fear.

Holy Bible, Psalms 27:3

Christianity

God hath not given us the spirit of fear; but of power, and of love, and of a sound mind.

Holy Bible, 2 Timothy 1:7

A great fear, when it is ill-managed, is the parent of superstition, but a discrete and well-guided fear produces religion.

Jeremy Taylor, *The Rule and Exercise of Holy Living*

No coward soul is mine,
No trembler in the world's storm-troubled sphere;
I see Heaven's glories shine,
And faith shines equal, armoring me from fear.

Charlotte Bronte, "Last Lines"

Private Enemy Number One is fear.

John A. Redhead, *Putting Your Faith to Work*

Hinduism

He who knows the joy of Brahman, which words cannot express and the mind cannot reach, is free from fear.

Upanishads, Taittiriya

Let our first act each morning be the following resolve: I shall not fear anyone on earth. I shall fear only God.

Mohandas K. Gandhi, *The Story of My Experiments with Truth*

Islam

The greatest obstacle to love is fear. It has been the source of all defects in human behavior throughout the ages.

Mahmoud Mohamed Taha, *The Second Message of Islam*

Judaism

He who has been bitten by a snake is frightened by a rope.

Talmud, Kohelet Rabbah 7:4

Unitarianism

There is such a thing as hell on earth. For the most part, it is populated by people who fear so deeply that they cannot love.

F. Forrester Church, *Entertaining Angels*

FOOLISHNESS

Christianity/Judaism

The way of a fool is right in his own eyes: but he that hearkeneth unto counsel is wise.

Holy Bible, Proverbs 12:15

A fool's mouth is his destruction.

Holy Bible, Proverbs 18:7

Christianity

I will say to my soul, Soul, thou hast much goods laid up for many years; take thine ease, eat, drink, and be merry.

But God said, unto him, Thou fool, this night thy soul shall be required of thee.

Holy Bible, Luke 12:19-20

Man is so made that by dint of telling him he is a fool he ends by believing it; and by dint of repeating it to himself he teaches himself to believe it.

Blaise Pascal, *Pensées*

The fool shall not enter into heaven be he ever so holy.

William Blake

This much is certain, that [foolishness] is a moral rather than an intellectual defect. There are people who are mentally agile but foolish, and people who are mentally slow but very far from foolish—a discovery that we make to our surprise as a result of particular situations.

Dietrich Bonhoeffer, *Letters and Papers from Prison*

Hinduism

Those abiding in the midst of ignorance,
Self-wise, thinking themselves learned,
Running hither and thither, go around deluded,
Like blind men led by one who is himself blind.

Upanishads, Katha

Islam

The harshest of all voices is the braying of an ass.

Koran, 31:19

Judaism

People say, "You can do nothing with a fool. Weep before him or laugh with him, it will make no difference."

Talmud, Sanhedrin 103a

FORGIVENESS

Christianity/Judaism

Blessed is he whose transgression is forgiven, whose sin is covered.

Holy Bible, Psalms 32:1

Christianity

Forgive, and ye shall be forgiven.

Holy Bible, Luke 6:37

Father, forgive them; for they know not what they do.

Holy Bible, Luke 23:34

Pardon one another so that later on you will not remember the injury. The recollection of an injury is . . . a rusty arrow and poison for the soul.

St. Francis of Paola

It is easier to forgive an enemy than to forgive a friend.

William Blake, *Jerusalem*

You ought certainly to forgive them, as a Christian, but never to admit them in your sight, or allow their names to be mentioned in your hearing.

Jane Austen, *Pride and Prejudice*

If we really want . . . to learn how to forgive, perhaps we had better start with something easier than the Gestapo.

C.S. Lewis, *Mere Christianity*

The only people . . . who can be trusted with forgiveness are those who at the same time acknowledge their solidity in sin with the forgiven. Otherwise, forgiveness, like justice, is an instrument of oppression.

A. Boyce Gibson, *The Religion of Dostoyevsky*

Teach your children how to forgive, make your homes places of love and forgiveness; make your streets and neighborhoods centers of peace and reconciliation.

Pope John Paul II, Speech at Drogheda, Ireland, September 29, 1979

Hinduism

If I treated Thee disrespectfully, to make sport of Thee,
    In the course of amusement, resting, sitting, or eating,
Either alone, O unshaken one, or in the presence of others,
    For that I beg forgiveness of Thee, the immeasurable one.

Bhagavad Gita, 11:42

Islam

He who forgives, and is reconciled unto his enemy, shall receive his reward from Allah.

Koran, 42:40

If you do not make mistakes and then ask for forgiveness, Allah shall replace you by people who make mistakes, ask for forgiveness, and are forgiven.

Muhammad

O God, Thou Who knowest all secrets!
I know that Thou art Omnipotent, Omniscient.
Thy infinite mercy, I am sure,
Will not deny me forgiveness for my sins.

Ismail Pasha Sabri, *A Rosary of Islam Readings*

Judaism

It is fitting for a great God to forgive great sinners.

Talmud, Wayyikra Rabbah 5, end

FREEDOM

Agnosticism

I am not so much for the freedom of religion as I am for the religion of freedom.

Robert G. Ingersoll

Buddhism

The fundamental aim of Buddhism is to attain emancipation from all bondage arising from the duality of birth and death.

Masao Abe, "God, Emptiness, and the True Self"

Christianity/Judaism

Let my people go.

Holy Bible, Exodus 5:1

Christianity

Stand fast . . . in the liberty wherewith Christ hath made us free, and be not entangled again with the yoke of bondage.

Holy Bible, Galatians 5:1

Long may our land be bright
With freedom's holy light;
Protect us by Thy might,
    Great God, our King.

Samuel Francis Smith, "America"

Liberty is the soul's right to breathe.

Henry Ward Beecher, Proverbs from Plymouth Pulpit

In the beauty of the lilies Christ was born across the sea,
With a glory in His bosom that transfigures you and me;
As He died to make men holy, let us die to make men free,
    While God is marching on.

Julia Ward Howe, "Battle Hymn of the Republic"

The gift of freedom implies the danger of servitude.

Paul Tillich, The Eternal Now

Man is free only in his constituted nature. A fish is free only as a fish: its bony structure and its habitat define its freedom. It cannot fly like an eagle or walk like a man; and if it should leap out of the pond "into a wider world," it would not be free: it would be dead.

George A. Buttrick, *Christ and History*

[The Cistercian and Carthusian monks] were poor, they had nothing, and therefore they were free and possessed everything, and everything they touched struck off something of the fire of divinity.

Thomas Merton, *The Seven Storey Mountain*

When we let freedom ring, when we let it ring from every village and every hamlet, from every state and every city, we will be able to speed up that day when all of God's children, black men and white men, Jews and Gentiles, Protestants and Catholics, will be able to join hands and sing in the words of the old Negro spiritual, "Free at last! Free at last! Thank God Almighty, we are free at last!"

Martin Luther King, Jr., Speech at the Lincoln Memorial, August 28, 1963

Hinduism

By knowing God one is released from all fetters.

Upanishads, Svetasvatara

Judaism

It is dangerous to take human freedom for granted, to regard it as a prerogative rather than as an obligation, as an ultimate fact rather than as an ultimate goal. It is the beginning of wisdom to be amazed at the fact of our being free.

Abraham Joshua Heschel, *The Insecurity of Freedom*

FRIENDSHIP

Buddhism

Those who cannot enlighten themselves should have good and learned friends to show them the way to see their nature.

The Platform Scripture

Christianity/Judaism

A man that hath friends must show himself friendly.

Holy Bible, Proverbs 18:24

A faithful friend is the medicine of life.

The Apocrypha, Ecclesiasticus 6:16

Christianity

Greater love hath no man than this, that a man lay down his life for his friends.

Holy Bible, John 15:13

How often have I found no friendship where I thought I should have found it, and how often have I found it where I least presumed it to be.

Thomas à Kempis, *The Imitation of Christ*

For those who dwell in the world and desire to embrace true virtue, it is necessary to unite themselves together by a holy and sacred friendship. By this means they encourage, assist, and conduct one another to good deeds.

St. Francis de Sales, *Introduction to the Devout Life*

The insight of a true friend is more useful than the goodwill of others: therefore gain [friends] by choice, not by chance.

Baltasar Gracian, *The Art of Worldly Wisdom*

Some friendships are made by nature, some by contract, some by interest, and some by souls.

Jeremy Taylor

I wager that if all men knew what each said of the other there would not be left four friends in the world.

Blaise Pascal, *Pensées*

Every man should have a fair-sized cemetery in which to bury the faults of his friends.

Henry Ward Beecher

Pure friendship is an image of the original and perfect friendship that belongs to the Trinity and is the very essence of God.

Simone Weil, *Waiting for God*

Hinduism

What has become of those former friendships
When we two held erstwhile unbroken converse?

Rig-Veda

Islam

He who has a thousand friends has not a friend to spare.
And he who has one enemy will meet him everywhere.

Ali Ibn Abi Talib, *Sentences*

Judaism

In choosing a friend, go up a step.

Talmud, Yebamot 63a

Rabbi Joshua, when asked by his teacher to discover the best and worst thing in a man's striving toward self-improvement, replied that the best thing is to have a good friend and the worst is to have a bad friend.

Louis Jacobs, *What Does Judaism Say About* . . . ?

GIFTS

Christianity/Judaism

He that giveth unto the poor shall not lack.

Holy Bible, Proverbs 28:27

Christianity

It is more blessed to give than to receive.

Holy Bible, Acts 20:35

God loveth a cheerful giver.

Holy Bible, 2 Corinthians 9:7

Every good gift and every perfect gift is from above.

Holy Bible, James 1:17

Never look a gift horse in the mouth.

St. Jerome, "On the Epistle to the Ephesians"

A man there was, though some did count him mad,
The more he cast away the more he had.

John Bunyan, *The Pilgrim's Progress*

A cheerful giver does not count the cost of what he gives. His heart is set on pleasing and cheering him to whom the gift is given.

St. Julian of Norwich, *Revelations of Divine Love*

God's gifts put man's best dreams to shame.

Elizabeth Barrett Browning, *Sonnets from the Portuguese*

Hinduism

On what are the gifts to the priests based?
On faith, for when one has faith, then one gives to the priests.

Upanishads, Brihadaranyaka

Islam

Behold! You are called upon to give to the cause of Allah. Some of you are stingy; yet whoever is stingy to this cause is stingy at the expense of his own soul. Indeed, Allah will exchange you for others.

Koran, 47:38

Poetics

You often say, "I would give, but only to the deserving."
The trees in your orchard say not so, nor the flocks in your pastures.
They give that they may live, for to withhold is to perish.

Kahlil Gibran, *The Prophet*

GOAL

Christianity

Then said one unto him, Lord, are there few that be saved? And he said unto them,

Strive to enter in at the strait gate: for many, I say unto you, will seek to enter in, and shall not be able.

Holy Bible, Luke 13:23-24

Dost thou wish to rise? Begin by descending. You plan a tower that shall pierce the clouds? Lay first the foundations on humility.

St. Augustine

Ah, but a man's reach should exceed his grasp,
Or what's a heaven for?

Robert Browning, "Andrea del Sarto"

A lecturer recently, with an engagement to speak in a certain city, arrived on a train that was late. He jumped from the train into a taxi and said to the chauffeur, "Drive fast, step on it!" And the driver did. He stepped on it. And when, after some fifteen minutes, speeding through the streets and skidding around corners, the lecturer said, "Well, aren't we about there?" the taxi driver said, "I don't know, sir. You never told me where we were to go."

Harry Emerson Fosdick, Riverside Sermons

It is possible to be defeated by one's secondary successes. Thus the good becomes the enemy of the best and we settle for lesser goals than the heights we might have reached.

Vance Havner, The Vance Havner Quotebook

The goal of the Christian life is not to save your soul but to transcend yourself, to vindicate the human struggle of which all of us are a part, to keep hope advancing.

William Sloane Coffin, Living the Truth in a World of Illusions

Hinduism

I would attain to that . . . dear dominion
Where men devoted to the gods do revel.

Rig-Veda

Humanism

We turn toward God only to obtain the impossible.

Albert Camus, The Myth of Sisyphus

Islam

For man, everything is temporary, changing, perishing and dying; yet this eternal movement [toward Allah] is continuous and the direction is always there!

Ali Shiarti, Hajj

Mormonism

This is the place!

Brigham Young

[Young exclaimed this upon first seeing the region of the Great Salt Lake.]

Taoism

An ordinary person lacks will power, fortitude, and strength. An unusual man is one of supreme determination. Once he puts his mind to it, anything can be done. The sages say a rock can come alive if one worships it with total belief.

Deng Ming-Dao, *Seven Bamboo Tablets of the Cloudy Satchel*

GOD

Christianity/Judaism

The eternal God is thy refuge.

Holy Bible, Deuteronomy 33:27

Arise, call upon thy god.

Holy Bible, Jonah 1:6

Christianity

Well, Master, thou hast said the truth: for there is one God; and there is none other but he.

Holy Bible, Mark 12:32

God is love; and he that dwelleth in love dwelleth in God, and God in him.

Holy Bible, 1 John 4:16

The glory of God is man fully alive.

St. Irenaeus, *Against Heresies*

Almost everything said of God is unworthy, for the very reason that it is capable of being said.

St. Gregory the Great, *Magna moralia*

The more God is in all things, the more He is outside them.

Meister Eckhart

Man considers the actions, but God weighs the intentions.

Thomas à Kempis, *The Imitation of Christ*

The majesty of God in itself goes beyond the capacity of human understanding and cannot be comprehended by it . . . .we must adore its loftiness rather than investigate it, so that we do not remain overwhelmed by so great a splendor.

John Calvin, *Instruction in Faith*

Inconceivable that God should exist, and inconceivable that He should not exist.

> Blaise Pascal, *Pensées*

God is a spirit, a fire, an essence and a light; and yet again he is none of these things.

> Angelus Silesius, *Cherubic Pilgrim*

Praise God, from whom all blessings flow;
Praise Him, all creatures here below;
Praise Him above, ye heavenly host;
Praise Father, Son, and Holy Ghost.

> Thomas Ken, "Morning Hymn" and "Evening Hymn"

The usual conception of God as one single being outside of the world and behind the world is not the beginning and the end of religion. . . . The true nature of religion is neither this idea nor any other, but immediate consciousness of the Deity as He is found in ourselves and in the world.

> Friedrich Schleiermacher, *On Religion*

The word "God" is a Theology in itself, indivisibly one, inexhaustibly various.

> John Henry Newman, *The Idea of a University*

I fled Him down the nights and down the days;
    I fled Him down the arches of the years;
I fled Him down the labyrinthine ways
    Of my own mind; and in the midst of tears
I hid from Him.

> Francis Thompson, "The Hound of Heaven"

We must look for God where He *could* be found—not in the wide stellar spaces, not "in eagle's wing or insect's eye," not at the end of a logical syllogism. If He is to be found at all we must look for him in the spiritual realm.

> Rufus M. Jones, *Social Law in the Spiritual World*

Man cannot of himself really believe in God. It is because man cannot do that that God reveals himself.

> Karl Barth, *Credo*

Even bein' Gawd ain't no bed of roses.

> Marc Connelly, *The Green Pastures*, Act 2, Sc. 6

The word *God* in our Anglo-Saxon speech comes from the same root as the word *good*. The "proof" of God is given in subtle ways, not by an onrush of theological armies. It comes in our thankfulness for a fine summer day, for we do not then thank trees and soil (that would be ludicrous) but we are grateful to—Whom?

George A. Buttrick, *God, Pain, and Evil*

I [Screwtape, a senior official in Satan's "Lowerarchy"] have known cases where what the patient [a Christian] called his "God" was actually *located*—up and to the left at the corner of the bedroom ceiling, or inside his own head, or in a crucifix on the wall. But whatever the nature of the composite object, you [a junior devil on earth] must keep him praying to it—to the thing that he has made, not to the Person who has made him.

C. S. Lewis, *The Screwtape Letters*

To ask for a proof of the existence of God is on a par with asking for a proof of the existence of beauty. If God does not lie at the end of a telescope, neither does he lie at the end of any syllogism.

Walter T. Stace, *Time and Eternity*

Millions . . . will readily enough affirm that there is a God, but His existence or nonexistence is actually low on the totem pole of their concerns.

James A. Pike, *If This Be Heresy*

Christian Science

God is incorporeal, divine, supreme, infinite Mind, Spirit, Soul, Principle, Life, Truth, Love.

Mary Baker Eddy, *Science and Health*

Cosmic

God is subtle, but he is not malicious.

Albert Einstein

Deism

If God did not exist, it would be necessary to invent him.

Voltaire, *"A l'Auteur du Livre des Trois Imposteurs"*

It does me no injury for my neighbor to say there are twenty gods or no God. It neither picks my pocket nor breaks my leg.

Thomas Jefferson, *Notes on the State of Virginia*

Hinduism

Grasping without hands, hasting without feet, he sees without eyes, he hears without ears. He knows what can be known, but no one knows him.

Upanishads, Svetasvatara

I am the father of this world,
    The mother, the establisher, the grandsire,
The object of knowledge, the purifier, the sacred syllable *om*,
    The verse of praise, the chant, and the sacrificial formula;

Bhagavad Gita, 9:17–18

In wild and lonely places, at any time, one may chance on the Great God [Shiva], for such are His most favored haunts. Once seen, there is no mistaking Him. Yet He has no look of being rich or powerful. His skin is covered with white wood-ashes. His clothing is but the religious wanderer's yellow cloth. The coils of matted hair are piled high on the top of His head. In one hand He carries the begging-bowl, and in the other His tall staff, crowned with the trident. And sometimes He goes from door to door at midday, asking alms.

Sister Nivedita, *Cradle Tales of Hinduism*

From a very early period a Hindu was conscious of the fact that the multitudinous deities of his pantheon really illustrate the various ways of describing one single God, the eternally existent One Being with his manifold attributes and manifestations.

Jitendra Nath Banerjea, "The Hindu Concept of God"

Islam

In the name of Allah, Most Gracious, Most Merciful.
Praise be to Allah, the Cherisher and Sustainer of the worlds;
Most Gracious, Most Merciful;
Lord of the Day of Judgment.
Thee do we worship, and Thine aid we seek.

Koran, 1:1-5

Who has made the earth your couch, and the heavens your canopy, and sent down rain from the heavens, and brought forth therewith fruits for your sustenance?
    Then set not up rivals unto God when ye know the truth.

Koran, 2:22

If the world had two gods, it would surely go to ruin—this is the first premise. Now it is known that it has not gone to ruin—this is the second premise. From these premises the conclusion must of necessity follow, that is, the denial of two gods.

Al-Ghazali, *The Just Balance*

Judaism

All attributes ascribed to God are attributes of His acts, and do not imply that God has any qualities.

Maimonides, *Guide of the Perplexed*

I believe with perfect faith that the Creator, blessed be his name, is not a body, and that he is free from all the accidents of matter, and that he has not any form whatsoever.

Maimonides, *Thirteen Principles*

The only God worth talking about is a God that cannot be talked about.

Walter Kaufmann, *I and Thou: A Prologue*

Antiquity arrived at monism, but no more. World and man have to become God's nature, have to submit to apotheosis, but God never lowers himself to them. He does not give of himself, does not love, does not have to love. For he keeps his physis to himself, and, therefore remains what he is: the metaphysical.

Franz Rosenzweig, *The Star of Redemption*

Nonsectarian

Suppose it were true that God was really up there, a "lure for our feelings," as Whitehead, not to mention Aristotle, had fondly maintained—bespectacled old Jahweh, scratching his chin through his mountains of beard.

John Gardner, *Mickelsson's Ghosts*

Pantheism

In order to make Himself known to men, God can and need use neither words nor miracles, nor any other created thing, but only Himself.

Spinoza, *The Book of God*

Platonism

God is a being of perfect simplicity and truth, both in deed and word, and neither changes in himself nor imposes upon others.

Plato, *Republic*

Secularism

There was a day when Jupiter was the king of the gods, and any man who doubted his puissance was *ipso facto* a barbarian and an ignoramus. But where in all the world is there a man who worships Jupiter today?

H.L. Mencken, "Memorial Service"

Stoicism

He is all mind. His being infinite—
All that we see and all that we do not see.
The Lord of heaven and earth, the God of Gods.
Without Him nothing is. Yet what He is
We know not!

Seneca, "The End of Being"

Any one thing in the creation is sufficient to demonstrate a Providence to a humble and grateful mind.

Epictetus, *Discourses*

Unitarianism

Without God our existence has no support, our life no aim, our improvements no permanence, our best labors no sure and enduring results, our spiritual weakness no power to lean upon, and our noblest aspirations and desires no pledge of being realized in a better state.

William Ellery Channing, *The Liberal Gospel*

GOOD AND EVIL

Christianity/Judaism

Your eyes shall be opened, and ye shall be as gods, knowing good and evil.

Holy Bible, Genesis 3:5

Woe unto them that call evil good, and good evil.

Holy Bible, Isaiah 5:20

Christianity

Abhor that which is evil; cleave to that which is good.

Holy Bible, Romans 12:9

Evil cannot exist but in good; sheer evil is impossible.

St. Thomas Aquinas, *Summa Contra Gentiles*

Man has always been dexterous at confusing evil with good. That was Adam's and Eve's problem, and it is our problem today. If evil were not made to appear attractive, there would be no such thing as temptation.

Billy Graham, *Till Armageddon*

Confucianism

Good and evil do not befall men without reason. Heaven sends them happiness or misery according to their conduct.

Confucius, *The Book of History*

Deism

Reason alone teaches us to know good and evil.

Jean Jacques Rousseau, *Emile*

Hinduism

According to how one acts, according to how one conducts himself, so does he become. The doer of good becomes good. The doer of evil becomes evil.

Upanishads, Brihadaranyaka

Islam

Good and evil deeds are not alike. Repel evil with what is good; then he who is your enemy will become your bosom friend.

Koran, 41:34

Judaism

Since those who claim that evil is good and good is evil have grown numerous, troubles have increased in the world.

Talmud, Sotah 47b

The Creator does not decree either that a man shall be good or that he shall be wicked. Accordingly, it follows that it is the sinner who has inflicted injury on himself; and he should, therefore, weep for and bewail what he has done to his soul.

Maimonides, *Mishneh Torah*

GOODNESS

Buddhism

Let no man think lightly of good: "It cannot be for me." Drop by drop is the pitcher filled, and little by little the wise man is filled with merit.

Dhammapada

Christianity/Judaism

Thou crownest the year with thy goodness.

Holy Bible, Psalms 65:11

Christianity

Behold the goodness and severity of God.

Holy Bible, Romans 11:22

God plays and laughs in good deeds, whereas all other deeds, which do not make for the glory of God, are like ashes before him.

Meister Eckhart, *Sermons*

It is very certain that all things God has made are good; and no less certain that they are not all equally good.

Etienne Gilson, *The Spirit of Medieval Philosophy*

Confucianism

The Master said, "Clever talk and a pretentious manner are seldom found in the Good."

Confucius, *Analects*

Mencius said, "If you let people follow their feelings, they will be able to do good. This is what is meant by saying that Human nature is good."

Mencius, *The Book of Mencius*

Human nature is disposed to do good, just as water flows downwards. There is no man that does not show this tendency to goodness.

Mencius, *The Book of Mencius*

Hinduism

Those that abide in goodness go on high.

Bhagavad Gita, 14:18

Judaism

Like the Ark of the Covenant, the good man should be golden within as well as without.

Talmud, Yoma 72b

Stoicism

Seek not good from without; seek it within yourselves or you will never find it.

Epictetus, *Discourses*

Unitarianism

Goodness is the only investment that never fails.

Henry David Thoreau, *Walden*

GOVERNMENT

Agnosticism

In all ages, hypocrites, called priests, have put crowns upon the heads of thieves, called kings.

Robert G. Ingersoll, *Prose Poems and Selections*

Christianity/Judaism

Is it fit to say to a king, thou art wicked? and to princes, ye are ungodly?

Holy Bible, Job 34:18

Curse not the king, no not in thy thought; . . . for a bird in the air shall carry the voice, and that which hath wings shall tell the matter.

Holy Bible, Ecclesiastes 10:20

Christianity

Render therefore unto Caesar the things which are Caesar's; and unto God the things that are God's.

Holy Bible, Matthew 22:21

A pagan or antichristian pilot may be as skillful to carry the ship to its desired port as any Christian mariner or pilot in the world, and may perform that work with as much safety and speed.

Roger Williams, *The Bloody Tenet of Persecution*

A civil ruler dabbling in religion is as reprehensible as a clergyman dabbling in politics. Both render themselves odious as well as ridiculous.

James Cardinal Gibbons, *The Faith of Our Fathers*

The clearest expression of the dignity of government, one source of which is its historical existence, is its power, the sword which it wields. Even when the government incurs guilt and is open to ethical attack, its power is from God.

Dietrich Bonhoeffer, *Ethics*

Confucianism

When Tzu-hsia was Warden of Chu-fu, he sought advice about government. The Master said, "Do not try to hurry things. Ignore minor considerations. If you hurry things, your personality will not come into play. If you let yourself be distracted by minor considerations, nothing important will ever get finished."

Confucius, *Analects*

Tzu-lu asked about government. The Master said, "Lead them; encourage them!" Tzu-lu asked for a further maxim. The Master said, "Untiringly."

Confucius, *Analects*

An oppressive government is more to be feared than a tiger.

Confucius, *Analects*

Islam

No person, class or group, not even the entire population of the state as a whole, can lay claim to sovereignty. God alone is the real sovereign; all others are merely His subjects.

Abu'l A'la Mawdudi, *Islamic Law and Constitution*

An Islamic state cannot be isolated from society because Islam is a comprehensive, integrated way of life. The division between private and public, the state and society, that is familiar in Western culture, has not been known in Islam.

Hassan al-Turabi, "The Islamic State"

Judaism

Just as the larger fish in the sea swallow the smaller, so also is it with men. If not for the fear of government, the stronger would swallow the weaker.

Talmud, Abodah Zarah 4a

Be sure that thou prayest for the well-being of the government, for it is respect for authority that saves men from swallowing up each other alive.

Talmud, Aboth 3:2

GRACE

Christianity/Judaism

In thy light shall we see light.

Holy Bible, Psalms 36:9

Christianity

By grace are ye saved through faith; and that not of yourselves: it is the gift of God:
Not of works, lest any man should boast.

Holy Bible, Ephesians 2:8-9

What is grace? I know until you ask me; when you ask me, I do not know.

St. Augustine

He who aspires to the grace of God must be pure, with a heart as innocent as a child's. Purity of heart is to God like a perfume sweet and agreeable.

St. Nicholas of Flue

He who the sword of Heaven will bear
Should be as holy as severe,
Pattern in himself to know,
Grace to stand, and virtue go.

William Shakespeare, *Measure for Measure*, Act. 3, Sc. 1

[Note: Henry Sebastian Bowden in *The Religion of Shakespeare* remarks: "The last line is noted by the Cambridge (Shakespeare) editors as corrupt. It is not so. The meaning is clear. The man should have the pattern or idea of holiness in himself to enable him to stand; and virtue to enable him to advance."]

Amazing grace! how sweet the sound,
That saved a wretch like me;
I once was lost, but now I'm found;
Was blind, but now I see.

'Twas grace that taught my heart to fear,
And grace my fear relieved;
How precious did that grace appear
The hour I first believed.

Through many dangers, toils and snares
    I have already come,
'Tis grace that brought me safe thus far,
    And grace will lead me home.

John Newton, "Amazing Grace"

It is becoming impossible for those who mix at all with their fellow-men
to believe that the grace of God is distributed denominationally.

William Ralph Inge, "Our Present Discontents"

Grace is forgiveness of sins.

Karl Barth, *Credo*

Don't be so morbid about the fact that you're selfish; don't deny that you
are self-regarding, but work in life and hope that by grace—this perhaps
is the door to the real answer—you will be redeemed. *By grace.*

Reinhold Niebuhr, *Justice and Mercy*

The promise of grace is not to be squandered. . . . There are those who
are not worthy of the sanctuary. . . . Grace may not be proclaimed to
anyone who does not recognize or distinguish or desire it.

Dietrich Bonhoeffer, *The Way to Freedom*

Grace is not a strange, magic substance which is subtly filtered into our
souls to act as a kind of spiritual penicillin. Grace is unity, oneness within
ourselves, oneness with God.

Thomas Merton, *The New Man*

Hinduism

Bowing and prostrating my body,
    I beg grace of Thee, the Lord to be revered:
As a father to his son, as a friend to his friend,
    As a lover to his beloved, be pleased to show mercy,
        O God!

Bhagavad Gita, 11:44

Man himself, and not any extraneous power, is responsible for his own
emancipation. This view is the very antithesis of the doctrine of God's
grace.

R. N. Dandekar, "The Role of Man in Hinduism"

Islam

Show us the straight way,
The way of those on whom Thou hast bestowed
Thy Grace, not of those whose portion
Is wrath, nor of those who go astray.

Koran, 1:6-7

Judaism

Rabbi Akiba said: Everything is foreseen, yet freedom is given; the world is judged by grace, yet all is according to the amount of good works.

Talmud, Aboth 3:19

GREATNESS

Christianity/Judaism

There were giants in the earth in those days.

Holy Bible, Genesis 6:4

Great men are not always wise.

Holy Bible, Job 32:9

Christianity

Choose an heroic ideal; but rather to emulate than to imitate. There are exemplars of greatness, living texts of honor.... Nothing arouses ambition so much in the heart as the trumpet-clang of another's fame.

Baltasar Gracian, *The Art of Worldly Wisdom*

Greatness is a spiritual condition worthy to excite love, interest, and admiration.

Matthew Arnold, *Culture and Anarchy*

Greatness ... appears to be not so much a certain size as a certain quality of human lives. It may be present in lives whose range is very small.

Phillips Brooks, "Purpose and Use of Comfort"

We can do no great things—only small things with great love.

Mother Teresa of Calcutta, *Life in the Spirit*

A man's greatness is not determined by his talent or wealth, but rather by what it takes to discourage him.

Jerry Falwell, *Finding Inner Peace and Strength*

Confucianism

The superior man is quiet and calm, waiting for the appointments of heaven, while the mean man walks in dangerous paths, looking for lucky occurrences.

Confucius

Hinduism

Here on earth people call cows and horses, elephants and gold, slaves and wives, fields and abodes "greatness." I do not speak thus.

Upanishads, Chandogya

Judaism

"Who is a hero?" the Jewish sages asked. Their answer: "He who masters himself."

Sidney Greenberg, *Say Yes to Life*

Unitarianism

Genuine greatness is marked by . . . a hearty interest in others, a feeling of brotherhood with the human family, and respect for every intellectual and immortal being as capable of progress toward its own elevation.

William Ellery Channing, *Works of . . .*

GREED

Christianity/Judaism

He that is greedy of gain troubleth his own house.

Holy Bible, Proverbs 15:27

Christianity

Riches are the instrument of all vices, because they render us capable of putting even our worst desires into execution.

St. Ambrose

Surely ivory and gold and riches are good creations of God, permitted, indeed appointed, for men's use by God's providence. . . . But where there is plenty, to wallow in delights, to gorge oneself, to intoxicate mind and heart with present pleasures and be always panting after new ones—such are very far removed from a lawful use of God's gifts.

John Calvin, *Institutes of the Christian Religion*

Our souls may sooner surfeit than be satisfied with earthly things. He that first thought ten thousand pounds too much for any one man will afterwards think ten millions too little for himself.

Thomas Fuller, *The Holy State and the Profane State*

Hinduism

It is well known that when greed has for its object material gain then it can have no end. It is like the chasing of the horizon by a lunatic. To go on in a competition multiplying millions becomes a steeplechase of insensate futility that has obstacles but no goal.

Rabindranath Tagore, *The Religion of Man*

Islam

Nothing destroys one's respect in the hearts of others more than greed.

Muhammad Taqi

Judaism

Short is the way from need to greed.

Abraham Joshua Heschel, *The Insecurity of Freedom*

Nonsectarian

Greed is a bottomless pit which exhausts the person in an endless effort to satisfy the need without ever reaching satisfaction.

Erich Fromm, *Escape from Freedom*

Taoism

There is no greater disaster than greed.

Lao-tzu, *Tao-te ching*

HAPPINESS

Buddhism

Let us live happily, though we call nothing our own. Let us be like God, feeding on love.

Dhammapada

Christianity/Judaism

Happy is the man whom God correcteth: therefore despise not thou the chastening of the Almighty.

Holy Bible, Job 5:17

Christianity

Weeping may endure for a night, but joy cometh in the morning.

Holy Bible, Psalms 30:5

Since happiness is nothing other than the enjoyment of the highest good, and since the highest good is above, no one can be happy unless he rise above himself, not by an ascent of the body, but of the heart.

St. Bonaventure

Happiness is the natural life of man.

St. Thomas Aquinas

To enjoy true happiness we must travel into a very far country, and even out of ourselves.

Sir Thomas Browne, *Christian Morals*

Joy to the world! The Lord is come;
Let earth receive her King.
Let ev'ry heart prepare Him room,
And heav'n and nature sing.

Isaac Watts, "Psalm 98"

My children, the three acts of faith, hope, and charity contain all the happiness of man upon the earth.

St. John Vianney

If life were always merry,
    Our souls would seek relief,
And rest from weary laughter
    In the quiet arms of grief.

Henry Van Dyke, "If All the Skies"

Happiness is a mystery, like religion, and should never be rationalized.

G.K. Chesterton, *Heretics*

Since religion was so much a part of my life as a child, and since my childhood was so happy and so full of laughter and joy, I associate the two. Even my concept of Jesus goes along with this association of happiness and religion.

Minnie Pearl, *Minnie Pearl: An Autobiography*

Hinduism

He, having cast off in advance the bonds of death,
With sorrow overpassed, rejoices in the heaven-world.

Upanishads, Katha

Kantianism

Morality is not properly the doctrine of how we may make ourselves happy, but how we may make ourselves worthy of happiness.

Immanuel Kant, *Critique of Practical Reason*

Mormonism

Adam fell that men might be; and men are, that they might have joy.

Book of Mormon, 2 Nephi 2:25

Stoicism

Lead the good life, and habit will make it pleasant.

Epictetus, *Discourses*

Unitarianism

You shall have joy, or you shall have power, said God; you shall not have both.

Ralph Waldo Emerson, *Journals*

HEALTH

Christianity/Judaism

A merry heart doeth good like a medicine.

Holy Bible, Proverbs 17:22

There is no riches above a sound body.

The Apocrypha, Ecclesiacticus 30:16

Christianity

Drink no longer water, but use a little wine for thy stomach's sake.

Holy Bible, 1 Timothy 5:23

A man may be as proud as Lucifer, and yet, if he observes the laws of physical health, he will get his reward—that is, physical health. He will not get anything higher than that, but he will get that.

Henry Ward Beecher, "Sowing and Reaping"

God does not want you to be a nervous wreck—getting up on pep pills, living on tranquilizers, going to bed on sleeping pills.

Jerry Falwell, *Finding Inner Peace and Strength*

Christian Science

We classify disease as error, which nothing but Truth or Mind can heal, and this Mind must be divine, not human.

Mary Baker Eddy, *Science and Health with Key to the Scriptures*

The fundamental assumptions of Christian Science are opposite to those of medical theory. . . . All disease is essentially a mental condition [since] man, in his true nature, is essentially a spiritual being and not a material organism.

DeWitt John, *The Christian Science Way of Life*

Hinduism

Ward off from us disease and weakness.
By day and night, lovers of sweetness, guard us.

Rig-Veda

[Note: The "lovers of sweetness" are two Vedic gods, the Asvins, inseparable twins. They are fond of mead and soma, a plant-juice liquor.]

Judaism

God creates the cure before He sends the malady.

Talmud, Zohar i, 196a

Since by keeping the body in health and vigor one walks in the ways of God—it being impossible during sickness to have any understanding or knowledge of the Creator—it is a man's duty to avoid whatever is injurious to the body, and cultivate habits conducive to health and vigor.

Maimonides, *Mishneh Torah*

HEAVEN

Buddhism

All thy rafters are broken, thy ridgepole is sundered; thy mind, approaching Nirvana, has attained to extinction of all desires.

Dhammapada

Nirvana is where there is no birth, no extinction; it is seeing the state of suchness, absolutely transcending all the categories constructed by mind.

Lankavatara Sutra

Christianity/Judaism

This is none other but the house of God, and this is the gate of heaven.

Holy Bible, Genesis 28:17

Is not God in the height of heaven? and behold the height of the stars, how high they are!

Holy Bible, Job 22:12

Christianity

Hereafter ye shall see heaven open, and the angels of God ascending and descending upon the Son of man.

Holy Bible, John 1:51

We know that if our earthly house of this tabernacle were dissolved, we have a building of God, a house not made with hands, eternal in the heavens.

Holy Bible, 2 Corinthians 5:1

I would not give one moment of heaven for all the joy and riches in the world.

Martin Luther

If you confine Christ's dwelling to a local heaven, you are ignorant of that which is the greatest joy that can be: Christ dwells in the heart.

William Penn, *Fruits of an Active Life*

There is a land of pure delight,
    Where saints immortal reign;
Infinite day excludes the night,
    And pleasures banish pain.

Isaac Watts, "Hymn 66"

This world is all a fleeting show,
    To man's illusion given;
The smiles of joy, the tears of woe,
Deceitful shine, deceitful flow—
    There's nothing true but Heaven.

Thomas Moore, *Sacred Songs*

Things learned on earth, we shall practice in heaven.

Robert Browning, "Old Pictures in Florence"

Look for me in the nurseries of Heaven.

Francis Thompson, "To My Godchild"

One old Quaker is said to have asked another, "Friend, does thee think there will be any other than Quakers in heaven?" To which his fellow-Quaker replied, "Well, if there aren't, it would hardly pay to keep the place open."

Douglas V. Steere, *Quaker Spirituality*

The heaven of faith is not the heaven of the astronauts. . . . God does not dwell . . . in a local or spatial sense "above" the world.

Hans Küng, *Eternal Life?*

Confucianism

Yin and yang are established as the way of Heaven, the weak and the strong as the way of Earth, and humanity and righteousness as the way of man.

Book of Changes

Hinduism

The supreme heaven shines in the lotus of the heart. They enter there who struggle and aspire.

Upanishads, Kaivalya

With ritual worship [the faithful] seek to go to heaven;
They, attaining the meritorious world of the lord of the gods,
Taste in the sky the divine enjoyments of the gods.

Bhagavad Gita, 9:20

Islam

For those who reject Our revelations and treat them with arrogance, no opening will there be of the gates of heaven, nor will they enter the Garden, until the camel can pass through the eye of a needle: Such is Our reward for those in sin.

Koran, 7:40

Allah will . . . reward [the righteous] with garments of silk. Reclining upon soft couches, they will feel neither the sun's burning heat nor the bitter cold. Trees will spread their shade over them, and bunches of fruit will hang low.

Koran, 76:11-14

Judaism

No one partakes of the enjoyments of the World to Come because of his father's merits.

Talmud, Midrash Tehillim 146,2

This world is only the vestibule to another; you must prepare yourself in the vestibule so that you may enter the banquet hall.

Talmud, Aboth 4,21

"God separated the light," meaning that he set it apart at creation and put it away for safekeeping so that his pious ones might enjoy it in the world to come . . . [where] the pious sit, with crowns on their heads, and behold the radiance of the manifest deity.

Franz Rosenzweig, *The Star of Redemption*

HELL

Christianity/Judaism

We have made a covenant with death, and with hell are we in agreement.

Holy Bible, Isaiah 28:15

Christianity

Wide is the gate, and broad is the way, that leadeth to destruction, and many there be which go in thereat.

Holy Bible, Matthew 7:13

Ye serpents, ye generation of vipers, how can ye escape the damnation of hell?

Holy Bible, Matthew 23:33

In the vale of darkness the happy host see the damned suffering pain as a punishment for their sins, the surging flame, and biting of the serpents with bitter jaws—a school of burning creatures. From that sight waxes for them a winsome joy, when they observe the others enduring the evil that they escaped through the mercy of the Lord.

Cynewulf

That the saints may enjoy their beatitude and the grace of God more abundantly, they are permitted to see the punishment of the damned in hell.

St. Thomas Aquinas, *Summa Theologica*

All hope abandon, ye who enter here.

Dante, *Divine Comedy: Inferno*

A city cast in darkness, burning with brimstone and noisome pitch and full of inhabitants who cannot make their escape. . . . The damned are in the abyss of hell . . . where they suffer unspeakable torments.

St. Francis de Sales, *Introduction to the Devout Life*

If there is no hell, a good many preachers are obtaining money under false pretenses.

Billy Sunday

The safest road to hell is the gradual one—the gentle slope, soft underfoot, without sudden turnings, without milestones, without signposts.

C.S. Lewis, *The Screwtape Letters*

Deism

Do not ask me whether the torments of the wicked will endure forever. I cannot tell, and I have no empty curiosity for the investigation of useless problems.

Jean Jacques Rousseau, *Emile*

Hinduism

This is of hell the threefold
    Gate, and ruins the soul:
Desire, wealth, and greed.

Bhagavad Gita, 16:21

Islam

You will be sent flames of fire and flashes of molten brass: there will be no one to help you.

Koran, 55:35

When the scoffers ask how dust and mouldering bones can be punished, the reply is that if God has power to call man to life the first time from a drop of water, He can as easily call him to life a second time to receive the rewards of his deeds.

Richard Bell, *The Origin of Islam in Its Christian Environment*

Judaism

The fire of Gehenna is sixty times as hot as the fire of this earth.

Talmud, Berakot

Gehenna, the hell where sinners roast for their misdeeds, is Gai Hinom, the Valley of Hinom, a small ravine in Jerusalem where idolators used to burn their children in sacrifice to Moloch. You can see Gehenna today from your balcony room in the King David Hotel overlooking the old city of Jerusalem. It is clearly too small to accommodate even a small fraction of the sinners of the moment, let alone those of previous generations.

Herman Wouk, *This Is My God*

HERESY

Agnosticism

Heresy is a cradle; orthodoxy a coffin.

Robert G. Ingersoll

Christianity

If forgers and malefactors are put to death by the secular power, there is much more reason for excommunicating and even putting to death one convicted of heresy.

St. Thomas Aquinas, Summa Theologica

By identifying the new learning with heresy we make orthodoxy synonymous with ignorance.

Erasmus

Every scratch in the hand is not a stab to the heart; nor doth every false opinion make a heretic.

Thomas Fuller, The Holy State and the Profane State

A man may be a heretic in the truth; . . . if he believes things only because his pastor says so, or the assembly so determines, . . . though his belief be true, yet the very truth he holds becomes his heresy.

John Milton, Areopagitica

There arises a jealousy and pregnant suspicion that they who persecute an opinion are destitute of sufficient arguments to confute it, and that the hangman is the best disputant.

Jeremy Taylor, The Liberty of Prophesying

A heretic in one generation would have been a saint if he had lived in another, and a heretic in one country would often be a hero in another.

Rufus M. Jones, The Church's Debt to Heretics

I did try to find a heresy of my own; and when I put the last touches to it I discovered it was orthodoxy.

G. K. Chesterton, Orthodoxy

Islam

He [a disbeliever] possesses wealth and children, but when Our revelations are recited to him, he says, "They are mere fables of the ancients." We will brand him on the nose!

Koran, 68:5

Judaism

There are those who . . . have adopted incorrect opinions. . . . Necessity at certain times impels killing them and blotting out the traces of their opinions lest they should lead astray the ways of others.

Maimonides, Guide of the Perplexed

HONESTY

Christianity

An honest man's the noblest work of God.

Alexander Pope, *An Essay on Man*

The Bible tells of both history's brokenness and history's redemption. . . . Compare this honesty with the Marxist dialectic ending in a stainless steel paradise. . . . Compare it with American faith in the natural goodness of man and the endlessness of material progress. Then be grateful for the honesty of the Bible story.

George A. Buttrick, *Christ and History*

Islam

Weigh therefore with fairness and scant not the balance.

Koran, 55:8

Judaism

Rabbi Safra . . . was approached to sell something he had and was offered a price which suited him, but [he] was unable at the time to signify his consent because he was reciting his prayers. . . . The buyer, under the impression that R. Safra had rejected his bid, kept on increasing the price, but R. Safra insisted on selling for the original price to which he had consented "in his heart."

Louis Jacobs, *What Does Judaism Say About . . . ?*

HOPE

Christianity/Judaism

To him that is joined to all the living there is hope: for a living dog is better than a dead lion.

Holy Bible, Ecclesiastes 9:4

Christianity

The promise, that he should be the heir of the world, was not to Abraham . . . through the law, but through the righteousness of faith. . . .
   Who against hope believed in hope.

Holy Bible, Romans 4:13, 18

Be always ready to give an answer to every man that asketh you a reason of the hope that is in you.

Holy Bible, 1 Peter 3:15

If you do not hope, you will not find what is beyond your hopes.

St. Clement of Alexandria

Never give out while there is hope; but hope not beyond reason, for that shows more desire than judgment.

William Penn, *Some Fruits of Solitude*

To have mature hope is to rejoice in the whole drama of human history, including the terrible anxieties of a nuclear age.

Reinhold Niebuhr, *Justice and Mercy*

What we call ideals are nothing but intricate plans based on hopes. . . . Religion itself is ultimately a loving hope; a hope that . . . there is a God, that there is a meaning in human suffering and in the disappointment of our individual, self-centered hopes.

Gordon W. Allport, *Waiting for the Lord*

Let me remind you . . . that a lot that goes by the name of hope is really wishful thinking. . . . God is . . . the only sure and certain ground for hope, either in this world or in the world to come.

J.B. Phillips, *Good News*

Hinduism

When kindled by hope . . . one longs for sons and cattle, for this world and the yonder. Reverence hope.

Upanishads, Chandogya

Judaism

True to the heart of Jewish religious belief, above both faith and reason, hope reigns supreme.

Milton Steinberg, *Anatomy of Faith*

Jews are borne along by a greater emotion than nostalgia, and that is hope. They are not merely pushed from Sinai, so many thousands of years behind them, but they are also pulled to the revelation which lies ahead.

Lionel Blue, *To Heaven, with Scribes and Pharisees*

HUMILITY

Christianity/Judaism

The meek shall inherit the earth.

Holy Bible, Psalms 37:11

The fear of the Lord is the instruction of wisdom; and before honor is humility.

Holy Bible, Proverbs 15:33

Christianity

Whosoever shall exalt himself shall be abased; and he that shall humble himself shall be exalted.

Holy Bible, Matthew 23:12

True humility does not make a show of herself or use many humble words; for she desires not only to conceal all other virtues, but most of all to conceal herself.

St. Francis de Sales, *Introduction to the Devout Life*

Humility is the great ornament and jewel of Christian religion.

Jeremy Taylor, *Holy Living*

He that is down needs fear no fall,
    He that is low, no pride;
He that is humble ever shall
    Have God to be his guide.

John Bunyan, "The Shepherd Boy's Song"

The tumult and the shouting dies,
    The captains and the kings depart;
Still stands thine ancient sacrifice,
    An humble and a contrite heart:
Lord God of Hosts, be with us yet,
Lest we forget, lest we forget.

Rudyard Kipling, "Recessional"

The very moment God sees us fully convinced of our nothingness, He reaches out His hand to us.

St. Thérèse de Lisieux

Humility moderates our estimate of what we know and will remind us that God gave to the wise more talents than others and more opportunities for developing those talents. But of him who has received much, much also will be expected. The intellectual leader has a tremendous responsibility thrust upon him, and woe to him if he uses his office of teaching to lead the young into error and conceit.

Fulton J. Sheen, *On Being Human*

These are the traits of character most sorely needed in our world today—a willingness to play second fiddle or, if you prefer, humility and that broad sympathy and sound common sense, without which the success of any great movement cannot be measured.

Peter Marshall, *Mr. Jones, Meet the Master*

It is part of the discipline of humility that we must not spare our hand where it can perform a service and that we do not assume that our schedule is our own to manage, but allow it to be arranged by God.

Dietrich Bonhoeffer, *Life Together*

Without humility, all the virtues are finite. Only humility makes them infinite.

Simone Weil, *The Simone Weil Reader*

The more you forget yourself, the more Jesus will think of you.

Mother Teresa of Calcutta, *Life in the Spirit*

Judaism

The proverb runs: How great that man would be were he not so arrogant.

Talmud, Kallah Rabbati 3

Rabbi Simeon ben Johai said, "A man should recite his virtues in a whisper and his faults in a shout."

Talmud, Sotah 32b

Humility . . . is, after all, a kind of pride. Only haughtiness and humility are contradictory. . . . Humility rests secure in the feeling of being sheltered. It knows that nothing can befall it.

Franz Rosenzweig, *The Star of Redemption*

Stoicism

Nothing is more scandalous than a man who is proud of his humility.

Marcus Aurelius, *Meditations*

HUMOR

Christianity

I have never understood why it should be considered derogatory to the Creator to suppose that He has a sense of humor.

William Ralph Inge, *A Rustic Moralist*

No somber God could have made a bullfrog or a giraffe.

George A. Buttrick, *Sermons Preached in a University Church*

A profound book on laughter might be almost a final theology.

George A. Buttrick, *God, Pain, and Evil*

Humor reminds us that we are not gods nor goddesses.

Bernard Ramm, *After Fundamentalism*

While the [Christian] faith takes care of the ultimate incongruities of life, humor does nicely with the intermediate ones.

William Sloane Coffin, *Living the Truth in a World of Illusions*

Considering the fact that Christians have been raised to celebrate a "Merry Christmas" and a "Happy Easter," I have always wondered why Christian humorist-writers are as rare as desert penguins.

Cal Samra, *The Joyful Christ*

Judaism

If one man says to thee, "Thou art a donkey," do not mind; if two speak thus, purchase a saddle for thyself.

Talmud, Bereshit Rabbah 74:2

To the question "Why does the Jew always answer a question with a question?" the traditional answer is: "Why not?"

Louis Jacobs, *What Does Judaism Say About . . . ?*

How can I believe in God when just last week I got my tongue caught in the roller of an electric typewriter.

Woody Allen, "Selections from the Allen Notebooks"

Platonism

Even the gods love their jokes.

Plato, *Cratylus*

Taoism

There was a faith-healer of Deal,
Who said, "Although pain is not real,
    When the point of a pin
    Goes into my skin,
I dislike what I fancy I feel."

Alan Watts, Tao: The Watercourse Way

HYPOCRISY

Buddhism

To preach religion and not to practice it is to be like a parrot saying a prayer.

The Supreme Path, the Rosary of Precious Gems

Christianity/Judaism

Knowest thou not this of old, since man was placed upon the earth,
    That the triumphing of the wicked is short, and the joy of the hypocrite but for a moment?

Holy Bible, Job 20:4-5

Christianity

O ye hypocrites, ye can discern the face of the sky; but can ye not discern the signs of the times?

Holy Bible, Matthew 16:3

This people honoreth me with their lips, but their heart is far from me.

Holy Bible, Mark 7:6

I conjure you to beware of deceitful men, especially impious priests, of whom the Lord has said, they are outwardly dressed in sheep's clothing, while within they are ravening wolves.

John Huss, Letters

Those who act in order that they may be seen by men and secure praise during their lifetime are hypocrites. It must therefore follow that . . . choral or spoken church services that are performed without true intent but only for reward are carried out either for the sake of reputation or for profit.

Huldrych Zwingli, "Sixty-seven Theses" (Nos. 45, 46)

If God could convert the preachers, the world would be saved. Most of them are a lot of evolutionary hot-air merchants.

Billy Sunday

You [a junior devil] should always try to make the patient [a Christian] abandon the people or food or books he really likes in favor of the "best" people, the "right" food, the "important" books. I [Screwtape, a senior official in Satan's "Lowerarchy"] have known a human defended from strong temptations to social ambition by a still stronger taste for tripe and onions.

C.S. Lewis, *The Screwtape Letters*

Hinduism

Avenging spies pursue men's falsehoods closely.

Rig-Veda

Judaism

God hates the man who says one thing with his mouth and another with his mind.

Talmud, Pesahim 113b

It is easier to rule the entire world than to sit before two insincere students of the Torah.

Talmud, Abot de-R. Nathan 25

IMMORTALITY

Buddhism

If in this present life we can never hope for union,
Then we shall first keep house in the Lotus Palace beyond.

Lafcadio Hearn, "Buddhist Allusions in Japanese Folksongs"

Christianity/Judaism

Surely goodness and mercy shall follow me all the days of my life: and I will dwell in the house of the Lord for ever.

Holy Bible, Psalms 23:6

Christianity

This is the promise that He hath promised us, even eternal life.

Holy Bible, 1 John 2:25

What reason have atheists for saying that we cannot rise again? Which is the more difficult—to be born or to rise again? . . . Is it more difficult to come into being than to return to it?

Blaise Pascal, *Pensées*

You are not born to time. Made out of the dust, you do not belong to the dust. Begun, you shall never end. God has great things for you, and all he asks is that, in the school where he is teaching you, you will be patient, believe in him, hope on, and be trustful.

Henry Ward Beecher, "Working and Waiting"

The road is wide and bright as crystal, and the sun is at the end of it.

Fyodor Dostoyevsky, *The Brothers Karamazov*

If my bark sink
    'Tis to another sea.
Mortality's ground floor
    Is immortality.

Emily Dickinson, "If My Bark Sink"

Our hearts tell us of a higher form of existence, in which the doom of death is not merely deferred but abolished. . . . Most firmly do I believe that this faith in immortality, though formless and impalpable as the air we breathe, . . . is nonetheless enthroned in the center of our being.

William Ralph Inge, *Wit and Wisdom of Dean Inge*

Both free enterprise and the labor movement at their best believe in the worth of an individual. But such a faith is nonsense if men are cheap candles blown out at death, or drops of water absorbed into some vague ocean of being . . . ; any real faith . . . rests on faith in the life everlasting.

George A. Buttrick, *So We Believe, So We Pray*

In the here-and-now [the Christian] must certainly do all the good he can; certainly he is called to a life of self-giving love, of compassion and service. But he is forever delivered from being such a fool as to suppose that this life is everything and that all his hopes and dreams are finished when his body dies.

J.B. Phillips, *Good News*

Hinduism

From the unreal lead me to the real!
From darkness lead me to light!
From death lead me to immortality!

Upanishads, Brihadaranyaka

Islam

Those that believe in Allah and do what is right shall be forgiven their sins and admitted to gardens watered by running streams, where they shall dwell forever.

Koran, 64:9

Judaism

I believe with perfect faith that there will be a revival of the dead at the time when it shall please the Creator.

Maimonides, *Commentary to Mishnah: Sanhedrin*

It is the *idea* of immortality, not its detailed blueprinting, that is of supreme importance.

Hyman J. Schachtel, *The Shadowed Valley*

The ideal of eternal life is not the private domain of a small spiritual elite or some particularly gifted individuals, but is the public domain of all Israel.

Joseph B. Soloveitchik, *Halakhic Man*

Zoroastrianism

For the first three nights after the breath has left the body the soul hovers about the lifeless frame and experiences joy or sorrow according to the deeds done in this life. On the dawn of the fourth day the soul takes flight from earth amid the waftings of a perfumed breeze or stifled by a blast of stench, according as the individual has been righteous or wicked. It is then met either by a beauteous maiden or by a hideous hag.

A.V. Williams Jackson, *Zoroastrian Studies*

INQUIRY

Christianity/Judaism

I gave my heart to seek and search out by wisdom concerning all things that are done under heaven.

Holy Bible, Ecclesiastes 1:13

Christianity

Ye rejoice with joy unspeakable and full of glory:
Receiving the end of your faith, even the salvation of your souls.
Of which salvation the prophets have inquired and searched diligently.

Holy Bible, 1 Peter 1:8-10

Search thine own heart. What paineth thee
In others in thyself may be.

John Greenleaf Whittier, "The Chapel of the Hermits"

Cosmic

I want to know how God created this world. I am not interested in this or that phenomenon. I want to know His thoughts. The rest are details.

Albert Einstein

Hinduism

Do not question too much, lest your head fall off. In truth, you are questioning too much about a divinity about which further questions cannot be asked.

Upanishads, Brihadaranyaka

Islam

To reflect on the essence of the Creator . . . is forbidden to the human intellect because of the severance of all relation between the two existences.

Muhammad 'Abduh, *Risalat at-Tawhid*

Judaism

Artists and philosophers like to imagine the thinker with a stern face, a profound look which penetrates into the unseen, and a noble bearing—an eagle preparing for flight. Not at all. A thinking man is one who has lost his balance, in the vulgar, not in the tragic sense. Hands raking the air, feet flying, face scared and bewildered, he is a caricature of helplessness and pitiable perplexity.

Lev Shestov, *All Things Are Possible*

Kantianism

Two things fill the mind with ever-increasing wonder and awe, the more often and the more intensely the mind of thought is drawn to them: the starry heavens above me and the moral law within me.

Immanuel Kant, *Critique of Practical Reason*

JUSTICE

Christianity/Judaism

Eye for eye, tooth for tooth, hand for hand, foot for foot.

Holy Bible, Exodus 21:24

The judgments of the Lord are true and righteous altogether.

Holy Bible, Psalms 19:9

Let judgment run down as waters, and righteousness as a mighty stream.

Holy Bible, Amos 5:24

Christianity

Judge not, that ye be not judged.

Holy Bible, Matthew 7:1

Justice is that virtue that assigns to every man his due.

St. Augustine, *The City of God*

Justice will not condemn even the Devil himself wrongly.

Thomas Fuller, *Gnomologia*

The disinherited of every age have dreamt of a just society.

Reinhold Niebuhr, *Moral Man and Immoral Society*

Injustice anywhere is a threat to justice everywhere.

Martin Luther King, Jr., "Letter from the Birmingham Jail"

Islam

One day the earth will be changed to a different earth, and so will be the
heavens, and men will be marshalled forth, before God, the one, the irresistible;
   And you will see the sinners that day bound together in fetters—
   Their garments of liquid pitch, and their faces covered with fire;
   That God may requite each soul according to its deserts; and verily God
is swift in calling to account.

Koran, 16:48-51

Absolute justice demands that men's incomes and rewards should . . .
vary, and that some have more than others—so long as human justice is
upheld by the provision of equal opportunity for all.

Syed Qutb, "Islamic Approach to Social Justice"

Judaism

Judgment delayed is judgment voided.

Talmud, Sanhedrin 95

If we compare our knowledge with that of the ancients, we appear very
wise. But we are no nearer to solving the riddle of eternal justice than
Cain was.

Lev Shestov, *All Things Are Possible*

It is tempting at one level to believe that bad things happen to people
(especially other people) because God is a righteous judge who gives them
exactly what they deserve. By believing that we keep the world orderly
and understandable. . . . But [this belief] has a number of serious limita-
tions. . . . It teaches people to blame themselves. It creates guilt when
there is no basis for guilt. It makes people hate God, even as it makes
them hate themselves. And most disturbing off all, it does not even fit
the facts.

Harold S. Kushner, *When Bad Things Happen to Good People*

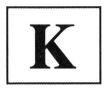

KINDNESS

Christianity/Judaism

Thou art a God ready to pardon, gracious and merciful, slow to anger, and of great kindness.

Holy Bible, Nehemiah 9:17

How excellent is thy loving-kindness, O God! therefore the children of men put their trust under the shadow of thy wing.

Holy Bible, Psalms 36:7

Christianity

Love ye your enemies and do good, and lend, hoping for nothing again; and your reward shall be great, and ye shall be the children of the Highest: for he is kind unto the unthankful and to the evil.

Holy Bible, Luke 6:35

That best portion of a good man's life,
His little, nameless, unremembered acts
Of kindness and of love.

William Wordsworth, "Lines Composed a Few Miles Above Tintern Abbey"

Kindness is always undeserved. And what rejoices man's heart is precisely what he is given as a sheer gift, . . . a gift which he has not deserved.

Rudolf Bultmann, *This World and the Beyond*

There are three rules of dealing with those who come to us: (1) Kindness, (2) Kindness, (3) Kindness.

Fulton J. Sheen

Be the living expression of God's kindness—kindness in your face, kindness in your eyes, kindness in your smile, kindness in your warm greeting.

Mother Teresa of Calcutta, *Life in the Spirit*

Islam

We have enjoined man to show kindness to his parents.

Koran, 46:15

If you see a blind man, kick him; why should you be kinder than God?

Iranian proverb

Judaism

The quiet, probably unnoticed sharing in a neighbor's joy, no less than in his sorrow, constitutes an act of kindness.

Morris Adler, *The World of the Talmud*

KNOWLEDGE

Buddhism

A dunce once searched for a fire with a lighted lantern.
Had he known what fire was,
He could have cooked his rice much sooner.

Mu-mon, *The Gateless Gate*

Even a common man by obtaining knowledge becomes a Buddha.

Japanese Buddhist proverb

Christianity/Judaism

A wise man is strong; yea, a man of knowledge increaseth strength.

Holy Bible, Proverbs 24:5

Christianity

Knowledge puffeth up.

Holy Bible, 1 Corinthians 8:1

[God] will have all men to be saved, and to come unto the knowledge of the truth.

Holy Bible, 1 Timothy 2:4

You cannot imagine how foolish people are. They have no sense of discernment, having lost it by putting their trust in their own knowledge. O stupid people, do you not see that you are not the source of your own knowledge?

St. Catherine of Siena

The more knowledge you have, the more grievously will you be judged for its misuse, if you do not live according to it.

Thomas à Kempis, *The Imitation of Christ*

Minister: What is the true and right knowledge of God?
Child: When we know Him in order that we may honor Him.

John Calvin, *The Geneva Catechism*

We know accurately only when we know little; with knowledge, doubt enters.

Goethe, *Maxims*

Knowledge is one thing, virtue is another.

John Henry Newman, *The Idea of a University*

When I say that *I know*, I do not mean that my body knows by means of the soul, or that the soul knows by means of the body; but that this concrete being "I," taken in its unity, performs an act of knowing.

Etienne Gilson, *The Spirit of Medieval Philosophy*

Knowledge is based on an original unity and involves a separation and a reunion of subject and object. In this respect knowledge is like love, as the late Greek thinkers knew. The Greek *gnosis*, "knowledge," had three meanings: sexual love, the knowledge of essences, and mystical union with the divine.

Paul Tillich, *My Search for Absolutes*

If we do not recognize the fragmentary character of knowledge we will be caught holding onto some old form of knowledge which is quite irrelevant to the responsibilities which we must face today.

Reinhold Niebuhr, *Justice and Mercy*

Confucianism

The Master said, "You, shall I teach you what knowledge is? When you know a thing, to recognize that you know it, and when you do not know a thing, to recognize that you do not know it. That is knowledge."

Confucius, *Analects*

If one's innate knowledge is clear, it will be all right either to try to obtain truth through personal realization in a quiet place or to discover it through training and polishing in the actual affairs of life.

Wang Yang-ming, *Instructions for Practical Living*

Hinduism

Knowledge is better than practice,
And meditation is superior to knowledge.

Bhagavad Gita, 12:12

Among all things, knowledge is the best thing: it cannot be stolen, nor can it be purchased, and it is imperishable.

Hitopadesa

Islam

We ascend from the ordering of the human domain to the description of its maker, which is knowledge; then again we ascend from knowledge to life, and from thence to the essence. This is the spiritual ascension, and these rules are the steps by which we ascend to the skies, and these principles are the stages of the ascent.

Al-Ghazali, *The Just Balance*

Judaism

Rabbi Eliezer said: . . . Warm yourself at the fire of the learned, but beware of their glowing coals, lest you get scorched. The bite of the learned is like the bite of a fox, their sting is like a scorpion's, their hiss like a serpent's, and all their words are like coals of fire.

Pirke Aboth

We are told in the language of Jewish myth that in his mother's womb man knows the universe and forgets it at birth.

Martin Buber, *I and Thou*

In the realm of the spiritual or intellectual . . . the fuller the "vessel," the more one can add to it. The daily, systematic indulgence of the intellect's hunger of knowledge is man's most effective defense against the ever-present onslaughts of boredom. As such it constitutes one of the great pillars of the good life.

Simon Greenberg, *A Jewish Philosophy and Pattern of Life*

Nonsectarian

I am convinced of what I *know*. Everything else is hypothesis, and beyond that I can leave a lot of things to the Unknown. They do not bother me.

Carl Jung, *Psychology and Religion*

Taoism

In Taoist thinking . . . the highest step to which thought can lead is to know that we do not know.

Erich Fromm, *The Art of Loving*

LANGUAGE

Buddhism

Words and sentences are produced by the law of causation and are mutually conditioning—they cannot express the highest Reality.

Lankavatara Sutra

Words cannot describe everything.
The heart's message cannot be delivered in words.
If one receives words literally, he will be lost.
If he tries to explain with words, he will not attain
    enlightenment in this life.

Mu-mon, *The Gateless Gate*

Christianity/Judaism

Therefore is the name of [the city] called Babel; because the Lord did there confound the language of all the earth.

Holy Bible, Genesis 11:9

Thou shalt not take the name of the Lord thy God in vain.

Holy Bible, Exodus 20:7

How forcible are right words!

Holy Bible, Job 6:25

A word fitly spoken is like apples of gold in pictures of silver.

Holy Bible, Proverbs 25:11

Christianity

I believe I was a child of God a long time before I really knew. The word *gospel* means "God's spell," or "good spell," or in other words "good news."

Dwight L. Moody, "Good News"

The Czech word *hus* means goose, and one of John Huss's friends, writing about him from Constance, said that the Goose was not yet cooked. Five centuries afterwards we still use that phrase in our vernacular, having long since forgotten its origin.

Harry Emerson Fosdick, *Great Voices of the Reformation*

Language falls down because it is derived from concrete experience and can be applied only with difficulty to religion, which is a stretching out for more adequate experience not yet existing as a definite and palpable state to which words are specifically appropriate.

Gordon W. Allport, *Waiting for the Lord*

Genuine words are being replaced by idle chatter. Words no longer possess any weight. There is too much talk.

Dietrich Bonhoeffer, *Ethics*

We celebrate Sunday, but we should not do so in order to forget that the same celebration is due on the other six days. Hence the Quakers call Sunday simply First-Day.

Jessamyn West, *The Quaker Reader*

When the United Nations was founded it was agreed the word *God* should be left out of its charter. The world has left God out of its planning.

Billy Graham, *Till Armageddon*

Confucianism

Confucius said, "In words all that matters is to express the meaning."

Confucius, *Analects*

Hinduism

Verily, sir, if a man meditate upon the syllable *Om* until the end of his life, what shall be his reward?. . .

With the syllable *Om* . . . the knower reaches that which is peaceful, unaging, immortal, fearless and supreme . . . he attains to Brahman!

Upanishads, Prasna

Water is called by different names by different people, one calling it *water,* another calling it *eau*, a third *aqua*, and another *pani*, so the one Sat-chit-ananda, the everlasting intelligent bliss, is invoked by some as *God*, by others as *Allah*, by some as *Jehovah*, by some as *Hari*, and by others as *Brahman.*

The Sayings of Shri Ramakrishna

Islam

We have put the Koran in Arabic so that you may understand it.

Koran, 43:3

The poetic force of the early portions of the Koran was not simply due to the stirrings of [Muhammad's] youthful imagination. These early portions are really very powerful. They are short, crisp, with a certain obscurity, probably designed; but for their purpose wonderfully expressive and impressive.

Richard Bell, *The Origin of Islam in Its Christian Environment*

"Islam" is an Arabic word. It means the act of resignation to God. The root word is *Slm*, pronounced *"salm,"* which means peace from which comes the word *"aslama"* which means he submitted, he resigned himself.

The Islamic Foundation, England

Judaism

Men love jargon. It is so palpable, tangible, visible, audible; it makes so obvious what one has learned; it satisfies the craving for results. It is impressive for the uninitiated. It makes one feel that one belongs. Jargon divides men into Us and Them.

Walter Kaufmann, *"I and Thou:* A Prologue"

One of the most imposing barriers that stands between the modern reader and the imaginative subtlety of biblical narrative is the extraordinary prominence of verbatim repetition in the Bible. . . . The extreme instance would be the description in Numbers 7:12–83 of the gifts brought to the sanctuary by the princes of the twelve tribes.

Robert Alter, The Art of Biblical Narrative

Taoism

The [Taoist] idea of teaching without words anticipated the Buddhist tradition of silent transmission of the mystic doctrine, especially in the Zen School. This is diametrically opposed to the Confucian ideal, according to which a superior man acts and "becomes the model of the world"; he speaks and "becomes the pattern of the world."

Wing-tsit Chan, A Source Book in Chinese Philosophy

LAW

Buddhism

He who considers all laws to be alike, void, devoid of particularity and individuality, not derived from an intelligent cause; nay, who discerns that nothingness is law;
   Such a one has great wisdom and sees the whole of the law entirely.

The Saddharma-Pundarika or The Lotus of the True Law

Christianity/Judaism

Ye shall have one manner of law, as well for the stranger, as for one of your own country: for I am the Lord your God.

Holy Bible, Leviticus 24:22

Christianity

And [Jesus] said, Woe unto you also, ye lawyers! for ye lade men with burdens grievous to be borne, and ye yourselves touch not the burdens with one of your fingers.

Holy Bible, Luke 12:46

Where no law is, there is no transgression.

Holy Bible, Romans 4:15

The law is good, if a man use it lawfully.

Holy Bible: 1 Timothy 1:8

Laws are not masters but servants, and he rules them who obeys them.

Henry Ward Beecher, Proverbs from Plymouth Pulpit

In the case of Natural Law, human reason has no share in the initiative and authority establishing the Law, either in making it exist or in making it known. How then does it know Natural Law? It knows it through inclination, . . . which is the work of God, and not by its own rational effort.

Jacques Maritain, *Moral Principles of Action*

If we have not heard the Gospel, we shall never hear the Law. The law that we think we hear without the Gospel is certainly not God's Law.

Karl Barth, *Credo*

Too much law means the obliteration of the individual; too much individualism means the weakening of law.

William Barclay, *Ethics in a Permissive Society*

[According to Jesus] there is to be no more of the old-style legalistic piety. Possession of the [Hebrew] law and correct observance of the law do not guarantee salvation. In the last resort the law is not decisive for salvation.

Hans Küng, *The Christian Challenge*

Hinduism

There is nothing higher than the law; a weak man controls a strong man by law, just as if by a king.

Upanishads, Brihadaranyaka

Whoso neglects the law's injunction,
    And lives according to his own willful desires,
He does not attain perfection,
    Nor bliss, nor the highest goal.

Bhagavad Gita, 16:23

Islam

As to the thief, male or female, cut off his or her hands. It is a reward for the crime and an exemplary punishment from Allah. Allah is mighty and wise.

Koran, 5:38

It is an accepted principle in Islamic law that everything is allowed unless explicitly prohibited and not the other way round.

Sa'id Ramadan, *Islamic Law: Its Scope and Equity*

Judaism

Law in Judaism never became a discipline independent of religion and ethics. It is in the last analysis the instrument of religion and ethics.

Morris Adler, *The World of the Talmud*

The laws of our religion, though no policeman enforces them, form an organic whole, a living pattern of behavior for a community and for each individual in it. The symbols and rites of the faith are stamped on every important part of life: on food, on clothing, on shelter, on time, on sex, on speech.

Herman Wouk, *This Is My God*

Law has been, and still is, the most effective human way society has for the conservation of its values. And to argue that religion, which gives the ultimate validity to all our values, must deny itself the use of Law is to cripple religion and endanger its effectiveness.

Emanuel Rackman, *One Man's Judaism*

God pokes his nose into all the nooks and crannies of life. There are laws about birds' nests, and shopping-scales, infectious diseases and care of the environment.

Lionel Blue, *To Heaven, with Scribes and Pharisees*

Taoism

The more laws and orders are multiplied, the more theft and violence increase.

Lao-tzu, *Tao-te ching*

LEADERSHIP

Christianity/Judaism

And the Lord went before them by day in a pillar of a cloud, to lead them the way; and by night in a pillar of fire, to give them light.

Holy Bible, Exodus 13:21

Christianity

Can the blind lead the blind? shall they not both fall into the ditch?

Holy Bible, Luke: 6:39

No man can firmly command save he who has learned gladly to obey.

Thomas à Kempis, *The Imitation of Christ*

We glibly propose that what our age needs is "a great leader." But he might not even be recognized, let alone followed; and if he were followed, he would still fail if the crosscurrents of our time did not gather to carry his vessel on his course.

George A. Buttrick, *Christ and History*

The father, the teacher, and the statesman are not leaders by nature, but stewards of their office. Anyone who expects otherwise is not looking at reality, he is dreaming.

Dietrich Bonhoeffer, *No Rusty Swords*

Christ spent more than half His time with just twelve men, developing them into leaders who would carry on His work after He ascended to Heaven.

Billy Graham, *The Holy Spirit*

Confucianism

The princely man in dealing with others does not descend to anything low or improper. How unbending his valor! He stands in the middle, and leans not to either side.

Confucius

Mencius said, . . . "Let the ruler be humane, and all his people will be humane. Let the ruler be righteous, and all his people will be righteous. Let the ruler be correct, and all his people will be correct.

Mencius, *The Book of Mencius*

Hinduism

He, affluent, rides formost in his chariot,
Bestowing gifts and in assemblies lauded.

Rig-Veda

Judaism

In the place where there is already a leader, do not seek to become a leader. But in the place where there is no leader, strive thou to become a leader.

Talmud, Berakot 63a

Taoism

Handle a large kingdom with as gentle a touch
    as if you were cooking small fish.
If you manage people by letting them alone,
Ghosts of the dead shall not haunt you.

Lao-tzu, *Tao-te ching*

LIFE

Buddhism

Life is like the flame of a lamp exposed to the wind.

Japanese Buddhist proverb

Christianity/Judaism

The Lord God formed man of the dust of the ground, and breathed into his nostrils the breath of life; and man became a living soul.

Holy Bible, Genesis 2:7

Christianity

What is your life? It is even a vapor, that appeareth for a little time, and then vanisheth away.

Holy Bible, James 4:14

From dust I rise
    And out of nothing now awake,
These brighter regions which salute mine eyes,
    A gift from God I take.

Thomas Traherne, "The Salutation"

Life is real! Life is earnest!
And the grave is not its goal.

Henry Wadsworth Longfellow, "A Psalm of Life"

God asks no man whether he will accept life. That is not the choice. You *must* take it. The only choice is *how*.

Henry Ward Beecher, *Life Thoughts*

Life is not an illogicality; yet it is a trap for logicians. It looks just a little more mathematical and regular than it is; its exactitude is obvious, but its inexactitude is hidden; its wildness lies in wait.

G.K. Chesterton, *Orthodoxy*

Reverence for life comprises the whole ethic of love in its deepest and highest sense. It is the source of constant renewal for the individual and for mankind.

Albert Schweitzer, *Reverence for Life*

Life . . . is meant to superabound but not to explode. Those who are bursting with life are often merely plunging into death with an enormous splash.

Thomas Merton, *The New Man*

Life is a journey. . . . We who call ourselves Christians believe that the journey begins and ends with God. He created us at the beginning of life and He will welcome us home when this life is over.

Jerry Falwell, *Strength for the Journey*

Existentialism

Everything has been figured out except how to live.

Jean-Paul Sartre

Hinduism

Life, verily, is more than hope. Just as the spokes of a wheel are fastened in the hub, so on this vital breath everything is fastened.

Upanishads, Chandogya

Like grain a mortal ripens!
Like grain he is born hither again!

Upanishads, Katha

Islam

Coin for them a simile about this life. It is like the green herbs that flourish when watered by the rain, soon turning into stubble which the wind scatters abroad. Allah has power over all things.

Koran, 18:45

Judaism

All actual life is encounter.

Martin Buber, *I and Thou*

Unitarianism

To be human is to know and care and ask. To keep rattling the bars of experience hollering, "What's it for?" at the stones and stars, and making prisons and palaces out of the echoing answers.

Robert Fulghum, *All I Really Need to Know I Learned in Kindergarten*

LOVE

Buddhism

Hateful the wind or rain that ruins the bloom of flowers:
Even more hateful far [is he] who obstructs the way of love.

Lafcadio Hearn, "Buddhist Allusions in Japanese Folksongs"

Christianity/Judaism

Rise up, my love, my fair one, and come away.
For, lo, the winter is past, the rain is over and gone;
The flowers appear on the earth; the time of the singing of
Birds is come, and the voice of the turtle is heard in our land.

Holy Bible, Song of Solomon 2:10-12

Christianity

Thou shalt love thy neighbor as thyself.

Holy Bible, Matthew 22:39

Love your enemies, do good to them which hate you,
Bless them that curse you, and pray for them which despitefully use you.

Holy Bible, Luke 6:27-28

For God so loved the world, that he gave his only begotten Son, that whosoever believeth in him should not perish, but have everlasting life.

Holy Bible, John 3:16

Perfect love casteth out fear.

Holy Bible, 1 John 4:18

He who subjects himself to his neighbor in love can never be humiliated.

St. Basil the Great

When [St.] John tarried in Ephesus to extreme old age, and could only with difficulty be carried to the church in the arms of his disciples, and was unable to give utterance to many words, he used to say no more at their several meetings than this: "Little children, love one another." At length the disciples and fathers who were there, wearied with always hearing the same words, said: "Master, why dost thou always say this?" "It is the Lord's command," was his reply, "and if this alone be done, it is enough."

St. Jerome, *Commentary on Galatians*

Nothing . . . is sweeter than love; nothing higher, nothing stronger, nothing larger, nothing more joyful, nothing fuller, nothing better, in heaven or on earth.

Thomas à Kempis, *The Imitation of Christ*

The soul cannot live without love.

St. Francis de Sales

Love is the hardest lesson in Christianity.

William Penn

He prayeth best, who loveth best
   All things both great and small;
For the dear God who loveth us,
   He made and loveth all.

Samuel Taylor Coleridge, "The Rime of the Ancient Mariner"

The more we know of men, the less we love them. It is the contrary with God; the more we know of Him, the more we love Him.

St. John Vianney

Love alone is capable of uniting living beings in such a way as to complete and fulfill them, for it alone takes them and joins them by what is deepest within themselves.

Pierre Teilhard de Chardin, *The Phenomenon of Man*

The original and positive ethical basis for Christianity was love. . . . God is love. The soul is holy, able to know God, and therefore of ultimate significance. Love, as it is interpreted in the fourth Gospel, is the primary fact of the universe.

Herschel Baker, *The Image of Man*

We have to note very carefully the word the Christian ethic uses for love. It is the word *agape*. . . . It means an undefeatable attitude of goodwill; it means that no matter what the other man does to us we will never under any circumstances seek anything but his good.

William Barclay, *Ethics in a Permissive Society*

Human love fails and will always fail. God's love never fails.

Corrie ten Boom, *Not I, But Christ*

Only he who knows God knows what love is; it is not the other way round.

Dietrich Bonhoeffer, *Ethics*

Love is a fruit in season at all times, and within reach of every hand. Anyone may gather it, and no limit is set.

> Mother Teresa of Calcutta, *Life in the Spirit*

The plain truth is this: love is not a matter of getting what you want. Quite the contrary. The insistence on always having what you want, on always being satisfied, on always being fulfilled, makes love impossible. . . . Love is not a deal, it is a sacrifice.

> Thomas Merton, *Love and Living*

Love is the only force capable of transforming an enemy into a friend.

> Martin Luther King, Jr., *The Words of Martin Luther King*

However wonderful and glamorous a passion may be, if it is going to hurt someone else, even indirectly, it cannot be genuine love.

> J.B. Phillips, *Good News*

Yes, fear and self-righteousness, indifference and sentimentality kill; but love never dies, not with God, and not even with us.

> William Sloane Coffin, *Living the Truth in a World of Illusions*

Christian Science

Divine Love always has met and always will meet every human need.

> Mary Baker Eddy, *Science and Health with Key to the Scriptures*

Confucianism

Mencius said: To feed a person without loving him is to treat him like a pig. To love without respecting him is to treat him like a domestic pet.

> Mencius, *The Book of Mencius*

Hinduism

Do we not carry a rose to our beloved because in it is already embodied a message which, unlike our language of words, cannot be analyzed?

> Rabindranath Tagore, *The Religion of Man*

Judaism

Love is wholly sweet only when it is love for what is mortal. The secret of ultimate sweetness is bound up with the bitterness of death.

Franz Rosenzweig, *The Star of Redemption*

Nonsectarian

The religious form of love, that which is called the love of God, . . . springs from the need to overcome separateness and to achieve union.

Erich Fromm, *The Art of Loving*

Poetics

Think not you can direct the course of love, for love, if it finds you worthy, directs your course.

Kahlil Gibran, *The Prophet*

Taoism

By the accident of fortune a man may rule the world for a time, but by virtue of love he may rule the world forever.

Lao-tzu, *Tao-te ching*

If one forsakes love and courage, forsakes restraint and reserve power,
Forsakes following behind and rushes in front, he is doomed!
For love is victorious in attack and invulnerable in defense.
Heaven arms with love those it would not see destroyed.

Chuang-tzu

LOYALTY

Christianity/Judaism

Though he slay me, yet will I trust in him.

Holy Bible, Job 13:15

Christianity

No man can serve two masters: for he will either hate the one, and love the other; or else he will hold to the one, and despise the other.

Holy Bible, Matthew 6:24

When tempted to despair, I have only one resource: to throw myself at the foot of the Tabernacle like a little dog at the foot of his master.

St. John Vianney

Loyalty is a sentiment, not a law. It rests on love, not on restraint.

Sir Roger Casement, Speech at his trial for treason, 1916

My schoolmasters did not tell me that the Puritan stood for religious loyalty, which is true. They told me that he stood for religious liberty, which is a lie of that mountainous and monstrous order which ignorant traditionalists call a Whopper.

G.K. Chesterton, "On the Truth of Legends"

MAN

Agnosticism

An honest God is the noblest work of man.

Robert G. Ingersoll, "The Gods"

Christianity/Judaism

So God created man in his own image, in the image of God created he him.

Holy Bible, Genesis 1:27

When I consider thy heavens, the work of thy fingers, the moon and the stars, which thou hast ordained;
    What is man, that thou art mindful of him?

Holy Bible, Psalms 8:3-4

Christianity

Then came Jesus forth, wearing the crown of thorns, and the purple robe. And Pilate saith unto them, Behold the man!

Holy Bible, John 19:5

Cursed is every one who placeth his hope in man.

St. Augustine, *On the Christian Conflict*

To whatever part of man we turn our eyes, it is impossible to see anything that is not impure, profane, and abominable to God.

John Calvin, *Instruction in Faith*

What a piece of work is a man! How noble in reason! how infinite in
faculties! in form and moving how express and admirable! in action how
like an angel! in apprehension how like a god!

William Shakespeare, *Hamlet*, Act 2, Sc. 2

What a monster . . . is man. What a novelty, what a portent, what a chaos,
what a contradiction, what a prodigy! Universal judge, and helpless worm;
trustee of truth, and sink of uncertainty and error.

Blaise Pascal, *Pensées*

Man as we know him is a poor creature; but he is half way between an
ape and a god, and he is traveling in the right direction.

William Ralph Inge, *Outspoken Essays*

Man has more grandeur than the Milky Way; but how easy evil is for him.

Jacques Maritain, *Moral Philosophy*

The high estimate of the human stature implied in the concept of "image of
God" stands in paradoxical juxtaposition to the low estimate of human virtue
in Christian thought. Man is a sinner. His sin is defined as rebellion against
God.

Reinhold Niebuhr, *The Nature and Destiny of Man*

Confucianism

Man occupies the most honored position in the scheme of things because
he combines in him the principles of all species. If he honors his own
position and enhances his honor, he can make all species serve him.

Shao Yung, *Supreme Principles Governing the World*

Deism

Man is not one; . . . I feel myself at once a slave and a free man; I perceive
what is right, I love it, and I do what is wrong; I am active when I listen
to the voice of reason; I am passive when I am carried away by my passions.

Jean Jacques Rousseau, *Emile*

Islam

Man is both the fruit of the universe and its elite, a king who must
rule wisely, competently, and fairly. God, in His grace, has permitted
man to be His viceregent.

Mahmoud Mohamed Taha, *The Second Message of Islam*

Judaism

The ideal man has the strength of a male and the compassion of a female.

Talmud, Zohar iv, 145b

Even the form in which we ask the question about man is biased by our conception of man as a thing. We ask: *What* is man? Yet the true question should be: *Who* is man? As a thing man is explicable; as a person he is both a mystery and a surprise. As a thing he is finite; as a person he is inexhaustible.

Abraham Joshua Heschel, *Who Is Man?*

Man, in one respect, is a mere random example of the biological species—species man—an image of the universal, a shadow of true existence. In another respect he is a man of God, possessor of an individual . . . authentic existence.

Joseph B. Soloveitchik, *Halakhic Man*

Stoicism

Man is a reasoning animal.

Seneca, *Epistles*

Unitarianism

Man is a god in ruins.

Ralph Waldo Emerson, *Nature*

MARRIAGE

Christianity/Judaism

And Adam said, This is now bone of my bones, and flesh of my flesh: she shall be called Woman. . . .
  Therefore shall a man leave his father and his mother, and shall cleave unto his wife, and they shall be one flesh.

Holy Bible, Genesis 2:23-24

Christianity

It is better to marry than to burn.

Holy Bible, 1 Corinthians 7:9

Those whom God hath joined together let no man put asunder.

Book of Common Prayer

To have and to hold from this day forward, for better, for worse, for richer, for poorer, in sickness and in health, to love and to cherish, till death do us part.

Book of Common Prayer

One was never married, and that's his hell; another is, and that's his plague.

Robert Burton, *The Anatomy of Melancholy*

I had always entertained so high a regard for marriage, as it was a divine institution, that I held it not lawful to make it a sort of political trade, to rise in the world by.

Thomas Ellwood, *The History of the Life of Thomas Ellwood*

Adam could not be happy even in Paradise without Eve.

John Lubbock, *Peace and Happiness*

A man denounces marriage as a lie, and then denounces aristocratic profligates for treating it as a lie.

G.K. Chesterton, *Orthodoxy*

In true married love it is not so much that two hearts walk side by side through life. Rather the two hearts form one heart. That is why death is not the separation of two hearts, but rather the tearing apart of one heart. It is this that makes the bitterness of grief.

Fulton J. Sheen, *Three to Get Married*

We are quite right in saying that marriage is based on love; we find this truth in the gospel. However, we must immediately add that true love makes us capable of taking on the tasks and problems of married and family life and that if it does not give us this capacity it cannot be called love.

Pope John Paul II, *The Word Made Flesh*

Hinduism

Though destitute of virtues, or seeking pleasure, or devoid of good qualities, yet a husband must be constantly worshipped as a god by a faithful wife.

Laws of Manu

Islam

Marry those among you who are single, including the virtuous ones among your male and female slaves.

Koran, 24:32

Poetics

Let there be spaces in your togetherness,
And let the winds of the heavens dance between you.

Kahlil Gibran, The Prophet

MATURITY

Christianity

When I was a child, I spake as a child, I understood as a child, I thought as a child: but when I became a man, I put away childish things.

Holy Bible, 1 Corinthians 13:11

Maturity can be recognized in the slowness with which a man believes.

Baltasar Gracian, The Art of Worldly Wisdom

We were all given youthful enthusiasm for many things and goals. But all this enthusiasm . . . cannot be used and increased. Most of the objects of our early enthusiasm must be sacrificed for a few, and those few approached soberly. No maturity is possible without this sacrifice.

Paul Tillich, The Eternal Now

Maturity is never merely a matter of age, but one of development. A mature sentiment has a way of handling doubt, of realizing . . . that personal commitment is possible even without absolute certainty, that a person can be half-sure without being half-hearted.

Gordon W. Allport, Waiting for the Lord

Confucianism

Mencius said, "The five kinds of grain are considered good plants, but if they are not ripe, they are worse than poor grains. So the value of humanity depends on its being brought to maturity."

Mencius, The Book of Mencius

Islam

Society suffers from a state in which most of its members are either adolescents or children, and there are few mature members capable of facing up to the truth. . . . A society characterized by wishful thinking and failure to distinguish between conflicting desires on a rational long-term basis is in need of guidance.

Mahmoud Mohamed Taha, The Second Message of Islam

MERCY

Christianity/Judaism

The mercy of the Lord is from everlasting to everlasting upon them that fear him.

Holy Bible, Psalms 103:17

He that hath mercy on the poor, happy is he.

Holy Bible, Proverbs 14:21

Christianity

Blessed are the merciful: for they shall obtain mercy.

Holy Bible, Matthew 5:7

God be merciful to me a sinner.

Holy Bible, Luke 18:13

If mercy were a sin, I believe I could not keep from committing it.

St. Bernard of Clairvaux

The more merciful acts thou dost, the more mercy thou wilt receive.

William Penn, *Some Fruits of Solitude*

Where Mercy, Love, and Pity dwell,
There God is dwelling too.

William Blake, "The Divine Image"

We hand folks over to God's mercy, and show none ourselves.

George Eliot, *Adam Bede*

Here lie I, Martin Elginbrodde:
Hae mercy o' my soul, Lord God;
As I wad do, were I Lord God,
And ye were Martin Elginbrodde.

George Macdonald, *David Elginbrod*

Mercy is a specifically divine attribute. There is no human mercy. Mercy implies an infinite distance.

Simone Weil, *First and Last Notebooks*

When we live at each other's mercy, we had better learn to be merciful.

William Sloane Coffin, *Living the Truth in a World of Illusions*

Islam

Swift is thy Lord in retribution; yet He is forgiving and merciful.

Koran, 6:165

Judaism

In the beginning God wished to render justice, but when He observed that the world could not rest on justice alone, He rendered mercy.

Talmud, Rosh Hashanah 17

Unitarianism

The essential and unbounded mercy of my Creator is the foundation of my hope, and a broader and surer one the universe cannot give me.

William Ellery Channing, *Works of . . .*

MIRACLES

Atheism

Miracles are propitious accidents, the natural causes of which are too complicated to be readily understood.

George Santayana, *Introduction to the Ethics of Spinoza*

Buddhism

There is no miracle in true doctrine.

Japanese Buddhist proverb

Christianity/Judaism

If the Lord be with us, why then is all this befallen us? and where be all his miracles which our fathers told us of?

Holy Bible, Judges 6:13

Christianity

When they wanted wine, the mother of Jesus saith unto him, They have no wine. . . .

Jesus saith unto them, Fill the waterpots with water. And they filled them up to the brim.

And he saith unto them, Draw out now, and bear unto the governor of the feast. And they bare it.

[Whereupon] the ruler of the feast . . . tasted the water that was made wine.

Holy Bible, John 2:3,7-9

Why, they ask, do not those miracles, which you preach of as past events, happen nowadays? I might reply that they were necessary before the world believed, to bring the world to believe.

St. Augustine, *The City of God*

Miracles are the swaddling clothes of infant churches.

Thomas Fuller, *Church History*

If there were no false miracles, there would be certainty.

Blaise Pascal, *Pensees*

The laws of nature had sometimes been suspended by their Divine Author; and since what had happened once might happen again, a certain probability, at least no kind of improbability, was attached to the idea . . . of miraculous intervention in later times.

John Henry Newman, *Apologia pro vita sua*

The most serious doubt that has been thrown on the authenticity of the miracles is the fact that most of the witnesses in regard to them were fishermen.

Arthur Brinstead, *Pitcher's Proverbs*

If in any human action upon the universe around us we admit that Will is producing a disturbance, then necessarily and inevitably we must admit that superior Will could make a greater disturbance, and that a Supreme Will creative of the universe could exercise a special influence upon any scale it chose.

Hilaire Belloc, "On Renan"

Miracles are God's signature, appended to his masterpiece of creation.

Ronald Knox, *Miracles*

If the world is really the medium of God's personal action, miracle is wholly normal.

D.E. Trueblood, *The Logic of Belief*

The church speaks of miracles because it speaks of God. Of eternity in time, of life in death, of love in hate, of forgiveness in sin, or salvation in suffering, of hope in despair.

Dietrich Bonhoeffer, *No Rusty Swords*

[Question:] Why are there no longer miracles?
[Answer:] Didn't the sun rise this morning?

Andrew M. Greeley, *The Catholic WHY? Book*

Jesus's cures have nothing to do with magic and sorcery, where the person is overpowered against his will. They are an appeal for faith, which itself sometimes appears to be the real miracle by comparison with which the cure is of secondary importance. The healing stories of the New Testament must be understood as stories of faith.

Hans Küng, *The Christian Challenge*

Confucianism

The Master never talked of prodigies, feats of strength, disorders or spirits.

Confucius, *Analects*

Islam

I have given credence to the veracity of Muhammad and of Moses, not through the splitting of the moon, or the changing of a rod into a snake. Such [demonstrations] lead to much delusion, and cannot be trusted.

Al-Ghazali, *The Just Balance*

Judaism

A miracle cannot prove what is impossible; it is useful only to confirm what is possible.

Maimonides, *Guide of the Perplexed*

We are terrified by . . . every inexplicable miracle, we are afraid of discovering a break in the course of historical phenomena. We devote all our efforts to banishing out of life everything "sudden," "spontaneous," "unexpected." We describe all such things as chance, but chance in our tongue means something which, strictly speaking, cannot exist.

Lev Shestov, *In Job's Balances*

Miracles sometimes occur, but one has to work terribly hard for them.

Chaim Weizmann

If miracle is really the favorite child of belief, then its father has been neglecting his parental duties badly. . . . For at least a hundred years the child has been nothing but a source of embarrassment.

Franz Rosenzweig, *The Star of Redemption*

Nonsectarian

There is not to be found, in all history, any miracle attested by a sufficient number of men, of such unquestioned good sense, education, and learning, as to secure us against all delusion in themselves.

David Hume, "Concerning Human Understanding"

Unitarianism

The very word *miracle*, as pronounced by Christian churches, gives a false impression; it is a monster. It is not one with the blowing clover and the falling rain.

> Ralph Waldo Emerson, Address to the Harvard Divinity School

MONEY

Christianity/Judaism

A feast is made for laughter, and wine maketh merry: but money answereth all things.

> *Holy Bible*, Ecclesiastes 10:19

Christianity

Ye cannot serve God and mammon.

> *Holy Bible*, Matthew 6:24

Thy money perisheth with thee.

> *Holy Bible*, Acts 8:20

The love of money is the root of all evil.

> *Holy Bible*, 1 Timothy 6:10

Everything bows to money. It seems as if this was as powerful a saying among all peoples as it is now in general use: Everything bows to money. It is mentioned among Hebrew proverbs in Ecclesiastes, Chapter 10, and is well known in the same form in Greek and Latin alike.

> Erasmus, *Adages*

There is no divine authority for preaching that the soul flies out of purgatory immediately as the money clinks in the till.

> Martin Luther, *Disputation on the Power and Efficacy of Indulgences* ("95 Theses" [No. 27])

The love of money and the love of learning rarely meet.

> George Herbert, *Jacula Prudentum*

When I have money, I get rid of it quickly, lest it find a way into my heart.

> John Wesley

A philosopher was once asked by a vulgar fellow whether his philosophy had ever brought him in any money. The answer, intended to be intelligble to the questioner, was: "It has saved me a great many expenses."

William Ralph Inge, *Wit and Wisdom of Dean Inge*

It is strange and bizarre that the most serious conflict in the majority of middle-class marriages is over the use of money, even though these marriages have available more money than did almost any previous marriage in the history of mankind.

Andrew M. Greeley, *Life for a Wanderer*

Judaism

Rabbi Johanan said, "If one's father has bequeathed him a large sum of money, and he is eager to lose it, he should dress in fine linen garments, use costly glass utensils, and hire laborers without supervising them."

Talmud, Baba Metzia 29b

Nonsectarian

If Kroll's [a big department store] could go, the courthouse could go, the banks could go. When the money stopped, they could close down God Himself.

John Updike, *Rabbit at Rest*

Unitarianism

We [in the United States] estimate the skill of an artist like that of a peddler, not by the pictures he has made, but by the money.

Theodore Parker, "The Position and Duties of the American Scholar"

MUSIC

Christianity/Judaism

Praise him with the sound of the trumpet: praise him with the psaltery and harp.

Praise him with the timbrel and dance: praise him with stringed instruments and organs.

Praise him upon the loud cymbals.

Holy Bible, Psalms 150:2-5

Christianity

I have no pleasure in any man who despises music. It is no invention of ours; it is the gift of God. I place it next to theology.

Martin Luther

Sing spiritual canticles, for the Evil One by this means has often desisted from his operation.

St. Francis de Sales, *Introduction to the Devout Life*

Music strikes in me a deep fit of devotion, and a profound contemplation of the First Composer. There is something in it of divinity.

Sir Thomas Browne, *Religio Medici*

But, oh! what art can teach,
What human voice can reach
    The sacred organ's praise?
    Notes inspiring holy love,
Notes that wing their heavenly ways
    To mend the choirs above.

John Dryden, "A Song for St. Cecilia's Day"

Music, the greatest good that mortals know,
And all of heaven we have below.

Joseph Addison, "A Song for St. Cecilia's Day"

O, may I join the choir invisible
Of those immortal dead who live again
In minds made better by their presence . . .
Whose music is the gladness of the world.

George Eliot, "O May I Join the Choir Invisible"

I know not what I was playing,
    Or what I was dreaming then;
But I struck one chord of music,
    Like the sound of a great Amen.

Adelaide Anne Procter, "A Lost Chord"

[The original first line of this stanza was, "I do not know what I was playing." Arthur Sullivan, in setting the verse to music as "The Lost Chord," changed it to the more familiar line shown above.]

In exchange for mad jazz and concert music, we [Carmelite nuns] have the Gregorian chant whose only audience is God.

Mother Catherine Thomas, *My Beloved*

It would be a sad day for us if ever the music of church bells were to become silent in our villages and towns. For it is this music which calls us away from the world of visible things, the world of our scheming and talking, inviting us to gather ourselves together to hear the word of God which resounds from the invisible world of eternity.

Rudolf Bultmann, *This World and the Beyond*

Confucianism

The Master said, "Let a man be first incited by the Songs, then given a firm footing by the study of ritual, and finally perfected by music."

Confucius, *Analects*

Ancient music appeased the heart, but modern music enhances desires.

Chou Tun-i, *Penetrating the Book of Changes*

Hinduism

If one desires the world of song and music, merely out of his conception song and music arise. Possessed of that world of song and music, he is happy.

Upanishads, Chandogya

Judaism

There is a Temple in Heaven that is opened only through song.

Talmud, Tikkune Zohar 45a

Their religious consciousness was largely a musical box: the thrill of the ram's horn, the cadenza of a psalmic phrase, the jubilance of a festival "Amen."

Israel Zangwill, *Children of the Ghetto*

Stoicism

What can I do, a lame old man, but sing hymns to God?

Epictetus, *Discourses*

MYSTERY

Christianity/Judaism

There be three things which are too wonderful for me, yea, four which I know not:

The way of an eagle in the air; the way of a serpent upon a rock; the way of a ship in the midst of the sea; and the way of a man with a maid.

Holy Bible, Proverbs 30:18–19

Christianity

[Jesus Christ] hath abounded toward us in all wisdom . . .
Having made known unto us the mystery of his will.

Holy Bible, Ephesians 1:8-9

Mix a little mystery with everything, and the very mystery arouses veneration.

Baltasar Gracian, *The Art of Worldly Wisdom*

God moves in a mysterious way
    His wonders to perform;
He plants his footsteps in the sea
    And rides upon the storm.

William Cowper, "Light Shining out of Darkness"

As long as you have mystery you have health; when you destroy mystery you create morbidity. The ordinary man has always been sane because the ordinary man has always been a mystic. He has permitted the twilight.

G.K. Chesterton, *Orthodoxy*

Whenever we penetrate to the heart of things, we always find a mystery. Life and all that goes with it is unfathomable. . . . Knowledge of life is recognition of the mysterious.

Albert Schweitzer, *Reverence for Life*

I would rather live in a world where my life is surrounded by mystery than live in a world so small that my mind could comprehend it.

Harry Emerson Fosdick, *Riverside Sermons*

Islam

Man is unable to explain to himself the mystery of life, the mystery of birth and death, the mystery of infinity and eternity. His reasoning stops before impregnable walls.

Muhammad Asad, *Islam at the Crossroads*

Judaism

Silence hovers over all the mountain peaks. The world is aflame with grandeur. Each flower is an outpouring of love. Each being speaks for itself. Man alone can speak to all beings. Human living alone enacts the mystery as a drama.

Abraham Joshua Heschel, *Who Is Man?*

Existence plays a mischievous game with us, as though to tease and provoke us. In the midst of knowledge there yet once again arises the mystery; in the midst of contemplation the riddle gains new strength.

Joseph B. Soloveitchik, *Halakhic Man*

One does not need to fast for days and meditate for hours at a time to experience the sense of sublime mystery which constantly envelops us. All one need do is to notice intelligently, if even for a brief moment, a blossoming tree, a forest flooded with autumn colors, an infant smiling.

Simon Greenberg, *A Jewish Philosophy and Pattern of Life*

MYTH

Christianity

When a myth becomes a daydream it is judged, found wanting, and must be discarded. To cling to it when it has lost its creative function is to condemn oneself to mental illness. I do not say we must learn to live without myths . . . but we must at least get along without evasions. A daydream is an evasion.

Thomas Merton, *Conjectures of a Guilty Bystander*

If the creation story, the virgin birth, and the resurrection are only myths, then I'm myth-taken and myth-tified and myth-erable.

Vance Havner, *Pepper 'n' Salt*

The Gospels were . . . written for people thinking mythologically at a time of mythological thinking.

Hans Küng, *On Being a Christian*

Judaism

The Jew of antiquity cannot tell a story in any other way than mythically, for to him an event is worth telling only when it has been grasped in its divine significance.

Martin Buber, *On Judaism*

NATURE

Buddhism

Green onions flowering—
For a moment golden
Buddha was there.

Kawabata Bosha

Christianity/Judaism

Thou madest him to have dominion over the works of thy hands; thou
hast put all things under his feet:
    All sheep and oxen, yea, and the beasts of the field;
    The fowl of the air, and the fish of the sea, and whatsoever passeth
through the paths of the seas.

Holy Bible, Psalms 8:6-8

The earth is the Lord's, and the fulness thereof; the world, and they that
dwell therein.

Holy Bible, Psalms 24:1

Christianity

Why take ye thought for raiment? Consider the lilies of the field, how
they grow; they toil not, neither do they spin.
    And yet I say unto you, That even Solomon in all his glory was not
arrayed like one of these.

Holy Bible, Matthew 6:28-29

Believe one who has tried, you shall find a fuller satisfaction in the woods than in books. The trees and the rocks will teach you that which you cannot hear from masters.

St. Bernard of Clairvaux

All things are artificial, for nature is the art of God.

Sir Thomas Browne, *Religio Medici*

The world is certainly a great and stately volume of natural things, and may be not improperly styled the hieroglyphics of a better [one]. But, alas, how very few leaves of it do we seriously turn over!

William Penn, *Some Fruits of Solitude*

A robin redbreast in a cage
Puts all Heaven in a rage.

William Blake, "Auguries of Innocence"

In the summer in July we were hastening to the monastery of Our Lady for the holy festival. . . . We spent the night in the open country, and I waked up early in the morning, when all was still sleeping and the sun had not yet peeped out from behind the forest. . . . Everywhere beauty passing all utterance! All was still, the air was light; the grass grows—Grow, grass of God; the bird sings—Sing, bird of God; the babe cries in the woman's arms—God be with you, little man; grow and be happy, little babe. . . . Life is sweet.

Fyodor Dostoyevsky, *The Raw Youth*

Some keep Sunday going to church,
    I keep it staying at home,
With a bobolink for a choirster,
    And an orchard for a throne.

Emily Dickinson, "Some Keep Sunday Going to Church"

Glory be to God for dappled things—
    For skies of couple-color as a brinded cow;
    For rose-moles all in stipple upon trout that swim;
Fresh-firecoal chestnut-falls; finches' wings.

Gerard Manley Hopkins, "Pied Beauty"

A man loves Nature in the morning for her innocence and amiability, and at nightfall, if he is loving her still, it is for her darkness and her cruelty.

G.K. Chesterton, *Orthodoxy*

It is harder for us today to feel near to God among the streets and houses of the city than it is for countryfolk. For them the harvested fields bathed in the autumn mists speak of God and his goodness far more vividly than any human lips.

Albert Schweitzer, Reverence for Life

The work of man's hand passes away; but nature goes on its unvarying course throughout all ages, renewing its life with every spring and scattering lavishly its riches without ever becoming poorer.

Rudolf Bultmann, This World and the Beyond

Poems are made by fools like me,
But only God can make a tree.

Joyce Kilmer, "Trees"

[Benedetto] Croce astonishingly proposed: "Do you wish to understand the history of a blade of grass? First and foremost, try to make yourself into a blade of grass." I tried, and found myself scampering at the very sight of a lawn mower.

George A. Buttrick, Christ and History

The mastery of nature is vainly believed to be an adequate substitute for self-mastery.

Reinhold Niebuhr, Christian Century

Our bodies are . . . communities in relationship with the earth. Our bodily fluids carry the same chemicals as the primeval seas. . . . Our bones contain the sugar that once flowed in the sap of now-fossilized trees. The nitrogen which binds our bones together is the same as that which binds nitrates to the soil.

James M. Nelson, Between Two Gardens

Hinduism

Waters that come from heaven or run in channels
Dug out, or flow spontaneously from nature,
That, clear and pure, have as their goal the ocean:
Here may those waters, goddesses, preserve me.

Rig-Veda

The God who is in fire, who is in water, who has entered into the whole world, who is in plants, who is in trees—to that God be adoration!

Upanishads, Svetasvatara

Islam

The Koran, with its splendid insistence on nature as a realm of Divine "signs," is squarely confronted by the contemporary temptation to find in it no more than observable phenomena and natural law.

Kenneth Cragg, *Counsels in Contemporary Islam*

Taoism

Nature and her animals are innocent. We may think nature cruel and unmerciful when we find a deer's carcass or see a tree torn by a thunderstorm. This is nature's way and nature's logic. She lacks the wishful thinking and stupid sentimentality that humans possess.

Deng Ming-Dao, *The Seven Bamboo Tablets of the Cloudy Satchel*

Unitarianism

What person has ever come near to nature and not seen therein the revelation of God's spirit? Through all the physical universe there runs the all-pervading life of God—hence is every particle of this universe in itself a revelation of the Divine.

John Haynes Holmes, *The Old and the New*

OBEDIENCE

Christianity/Judaism

If ye be willing and obedient, ye shall eat the good of the land.

Holy Bible, Isaiah 1:19

Christianity

If ye love me, keep my commandments.

Holy Bible, John 14:15

Holy obedience puts to shame all natural and selfish desires. It mortifies our lower nature and makes it obey the spirit and our fellow men.

St. Francis of Assisi

Courage can be shown by any fool;
Obedience is the Christian's jewel.

Friedrich von Schiller

Obedience—not "Yes, but," but "Yes, Father."

Corrie ten Boom, *Not I, But Christ*

Obedience in the modern world is *not* the virtue that inclines us to respond blindly and unthinkingly to whatever our leader says; it is, rather, that virtue which inclines us to enter into a responsible, cooperative relationship with those who are our colleagues.

Andrew M. Greeley, *Life for a Wanderer*

Islam

Who has a better religion than he who submits himself entirely to Allah, intelligently and knowingly, and follows Abraham's perfect creed?

Koran, 4:125

Obey what is revealed you from your Lord. Allah is aware of all you do. And put your trust in Him, for He is your guardian and trustee.

Koran, 33:2-3

OLD AGE

Buddhism

Now the swinging bridge
Is quieted with creepers—
Like our tendrilled life.

Basho

Christianity/Judaism

With the ancient is wisdom; and in length of days understanding.

Holy Bible, Job 12:12

Cast me not off in the time of old age; forsake me not when my strength faileth.

Holy Bible, Psalms 71:9

Christianity

Elderly people are often much more romantic than young people, and sometimes even more adventurous, having begun to realize how many things they do not know.

G.K. Chesterton, "On the Pleasures of No Longer Being Very Young"

Old age comes from God, old age leads on to God, old age will not touch me only so far as He wills.

Pierre Teilhard de Chardin

Age creeps on, but we refuse to recognize it.
We enlist the help of the masseuse and the golf pro
        the dressmaker and the tailor
        creams and lotions
        hair dyes and plastic surgeons
all in an effort to keep alive the illusion
        that life here will go on forever.

Peter Marshall, "Go Down Death"

[Question:] Why do we try to prolong this life if happiness in the next life is the whole point of this life.

[Answer:] First of all, happiness in the next life is not the whole point of this life. . . . This life is not a shell game, not a shadow existence, not a test to be passed like the college boards which we have to get by to make it into college. This life has a value, a dignity, and a worth of its own.

Andrew M. Greeley, *The Catholic WHY? Book*

Hinduism

To us vouchsafe to see a hundred autumns:
May we attain to lives prolonged and happy.

Rig-Veda

Judaism

The unlearned lose the power of clear thinking as they grow old, but scholars gain in it as their years advance.

Talmud, Kinnim, end

One father finds it possible to sustain a dozen children, yet a dozen children find it impossible to sustain one father.

Abraham Joshua Heschel, *The Insecurity of Freedom*

OUTCOME

Atheism

The church and Sunday School had nurtured in [Elmer Gantry] a fear of religious machinery which he could never lose. . . .

In Bible stories, in the words of the great hymns, in the anecdotes which the various preachers quoted, he had his only knowledge of literature—

How familiar they were, how thrilling, how explanatory to Elmer of the purposes of life, how preparatory for his future usefulness and charm. . . .

He had, in fact, got everything from church and Sunday School, except, perhaps, any longing whatever for decency and kindness and reason.

Sinclair Lewis, *Elmer Gantry*

Christianity/Judaism

They have sown the wind, and they shall reap the whirlwind.

Holy Bible, Hosea 8:7

Christianity

Whatsoever a man soweth, that shall he also reap.

Holy Bible, Galatians 6:7

I cannot . . . excuse St. Barbara from undutifulness, and occasioning her own death. The matter this: Her father, being a pagan, commanded his workmen, building his house, to make two windows in a room. Barbara, knowing her father's pleasure, in his absence enjoined them to make three, that, seeing them, she might the better contemplate the mystery of the Holy Trinity. Methinks two windows might as well have raised her meditations, and the light arising from both would as properly have minded her of the Holy Spirit proceeding from the Father and the Son. Her father, enraged, at his return, thus came to the knowledge of her religion, and accused her to the magistrate; which cost her her life.

Thomas Fuller, *The Holy State and the Profane State*

Although the moral law in the abstract may be perfectly clear, its concrete application in difficult cases will always be full of risk, because we can never be quite sure that we fully understand the object of our choice, its real end, and all the circumstances surrounding it.

Thomas Merton, *Love and Living*

I say to you, young girl, don't go with that godless, God-forsaken, sneering young man that walks the streets smoking cigarettes. . . . Don't go to that dance. Don't you know that it is the most damnable, low-down institution on the face of God's earth, that it causes more ruin than anything else this side of hell?

Billy Sunday

While opening a new abbey at Foigny, the Cistercian brothers were attacked by a horde of flies. They were unable to swat them away. Finally [St. Bernard of Clairvaux] solemnly told the flies, "I hereby excommunicate you." The next day, the story goes, every single fly was found dead on the floor.

Cal Samra, *The Joyful Christ*

Hinduism

A man is the creator of his own fate. . . . Whether confined in a mountain fastness or lulling on the bosom of a sea . . . a man cannot fly from the effects of his own prior deeds.

Garuda Purana

Islam

Those who deny Allah's revelations shall be sternly punished; Allah is mighty and capable of revenge.

Koran, 3:4

I hear the clacking of the mill, but I do not see any flour.

Arab proverb

Judaism

"O Godhead, give me Truth!" the Hebrew cried.
His prayer was granted; he became the slave
Of the Idea, a pilgrim far and wide,
Cursed, hated, spurned, and scourged with none to save.

Emma Lazarus, "Gifts"

The Chinese poet relates that men did not want to hear the song that he was playing on his flute of jade; then he played it to the gods, and they inclined their ears; and ever since men, too, have listened to the song.

Martin Buber, *I and Thou*

Taoism

When we lose the Tao, we turn to virtue.
When we lose virtue, we turn to kindness.
When we lose kindness, we turn to morality.
When we lose morality, we turn to ritual.

Tao-te ching

PEACE

Christianity/Judaism

They shall beat their swords into plowshares, and their spears into pruninghooks: nation shall not lift up sword against nation, neither shall they learn war any more.

Holy Bible, Isaiah 2:4

Christianity

Blessed are the peacemakers: for they shall be called the children of God.

Holy Bible, Matthew 5:9

The peace of God, which passeth all understanding.

Holy Bible, Philippians 4:7

Christianity . . . aside, if the costs and fruits of war were well considered, peace with all its inconveniences is generally preferable.

William Penn, Preface to George Fox's *Journal*

I heard the bells on Christmas Day
Their old, familiar carols play,
And wild and sweet
The words repeat
Of peace on earth, good will to men!

Henry Wadsworth Longfellow, "Christmas Bells"

With malice toward none, with charity for all, with firmness in the right, as God gives us to see the right, let us...achieve and cherish a just and lasting peace among ourselves, and with all nations.

Abraham Lincoln, Second Inaugural Address, March 4, 1865

The time when "nation shall not lift up sword against nation, neither shall they learn war any more," will probably come at last, though no one can predict what the conditions will be which will make such a change possible.

William Ralph Inge, "The Indictment Against Christianity"

Freedom to have a world which is permanently at peace will not come so easily. It is not a gift but an achievement, an achievement which each one of us must devoutly desire and earnestly seek to promote and continually pray for.

John A. Redhead, *Putting Your Faith to Work*

Islam

If two parties among the believers fall into a quarrel, make peace between them. But if one of them commits aggression against the other, then all should fight against the one that transgresses until it complies with the judgment of Allah. When it complies, make peace between them with justice and fairness.

Koran, 49:9

Judaism

Great is peace! Peace is the name of God.

Talmud, Bemidbar Rabbah 11,18

Unitarianism

If ever there is truly peace on earth, goodwill to men, it will be because of women like Mother Teresa. Peace is not something you *wish* for; it's something you *make*, something you *do*, something you *are*, and something you *give away!*

Robert Fulghum, *All I Really Need to Know I Learned in Kindergarten*

PERFECTION

Buddhism

The perfect man penetrates the infinite with his wonderful mind, and the finite cannot obstruct him . . . therefore, he can mix with the impure and achieve purity, and since he is in accord with whatever he encounters, he sees the unity of things as he comes in contact with them.

Seng-chao, *Treatises*

Christianity/Judaism

I am the Almighty God; walk before me, and be thou perfect.

Holy Bible, Genesis 17:1

Ascribe ye greatness unto our God.
He is the Rock, his work is perfect.

Holy Bible, Deuteronomy 32:3-4

Christianity

Be ye therefore perfect, even as your Father which is in heaven is perfect.

Holy Bible, Matthew 5:48

If any man offend not in word, the same is a perfect man.

Holy Bible, James 3:2

True perfection consists in having but one fear, the loss of God's friendship.

St. Gregory of Nyssa

Every perfection in this life has some imperfection attached to it, and there is no knowledge in this world that is not mixed with some blindness or ignorance.

Thomas à Kempis, *The Imitation of Christ*

And there came many to dispute in Northumberland, and pleaded against perfection. But I declared unto them that Adam and Eve were perfect before they fell, and all that God made was perfect, and the imperfection came by the Devil and the Fall. And Christ that came to destroy the Devil said, "Be ye perfect."

George Fox, *Journal*

The Saviour, I suppose, did not expect that any human creature could be as perfect as the Father in heaven; but...he set that up as a standard, and he who did the most toward reaching that standard attained the highest degree of moral perfection.

Abraham Lincoln, Speech in Chicago, July 10, 1858

The Christian puts all the weight not on the perfection of the world as it stands, but on the putting right of what for whatever reason is far from perfect through the Christian practice of identification and sacrifice.

A. Boyce Gibson, *The Religion of Dostoyevsky*

Better to do something imperfectly than to do nothing flawlessly.

Robert H. Schuller, *Tough Times Never Last, But Tough People Do!*

Hinduism

Taking delight in his own special kind of action,
    A man attains perfection.

Bhagavad Gita, 18:45

Islam

Of all religious systems, Islam alone declares that individual perfection is possible in our earthly existence.

Muhammad Asad, *Islam at the Crossroads*

Unitarianism

Whether it be for riches or thinness, fitness or knowledge or fame, the desire for perfection shuts out all other people and pleasures one by one. It is an addiction like cocaine: ever more deadly in proportion to its purity.

F. Forrester Church, *Entertaining Angels*

PERSEVERANCE

Buddhism

Should various misfortunes assail thee, persevere in patience of body, speech, and mind.

The Supreme Path, the Rosary of Precious Gems

Christianity/Judaism

A just man falleth seven times, and riseth up again.

Holy Bible, Proverbs 24:16

Christianity

Behold, we count them happy which endure. Ye have heard of the patience of Job.

Holy Bible, James 5:11

The woman who stayed behind to seek Christ was the only one to see him. For perseverance is essential to any good deed, as the voice of truth tells us: "Whosoever perseveres to the end will be saved."

St. Gregory the Great

Confucianism

If one concentrates on one thing and does not get away from it . . . , he will possess strong, moving power.

Ch'eng I, *I-shu*

Islam

Allah is with those who patiently persevere.

Koran, 8:46

POLITICS

Aristotelianism

If men think that a ruler is religious and has a reverence for the gods, they are less afraid of suffering injustice at his hands.

Aristotle, *Politics*

Christianity/Judaism

It is not for kings to drink wine; nor for princes strong drink:
  Lest they drink and forget the law.

Holy Bible, Proverbs 31:4-5

Christianity

When Jesus . . . perceived that they would come and take him by force, to make him a king, he departed again into a mountain himself alone.

Holy Bible, John 6:15

In politics as in religion, it so happens that we have less charity for those that believe the half of our creed than for those that deny the whole of it.

Charles Caleb Colton, *Lacon*

He who will introduce into public affairs the principles of primitive Christianity will revolutionize the world.

Benjamin Franklin, *Works*

Set yourselves against all political falsehood. The most monstrous lies ever told in this country are during the elections. . . . Prominent candidates for office are denounced as renegade and inebriate. . . . O Christian men! frown upon the political falsehood! Remember that a political lie is as black as any other kind of lie.

Thomas DeWitt Talmage, "The Christian at the Ballot Box"

It was but the other day that a man sent me a letter asking me what matter one should put into a political speech. To which I answered, having an expert knowledge in this, that the whole art of a political speech is to put *nothing* into it.

Hilaire Belloc, "On Speeches"

Political and social concerns have absorbed the energies of religion to such a degree that for great numbers of Europeans and Americans religions and political ideals coincide.

Paul Tillich, *On the Boundary*

The realm of politics is the realm of waste. The Pharoahs at least built pyramids.

Thomas Merton, *Conjectures of a Guilty Bystander*

I am not a perfect servant. I am a public servant doing my best against the odds. As I develop and serve, be patient. God is not finished with me yet.

Jesse Jackson, Speech to the Democratic National Convention, July 17, 1984

Hinduism

I could not be leading a religious life unless I identified myself with the whole of mankind, and that I could not do unless I took part in politics.

Mohandas K. Gandhi, *Non-Violence in Peace and War*

Islam

Party politics may be seen as directly contradictory of the truth that in Islam the body of believers is the only "party." . . . It was as if orthodoxy had to consent to becoming a sect, or fundamentalism share a status with conflicting opinions.

Kenneth Cragg, *Counsels in Contemporary Islam*

The movement of Islamic resurgence . . . represents a reawakening of faith. This dimension is neglected in most of the Western writings; they assume that it is just a question of political and social rearrangements.

Khurshid Ahmad, "The Nature of Islamic Resurgence"

All public life in Islam is religious, being permeated by the experience of the divine.

Hassan al-Turabi, "The Islamic State"

Judaism

Any man who is seeking public office and allows his ambition to affect his religious affiliation is not worthy of the confidence of his fellow citizens.

Herbert H. Lehman, Governor of New York, 1933–43

Secularism

I see no way out of the world's misery but the way which would have been found by Christ's will if he had undertaken the work of a modern practical statesman.

George Bernard Shaw, *Androcles and the Lion,* Preface

Unitarianism

The question before the human race is whether the God of nature shall govern the world by his own laws, or whether priests and kings shall rule it by fictitious miracles.

John Adams, Letter to Thomas Jefferson, June 20, 1815

POWER

Atheism

The Pope! How many divisions has he got?

Joseph Stalin, Conversation with Pierre Laval, May 13, 1935

Christianity/Judaism

The Lord is my rock, and my fortress, and my deliverer.

Holy Bible, 2 Samuel 22:2

Thine, O Lord, is the greatness, and the power, and the glory, and the victory, and the majesty: for all that is in the heaven and in the earth is thine.

Holy Bible, 1 Chronicles 29:11

Christianity

For thine is the kingdom, and the power, and the glory for ever. Amen.

Holy Bible, Matthew 6:13

Jesus came and spake unto them, saying, All power is given unto me in heaven and in earth.

> *Holy Bible*, Matthew 22:18

A mighty fortress is our God,
  A bulwark never failing;
Our Helper He amid the flood
  Of mortal ills prevailing.

> Martin Luther, "Hymn"

I sing the mighty power of God,
  That made the mountains rise,
That spread the flowing seas abroad,
  And built the lofty skies.

> Isaac Watts, "I Sing the Mighty Power of God"

Mine eyes have seen the glory of the coming of the Lord:
He is trampling out the vintage where the grapes of wrath are stored;
He hath loosed the fateful lightning of His terrible swift sword;
His truth is marching on.

> Julia Ward Howe, "Battle Hymn of the Republic"

Power is a word often on the lips of Jesus; never used, it should be said, in the sense of extrinsic authority or the right to command and govern, but always in reference to an intrinsic and interior moral and spiritual energy of life.

> Rufus M. Jones, *Spiritual Energies in Daily Life*

As individuals, men believe that they ought to love and serve each other and establish justice between each other. As racial, economic, and national groups, they take for themselves whatever their power can command.

> Reinhold Niebuhr, *Moral Man and Immoral Society*

Goodness, armed with power, is corrupted; and pure love without power is destroyed.

> Reinhold Niebuhr, *Beyond Tragedy*

Power . . . is the supreme end for all those who have not understood.

> Simone Weil, *Gravity and Grace*

Power cannot, as some demand, simply be abolished. That is an illusion. But in the light of the Christian conscience power . . . can be used for service instead of domination.

> Hans Küng, *The Christian Challenge*

Hinduism

One man of strength causes a hundred men of understanding to tremble.

Upanishads, Chandogya

Power takes as ingratitude the writhing of its victims.

Rabindranath Tagore, *Stray Birds*

Islam

Anyone who seeks power [should understand that] power is Allah's alone.

Koran, 35:10

He is the best of men who dislikes power.

Muhammad

The lease of power to the states of Islam is a lease of life to her ideologies.

Kenneth Cragg, *Counsels in Contemporary Islam*

Judaism

Power abdicates only under the stress of counter-power.

Martin Buber, *Paths in Eutopia*

Taoism

He who is able to conquer others is powerful; he who is able to conquer himself is more powerful.

Lao-tzu, *Tao-te ching*

Unitarianism

Of all injuries and crimes, the most flagrant is chargeable on him who aims to establish dominion over his brethren.

William Ellery Channing, *Works of . . .*

PRAYER

Christianity/Judaism

As for me, I will call upon God; and the Lord shall save me.
Evening, and morning, and at noon, will I pray.

Holy Bible, Psalms 55:16-17

The sacrifice of the wicked is an abomination to the Lord: but the prayer of the upright is his delight.

Holy Bible, Proverbs 15:8

Christianity

When thou prayest, enter into thy closet, and when thou has shut thy door, pray to thy Father which is in secret; and thy Father which seeth in secret shall reward thee openly.

Holy Bible, Matthew 6:6

The effectual fervent prayer of a righteous man availeth much.

Holy Bible, James 5:16

Lord, teach us to pray.

Holy Bible, Luke 11:1

I would rather say five words devoutly with my heart than five thousand which my soul does not relish with affection and understanding.

St. Edmund the Martyr

However great may be the temptation, if we know how to use the weapon of prayer well, we shall come off conquerors at last, for prayer is more powerful than all the devils.

St. Bernard of Clairvaux

My words fly up, my thoughts remain below.
Words without thoughts never to heaven go.

William Shakespeare, *Hamlet*, Act 3, Sc. 3

He that will learn to pray, let him go to sea.

George Herbert, *Jacula Prudentum*

I went to my room and got down on my knees in prayer. Never before had I prayed with so much earnestness. I wish I could repeat my prayer. I felt that I must put all my trust in Almighty God. He gave our people the best country ever given to men. He alone could save it from destruction.

Abraham Lincoln, Letter to Major General Daniel V. Sickles after the
Battle of Gettysburg

More things are wrought by prayer
Than this world dreams of.

Alfred, Lord Tennyson, *Idylls of the King*

What a friend we have in Jesus,
All our sins and griefs to bear;

What a privilege to carry
Everything to God in prayer.
O what peace we often forfeit,
O what needless pain we bear,
All because we do not carry
Everything to God in prayer.

> Joseph Scriven, "What a Friend We Have in Jesus"

I bow my forehead to the dust,
    I veil my eyes for shame,
And urge, in trembling self-distrust,
    A prayer without a claim.

> John Greenleaf Whittier, "The Eternal Goodness"

Surely we may with reverence say that, in a true and deep sense, God Himself is the answer to prayer.

> Caroline Stephen, *Quaker Strongholds*

We cannot all argue, but we can all pray; we cannot all be leaders, but we can all be pleaders; we cannot all be mighty in rhetoric, but we can all be prevalent in prayer.

> Charles H. Spurgeon

Praying is spiritual work, and human nature does not like taxing, spiritual work. Human nature wants to sail to heaven under a pleasant breeze, and a full, smooth sea.

> E.M. Bounds, *Power Through Prayer*

God is not a cosmic bellboy for whom we can press a button to get things done.

> Harry Emerson Fosdick, *The Meaning of Prayer*

To wish to pray is a prayer in itself.

> Georges Bernanos, *The Diary of a Country Priest*

I flew thirty missions over Germany in a bomber. As the going got rougher I would just hope all the harder that we would get out of harm's way. Fear motivated the hoping, and where hoping ends and prayer begins I don't know.

> Gordon W. Allport, *The Individual and His Religion*

We forget that God sometimes has to say, "No."

> Peter Marshall, "Praying Is Dangerous Business"

Prayer to be fruitful must come from the heart and must be able to touch the heart of God.

Mother Teresa of Calcutta, *Life in the Spirit*

Christian Science

The prayer that reforms the sinner and heals the sick is an absolute faith that all things are possible to God.

Mary Baker Eddy, *Science and Health with Key to the Scriptures*

Confucianism

When people pray for rain, it rains. Why? I say: There is no need to ask why. It is the same as when it rains when no one prays for it.

Hsun-tzu, "On Nature"

Hinduism

Prayer is not an old woman's idle amusement. Properly understood and applied, it is the most potent instrument of action.

Mohandas K. Gandhi, *Non-Violence in Peace and War*

Islam

Enjoin prayer on thy people and be constant in its observance.

Koran, 20:132

A Muslim has to pray five times a day, before sunrise, between midday and afternoon, in the afternoon, immediately after sunset and between the time when the twilight is over and just before dawn.

The Islamic Foundation, England

Judaism

The Holy One, blessed be he, longs for the prayer of the righteous.

Mishnah, Jebamoth 64

An intoxicated person must not pray because he cannot concentrate. If he prays, his prayer is an abomination.

Maimonides, *Mishneh Torah*

In prayer man pours himself out, dependent without reservation, knowing that, incomprehensibly, he acts on God, albeit without exacting anything from God.

Martin Buber, *I and Thou*

Prayer, though it has no magic powers as such, nevertheless, by lighting the way for love, arrives at possibilities of magic effects. It can intervene in the divine system of the world.

Franz Rosenzweig, The Star of Redemption

Prayer is an invitation to God to intervene in our lives, to let His will prevail in our affairs.

Abraham Joshua Heschel, The Wisdom of Heschel

The key Jewish prayer [Shema] is . . . really not said to God at all, it is said to ourselves, and, above all, we say it to each other.

Lionel Blue, To Heaven, with Scribes and Pharisees

Poetics

For I remember stopping by the way
To watch a Potter thumping his wet Clay:
    And with its all-obliterated Tongue
It murmur'd—"Gently, Brother, gently, pray!"

Edward FitzGerald, The Rubaiyat of Omar Khayyam

Unitarianism

It is useless to think that God can be persuaded by our prayers to suspend one single law in our behalf . . . but it is only truth to say that, by our prayers, we bring ourselves into the knowledge and the love of God, and therewith gain more and better help than if suddenly every law in the universe were altered to our benefit.

John Haynes Holmes, The Messiah Pulpit

PREACHING

Buddhism

The priest who preaches foul doctrine shall be reborn as a fungus.

Japanese Buddhist proverb

Christianity/Judaism

The Lord hath anointed me to preach good tidings unto the meek.

Holy Bible, Isaiah 61:1

Christianity

From that time Jesus began to preach, and to say, Repent: for the kingdom
of heaven is at hand.

Holy Bible, Matthew 4:17

The parson of a country town was he
Who knew the straits of humble poverty;
But rich he was in holy thought and work,
Nor less in learning as became a clerk.
The word of Christ most truly did he preach,
And his parishoners devoutly teach.

Geoffrey Chaucer, *The Canterbury Tales*

He that has but one word of God before him and out of that cannot make
a sermon can never be a preacher.

Martin Luther, *Table Talk*

It was said of one who preached very well, and lived very ill, that when
he was out of the pulpit, it was a pity he should ever go into it; and when
he was in the pulpit, it was a pity he should ever come out of it.

Thomas Fuller, *The Holy State and the Profane State*

The preaching of divines helps to preserve well-inclined men in the course
of virtue, but seldom, or never, reclaims the vicious.

Jonathan Swift, *Thoughts on Various Subjects*

I must preach so that the most illiterate laborer can understand me.

St. Alphonsus Liguori

Truth from his lips prevail'd with double sway,
And fools, who came to scoff, remained to pray.

Oliver Goldsmith, "The Deserted Village"

There stands the messenger of truth: there stands
The legate of the skies!—His theme divine,
His office sacred, his credentials clear.

William Cowper, "The Task"

As a marksman aims at the target and its bull's-eye, and at nothing else, so
the preacher must have a definite point before him, which he has to hit.

John Henry Newman, *The Idea of a University*

The gospel of Christ does not move by popular waves. It has no self-propelling power. It moves as the men who have charge of it move. The preacher must live the gospel.

E.M. Bounds, *Power Through Prayer*

What is true of the artist's mission is no less true of the minister's. His business is making God real to men here—not entertaining them, or giving them a theory of society. It is no easy mission, that is clear enough, but it is the greatest one on earth.

Rufus M. Jones, *The Faith and Practice of the Quakers*

It is very difficult to preach the gospel honestly. It means to preach the severity of God to the proud, and the mercy of God to the brokenhearted.

Reinhold Niebuhr, *Justice and Mercy*

The preacher is not the spokesman of the congregation, but, if the expression may be allowed, he is the spokesman of God before the congregation.

Dietrich Bonhoeffer, *Ethics*

Some church services start at eleven o'clock sharp and end at twelve o'clock dull.

Vance Havner, *The Vance Havner Quotebook*

To me, preaching is raising to a conscious level the knowledge inherent in everyone's experience.

William Sloane Coffin, *Living the Truth in a World of Illusions*

Judaism

A generation ago the distinguished pulpit orator was called to the largest congregation and commanded the highest salary. But in our own day there has been a renewed tendency . . . to esteem a rabbi for his learning rather than for his eloquence.

Emanuel Rackman, *One Man's Judaism*

Unitarianism

The frightful engines of ecclesiastical councils, of diabolical malice, and Calvinistical good nature never failed to terrify me exceedingly whenever I thought of preaching.

John Adams, Letter to Richard Cranch, August 29, 1756

PREDICTION

Christianity/Judaism

When a prophet speaketh in the name of the Lord, if the thing follow not, nor come to pass . . . the Lord hath not spoken, but the prophet hath spoken it presumptuously.

Holy Bible, Deuteronomy 18:22

Behold, a virgin shall conceive, and bear a son, and shall call his name Immanuel.

Holy Bible, Isaiah 7:14

Christianity

A prophet is not without honor, save in his own country.

Holy Bible, Matthew 13:57

We see through a glass darkly.

Holy Bible, 1 Corinthians 13:12

Judaism

The most compelling reason no one can predict the future is that the future does not exist. You and I are not robots. We have freedom of will to determine the shape of tomorow by what we do today.

Sidney Greenberg, *Say Yes to Life*

PREPARATION

Christianity/Judaism

Prepare your hearts unto the Lord, and serve him only: and he will deliver you out of the hand of the Philistines.

Holy Bible, 1 Samuel 7:3

Christianity

Stand therefore, having your loins girt about with truth, and having on the breastplate of righteousness; And your feet shod with the preparation of the gospel of peace.

Holy Bible, Ephesians 6:14-15

To last an eternity requires an eternity of preparation. Only excellence counts; only achievement endures.

> Baltasar Gracian, *The Art of Worldly Wisdom*

One cannot build his house on rock after the storm breaks; that must be done before.

> Harry Emerson Fosdick, *Riverside Sermons*

Hinduism

Then Janasruti [a "pious dispenser" and seeker of truth] spoke to him: "Raikva [a Brahman], here are six hundred cows, and here is a gold necklace, and here is a chariot drawn by a she-mule. Now, sir, teach me that divinity . . . which you reverence."

> *Upanishads*, Chandogya

Islam

Trust in Allah—but tie your camel first.

> Muhammad

Judaism

The wise man knows at the commencement of a matter what its end will be.

> *Talmud*, Y. Sotah 5, end

PRIDE

Christianity/Judaism

Pride goeth before destruction, and a haughty spirit before a fall.

> *Holy Bible*, Proverbs 16:18

Christianity

An old man, very experienced in these matters, once spiritually admonished a proud brother who said in his blindness: "Forgive me, father, but I am not proud." "My son," said the wise old man, "What better proof of your pride could you have given than to claim you were not proud?"

> St. John Climacus

When I survey the wondrous Cross
    On which the Prince of Glory died,
My richest gain I count but loss,
    And pour contempt on all my pride.

> Isaac Watts, "When I Survey the Wondrous Cross"

The pride of the peacock is the glory of God.

> William Blake, "Proverbs of Hell"

God of our fathers, known of old,
    Lord of our far-flung battle line,
Beneath whose awful hand we hold
    Dominion over palm and pine:
Lord God of hosts, be with us yet,
    Lest we forget, lest we forget.

> Rudyard Kipling, "Recessional"

It is a fine thing to rise above pride, but you must have pride in order to do so.

> Georges Bernanos, *The Diary of a Country Priest*

Pride is a deep, insatiable need for unreality, an exorbitant demand that others believe the lie we have made ourselves believe about ourselves.

> Thomas Merton, *The New Man*

Confucianism

All around I see Nothing pretending to be Something,
Emptiness pretending to be Fullness.

> Confucius, *Analects*

Hinduism

If you think, "I know well," only slightly do you know!

> *Upanishads*, Kena

Islam

Do not turn thy cheek in scorn, nor walk insolently on the earth; Allah does not love an arrogant boaster.

> *Koran*, 31:18

Judaism

Why was man created on the sixth day? To teach that if he is ever swollen with pride, it can be said to him: A flea came ahead of thee in creation.

> *Talmud*, Sanhedrin 38a

Yes, I am a Jew, and when the ancestors of the right honorable gentleman were brutal savages in an unknown island, mine were priests in the temple of Solomon.

> Benjamin Disraeli, Reply in Parliament to Daniel O'Connell

PRIORITIES

Christianity/Judaism

I had rather be a doorkeeper in the house of my God, than to dwell in the tents of wickedness.

Holy Bible, Psalms 84:10

Christianity

We ought to obey God rather than men.

Holy Bible, Acts 5:29

'Tis mad idolatry
To make the service greater than the God.

William Shakespeare, *Troilus and Cressida*, Act 2, Sc. 2

God is more interested in the salvation of the human race than in the labor of philosophers.

Jacques Maritain, *Moral Philosophy*

People are always more important than things; men are always more important than money; workers are always more important than machines.

William Barclay, *Ethics in a Permissive Society*

Many people are religious only in moments of crisis; the rest of the time they rub along comfortably and godlessly, content to let their religious sentiment lie dormant.

Gordon W. Allport, *The Individual and His Religion*

Sure, they need us—our children, our employees, our parishoners—but not that badly. No one is indispensable—except to God.

William Sloane Coffin, *Living the Truth in a World of Illusions*

Hinduism

Janaka, king of Videh, . . . had a thousand cows enclosed in a pen, with ten gold coins attached to the horns of each one.

"Venerable Brahmans," said Janaka, "let the wisest one among you take away these cows."

None of the Brahmans dared to move, except for Yagnavalkya, who said to his pupil, "Samasravas, drive these cows home."

The Brahmans were infuriated. "How can he declare himself to be the best Brahman among us?" they cried.

Asvala, who was the priest to Janaka, asked: "Yagnavalkya, are you now the best Brahman here?"

"I give honor to the best Brahman," Yagnavalkya replied. "But I really want those cows."

Upanishads, Brihadaranyaka

Islam

Deep in the sea are riches beyond compare.
But if you seek safety, it is on the shore.

Saadi of Shiraz

Judaism

The sole purpose of the divine word was to single Israel out from among all other nations as God's special possession, to become holy unto Him before all other nations.

Moses Mendelssohn, *Jerusalem and Other Jewish Writings*

Men will sooner surrender their rights than their customs.

Moritz Guedemann, *Geschichte des Erziehungswesens*

To the outsider the attention which Judaism lavishes on food is excessive. But insiders know that the question of food involves, however clumsily, the meaning of ritual, the relevance of purity, and the survival of holiness. These details seem so small, almost trivial, but Judaism is a religion of detail.

Lionel Blue, *To Heaven, with Scribes and Pharisees*

A shoe manufacturer condensed [a] whole philosophy of life in a small sign that sat on his desk: "God first, shoes second."

Sidney Greenberg, *Say Yes to Life*

PROGRESS

Christianity

When I had drunk the spirit from Heaven . . . doubts began to be resolved, closed doors to be opened, dark places to be light; what before was difficult now seemed easy.

St. Cyprian of Carthage

Lead, kindly Light, amid the encircling gloom;
Lead thou me on!

> John Henry Newman, "Lead, Kindly Light"

There is no greater disloyalty to the great pioneers of human progress than to refuse to budge an inch from where they stood.

> William Ralph Inge, *Wit and Wisdom of Dean Inge*

Most certainly it is God himself who, in the course of centuries, awakens the great benefactors of humankind, and the great physicians, in ways that agree with the general rhythm of progress.

> Pierre Teilhard de Chardin, *The Divine Milieu*

All progress is precarious, and the solution of one problem brings us face to face with another problem.

> Martin Luther King, Jr., *Strength to Love*

Hinduism

From the dark I go to the varicolored. From the varicolored I go to the dark. Shaking off evil, as a horse his hairs; shaking off his body, as the moon releases itself from the mouth of Rahu [a dragon]; I, a perfected soul, pass into the uncreated Brahma-world—yea, into it I pass!

> *Upanishads*, Chandogya

Islam

Material progress . . . means the enjoyment of certain comforts and benefits of an advanced standard of living. Thus, if a man owns a grand car, a beautiful house, and nice furniture, he enjoys material progress. If he obtained these means at the expense of his freedom, then he is not civilized, even though he is materially advanced. . . . We strive today to achieve both material progress and civilization at one and the same time.

> Mahmoud Mohamed Taha, *The Second Message of Islam*

REALITY

Buddhism

One must know that all visible phenomena, being illusory, are unreal.

The Supreme Path, the Rosary of Precious Gems

There is only inner consciousness which produces what seems to be the external sphere.

Hsuan-tsang, *Ch'eng wei-shih lun*

Christianity/Judaism

The Lord seeth not as man seeth; for man looketh on the outward appearance, but the Lord looketh on the heart.

Holy Bible, 1 Samuel 16:7

Christianity

Judge not according to the appearance.

Holy Bible, John 7:24

Thought! Surely thoughts are true;
They please us as much as things can do:
    Nay, things are dead,
    And in themselves are severed
    From souls; nor can they fill the head
Without our thoughts.

Thomas Traherne, "Dreams"

To understand reality is not the same as to know about outward events. It is to perceive the essential nature of things. The best-informed man is not necessarily the wisest. Indeed there is a danger that precisely in the multiplicity of his knowledge he will lose sight of what is essential.

Dietrich Bonhoeffer, *Ethics*

Hinduism

In the heart of all things, of whatever there is in the universe, dwells the Lord. He alone is the reality.

Upanishads, Isha

Though the Vedic hymns are addressed to many gods, the Vedic seers in their search after truth very soon discovered that there is one Supreme Spirit of which the various gods worshipped by men are only partial manifestations. There is a Vedic passage which is often quoted in support of this statement, "Reality is one; sages speak of it in different ways."

D.S. Sarma, "The Nature and History of Hinduism"

Judaism

When we are confronted with the world of the mind, it is not originality that matters but reality. . . . This "for the first time" can be the concern only of a mole's stunted intellect, incapable of discerning the mind's never-ending history with its eternally new creations carved out of the eternally same matter.

Martin Buber, *On Judaism*

REASON

Christianity/Judaism

I desire to reason with God.

Holy Bible, Job 13:3

Should a wise man utter vain knowledge?
Should he reason with unprofitable talk?

Holy Bible, Job 15:2-3

Come now, and let us reason together.

Holy Bible, Isaiah 1:18

Christianity

What reason ye in your hearts?

Holy Bible, Luke 5:22

Those who are now counted authorities gained their reputation by following reason, not authority.

Adelard of Bath, *Questiones naturales*

We are generally more effectually persuaded by reasons we have ourselves discovered than by those which have occurred to others.

Blaise Pascal, *Pensees*

All we have a right to say is that individuals are occasionally guided by reason, crowds never.

William Ralph Inge, *Wit and Wisdom of Dean Inge*

It is idle to talk always of the alternative of reason and faith. Reason is itself a matter of faith. It is an act of faith to assert that our thoughts have any relation to reality at all.

G.K. Chesterton, *Orthodoxy*

A true faith both instigates the life of reason and provides it a home. That is why the great discoveries of science come not from reason alone, but from the deeps of the subconscious.

George A. Buttrick, *God, Pain, and Evil*

Reason is the instrument of our transcendence. Man lives in nature, yet transcends nature.

Reinhold Niebuhr, *Justice and Mercy*

It is almost impossible to convince anyone of the truth of religion through reason—and yet a whole science of apologetics has been built up for this purpose and has been used for centuries.

Fulton J. Sheen, *On Being Human*

Intellectual honesty in all things, including questions of belief, was the great achievement of emancipated reason and it has ever since been one of the indispensable moral requirements of Western man. Contempt for the age of rationalism is a suspicious sign of failure to feel the need for truthfulness.

Dietrich Bonhoeffer, *Ethics*

Confucianism

Confucius said, "He who learns but does not think is lost; he who thinks but does not learn is in danger."

Confucius, *Analects*

Hinduism

It is with the mind, truly, that one sees. It is with the mind that one hears. Desire, imagination, doubt, faith, lack of faith, steadfastness, lack of stead-fastness, shame, meditation, fear—all this is truly mind.

Upanishads, Brihadaranyaka

Islam

The Prophet has consecrated reason as the highest and noblest function of the human intellect. Our schoolmen and their servile followers have made its exercise a sin and a crime.

Ameer Ali, *The Spirit of Islam*

Great as this gift of reason is, by itself it does not and cannot suffice—for reason only operates within the framework of instinctive life conditioned as it is by the sensory apparatus. It has, therefore, its own limits, and beyond those limits it is dangerous to go.

Allahbukhsh K. Brohi, "The Qur'an and Its Impact on Human History"

Judaism

Precisely because reason is destined to guide man in his empiric existence, to protect him here on earth, it is essentially unable to guide us in our metaphysical wanderings.

Lev Shestov, *In Job's Balances*

The Talmud records that the Law was rarely decided in accordance with Rabbi Meir's opinion, though he was acknowledged by his contemporaries to be the most learned among them, because they suspected his brilliance. He could prove both sides of an issue with equal logical cogency.

Simon Greenberg, *A Jewish Philosophy and Pattern of Life*

RELATIONSHIPS

Christianity/Judaism

Am I my brother's keeper?

Holy Bible, Genesis 4:9

If a stranger sojourn with thee in your land, ye shall not vex him. But the stranger that dwellest with you shall be unto you as one born among you, and thou shalt love him as thyself; for ye were strangers in the land of Egypt.

Holy Bible, Leviticus 19:33-34

Christianity

I was a stranger and ye took me in.

Holy Bible, Matthew 25:35

Ye are no more strangers and foreigners, but fellow citizens with the saints, and of the household of God.

Holy Bible, Ephesians 2:19

To pass judgment on another is to usurp shamelessly a prerogative of God.

St. John Climacus

I am His daughter: He said so. Oh, infinite gentleness of my God! . . . Ocean of joy!

St. Margaret of Cortona

It is interesting that most of our relationships with other people are con- tacts, as one billiard ball contacts another billiard ball. We become like oranges in a box; we mingle with others externally, but we do not commune with others in a common task.

Fulton J. Sheen

We may understand far more than our primitive ancestors did about the physical processes of the universe...but we have to cope with social and interpersonal processes that are far more elaborate, far more powerful, and far more controlling than our ancestors would have dreamed possible.

Andrew M. Greeley, *The New Agenda*

Deism

Man's proper study is that of relationships. . . . When [in childhood] he begins to feel his moral being, he should study himself in relation to his fellowmen; this is the business of his whole life.

Jean Jacques Rousseau, *Emile*

Existentialism

Twenty-five signatures make the most frightful stupidity into an opinion.

Søren Kierkegaard, *The Present Age*

Islam

Many [Muslim intellectuals] think it is important to engage in dialogue with Christians, because they realize that there is a sense in which all believers in God are engaged in a common struggle against materialism, atheistic humanism and other anti-religious forces.

M. Montgomery Watt, *Islamic Philosophy and Theology*

Judaism

All real living is meeting.

Martin Buber, *I and Thou*

Jews in Utah, being non-Mormon, are theoretically subject to classification as Gentiles, which gave rise to the well-known remark that "Utah is the only place in the world where Jews are Gentiles."

John Gunther, *Inside U.S.A.*

A basic biblical perception about both human relations and relations between God and man is that love is unpredictable, arbitrary, at times perhaps seemingly unjust.

Robert Alter, *The Art of Biblical Narrative*

Nonsectarianism

It is highly moral people, unaware of their other side, who develop peculiar irritability and hellish moods which make them insupportable to their relatives.

Carl Jung, *Psychology and Religion*

RELIGION

Agnosticism

I do not consider it an insult, but rather a compliment, to be called an agnostic. I do not pretend to know, where many ignorant men are sure—that is all that agnosticism means.

Clarence Darrow, Argument at the Scopes trial, Dayton, Tennessee,
July 13, 1925.

Atheism

Religion . . . is the opium of the people.

Karl Marx, *Critique of the Hegelian Philosophy of Right*

Buddhism

Buddhism is not a system of dogmas nor a church building, but a way of life for people who are molded according to Buddhist discipline. Buddhism is pervasive but formless.

Kodo Matsunami, *Introducing Buddhism*

Christianity

Pure religion and undefiled before God is this, To visit the fatherless and widows in their affliction, and to keep himself unspotted from the world.

Holy Bible, James 1:27

As he sat, the eyes of his understanding began to open. He beheld no vision, but he saw and understood many things, spiritual as well as those concerning faith and learning. This took place with so great an illumination that these things appeared to be something altogether new.

St. Ignatius of Loyola

The religion of one seems madness unto another.

Sir Thomas Browne, *Urn Burial*

I see many religions, contrary to one another, and therefore all false save one.

Blaise Pascal, *Pensées*

Religion is nothing else but love of God and man.

William Penn, *Some Fruits of Solitude*

Religion is the best armor, but the worst cloak.

Thomas Fuller, *Gnomologia*

When I mention religion, I mean the Christian religion; and not only the Christian religion, but the Protestant religion; and not only the Protestant religion, but the Church of England.

Henry Fielding, *Tom Jones*

All sects seem to me to be right in what they assert and wrong in what they deny.

Goethe, *Conversations with Goethe*

The whole circumference of religion is infinite, and is not to be comprehended under one form, but only under the sum total of all forms. It is infinite, not merely because any single religious organization has a limited horizon . . . but more particularly because everyone is a person by himself, and is only to be moved in his own way, so that for everyone the elements of religion have . . . differences.

Friedrich Schleiermacher, *On Religion*

Man will wrangle for religion; write for it; fight for it; die for it; anything but live for it.

Charles Caleb Colton, *Lacon*

Religion is the fashionable substitute for belief.

Oscar Wilde, *The Picture of Dorian Gray*

A religion is not a proposition, but a system; it is a rite, a creed, a philosophy, a rule of duty, all at once.

John Henry Newman, *A Grammar of Assent*

Religion is not a popular error; it is a great instinctive truth, sensed by the people, expressed by the people.

Ernest Renan, *Les Apotres*

If your religion does not change you, then you should change your religion.

Elbert Hubbard, *The Roycroft Dictionary and Book of Epigrams*

We have to practice the difficult art of living in a world which we do not understand. Religion is the chief portion of this art. Truth is relative to our spiritual need; it has been said whatever helps our souls is true.

William Ralph Inge, "Willing and Knowing"

Whether religion is a pathway to reality or not, there seems at least no question that its springs lie deep down in the elemental nature of human life itself. It is not something foisted off on man by clever manipulators.

Rufus M. Jones, *Pathways to the Reality of God*

We know too much and are convinced of too little. Our literature is a substitute for religion, and so is religion.

T.S. Eliot, *A Dialogue on Dramatic Poetry*

Religion is always a citadel of hope, which is built on the edge of despair.

Reinhold Niebuhr, *Moral Man and Immoral Society*

Religion is the search for a value underlying all things, and as such is the most comprehensive of all the possible philosophies of life.

> Gordon W. Allport, *Personality, A Psychological Interpretation*

In the peasants' world there is no room for reason, religion, and history. There is no room for religion, because to them everything participates in divinity.

> Carlo Levi, *Christ Stopped at Eboli*

Confucianism

The Master said, "In the morning, hear the Way; in the evening, die content."

> Confucius, *Analects*

Confucius was the founder of a religion. He was a sagely king with spiritual intelligence. He was a counterpart of Heaven and Earth and nourished all things. All human beings, all events, and all moral principles are encompassed in his great Way.

> K'ang Yu-wei, *Book of Great Unity*

Cosmic

My religion consists of a humble admiration of the illimitable superior spirit who reveals himself in the slight details we are able to perceive with our frail and futile minds. That deeply emotional conviction of the presence of a superior reasoning power, which is revealed in the incomprehensible universe, forms my idea of God.

> Albert Einstein, quoted in *The New York Times* obituary,
> April 19, 1955

Deism

What more can men tell us? Far from throwing light upon the ideas of the Supreme Being, special doctrines seem to me to confuse these ideas . . . they add absurd contradictions, they make man proud, intolerant, and cruel.

> Jean Jacques Rousseau, *Emile*

Difference of opinion is advantageous in religion. The several sects perform the office of a *censor morum* over each other.

> Thomas Jefferson, *Notes on Virginia*

Hinduism

Even the highest theism is only a sort of glorified anthropomorphism, but we cannot do without it.

D.S. Sarma, "The Nature and History of Hindusim"

Islam

Religion is a candle inside a multicolored lantern. Everyone looks through a particular color, but the lantern is always there.

Mohammed Neguib, President of Egypt, Speech, December 31, 1953

The immense benefit which religion . . . confers upon man is the realization that he is, and never can cease to be, a well-planned unit in the eternal movement of Creation: a definite part in the infinite organism of universal destiny.

Muhammad Asad, *Islam at the Crossroads*

For the Muslim, Islam is more than a creed; it is his community, his nation, the locus in which he will attain his true individuality. . . . There is no bifurcation of the spiritual and the temporal.

John L. Esposito, *Voices of Resurgent Islam*

Islam is a universal religion and all Muslims, regardless of regional or national ties, belong to a single community of brotherhood.

Khurshid Ahmad, "The Nature of Islamic Resurgence"

Judaism

Judaism, the Bible, all the given religions are but evolutions of morality.

Kaufmann Kohler, "Evolution and Religion"

Every religion must . . . go back to the fundamental problem of optimism and pessimism, the problem of whether existence has a meaning and whether there is a world order which makes for the good.

Leo Baeck, *The Essence of Judaism*

Some religions do not regard our sojourn on earth as true life. . . . Judaism, on the contrary, teaches that what a man does now and here with holy intent is no less important, no less true . . . than life in the world to come.

Martin Buber, *Hasidism and Modern Man*

There may be different forms of religion, but religion is one, as is ethics. Each so-called religion is merely a particular vehicle of religion as such.

Mordecai M. Kaplan, *The Purpose and Meaning of Jewish Existence*

Nonsectarian

Religion, whatever it is, is a man's total reaction upon life.

William James, *The Varieties of Religious Experience*

Religion . . . shall mean for us, the feelings, acts, and experiences of individual men in their solitude, so far as they apprehend themselves to stand in relation to whatever they may consider the divine.

William James, *The Varieties of Religious Experience*

An adequate definition of religion is unattainable. It remains the supreme symbol of what is perhaps its most fundamental quality, which is mystery.

Herschel Baker, *The Image of Man*

Any religion, liberal or orthodox, theistic or nontheistic, must be not only intellectually credible and morally worthy of respect, but it must also be emotionally satisfying. . . . No wonder the liberal religions . . . exert so little influence even though their members are the most intelligent and most capable sections of the population.

Abraham H. Maslow, *Religions, Values, and Peak-Experiences*

Pantheism

I take a totally different view of God and Nature from that which the later Christians usually entertain, for I hold that God is the immanent, and not the extraneous, cause of all things. I say, All is in God; all lives and moves in God.

Spinoza, *Letters*

Pantheism seduces by its vistas of perfect universal union. But ultimately, if it were true, it would give us only fusion and unconsciousness; for, at the end of the evolution it claims to reveal, the elements of the world vanish in the God they create or by which they are absorbed.

Pierre Teilhard de Chardin, *The Divine Milieu*

Secularism

There is only one religion, though there are a hundred versions of it.

George Bernard Shaw, *Plays Pleasant and Unpleasant*

Taoism

Acting without design, occupying oneself without making a business of it, finding the great in what is small and the many in the few, repaying injury with kindness, effecting difficult things while they are easy, and managing great things in their beginnings: this is the method of Tao.

Lao-tzu, *Tao-tse ching*

Unitarianism

Religion gives life, strength, elevation to the mind, by connecting it with the Infinite Mind. . . . It is religion alone which nourishes patient, resolute hopes and efforts for our own souls.

William Ellery Channing, *The Liberal Gospel*

The test of a religion or philosophy is the number of things it can explain.

Ralph Waldo Emerson, *Journals*

Universalism

A religion that requires persecution to sustain it is of the devil's propagation.

Hosea Ballou

REPENTANCE

Christianity/Judaism

I abhor myself, and repent in dust and ashes.

Holy Bible, Job 42:6

Christianity

Repent ye: for the kingdom of heaven is at hand.

Holy Bible, Matthew 3:2

I am not come to call the righteous, but sinners to repentance.

Holy Bible, Matthew 9:13

Joy shall be in heaven over one sinner that repenteth, more than over ninety and nine just persons which need no repentance.

Holy Bible, Luke 15:7

God hath promised pardon to him that repenteth, but he has not promised repentance to him that sinneth.

St. Anselm

Confess yourself to heaven;
Repent what's past; avoid what is to come.

William Shakespeare, *Hamlet*, Act 3, Sc. 4

Once a man went to the village priest to confess his sins and receive absolution. He said: "I stole three sacks of potatoes." The priest listened and pointed to repentance and forgiveness.

When they had finished talking, the priest said: "I heard about that theft, but thought only two sacks were taken. You spoke of three."

"Yes," the man answered, "but tomorrow I am going to steal the third one."

Corrie ten Boom, *Not I, But Christ*

Islam

If you repent, it will be well with you; but if you turn away, know that you cannot escape Allah. You will pay a grievous penalty.

Koran, 9:3

Judaism

The desire to be another person, to be different than I am now, is the central motif of repentance.

Joseph B. Soloveitchik, *Halakhic Man*

Mormonism

Yea, come and go forth, and show unto your God that ye are willing to repent of your sins and enter into a covenant with him to keep his commandments, and witness it unto him this day by going into the waters of baptism.

Book of Mormon, Alma 7:15

REVELATION

Christianity/Judaism

The glory of the Lord shall be revealed, and all flesh shall see it together: for the mouth of the Lord hath spoken it.

Holy Bible, Isaiah 40:5

Christianity

[Jesus] saith unto them, But whom say ye that I am?

And Simon Peter answered and said, Thou art the Christ, the Son of the living God.

And Jesus answered and said unto him, Blessed art thou Simon . . . : for flesh and blood hath not revealed it unto thee, but my Father which is in heaven.

Holy Bible, Matthew 16:15-17

I am not ashamed of the gospel of Christ . . .
For therein is the righteousness of God revealed.

Holy Bible, Romans 1:16-17

I saw and felt the pure life of the Son made manifest in me; and the Father drew me to Him as to a living stone, and hath built my soul upon Him, and brought me to Mount Zion, and the holy city of our God; where the river of life sends forth its streams, which refresh and make glad the holy city, and all the tabernacles that are built on God's holy hill.

Isaac Penington, *Letters*

I saw on earth another light
    Than that which lit my eye
Come forth as from my soul within,
    And from a higher sky.

Jones Very, "The Light from Within"

God's revelation does not need the light of human genius, the polish and strength of human culture, the brilliancy of human thought, the force of human brains to adorn or enforce it. But it does demand the simplicity, docility, humility, and faith of a child's heart.

E.M. Bounds, *Power Through Prayer*

The word of God came unto me,
Sitting alone among the multitudes;
And my blind eyes were touched with light.
And there was laid upon my lips a flame of fire.

Helen Keller, "In the Garden of the Lord"

Knowledge of revelation does not always begin with clarity. It may increase in clarity; it should do so. It may, however, diminish also in clarity. But under all circumstances, it begins with certitude. . . . Doubt and despair, human unbelief, and even a sea of uncertainties on our part, will not be able to change the certitude of His presence.

Karl Barth, *God in Action*

With the approach of death I care less and less about religion and truth. One hasn't long to wait for revelation and darkness.

Graham Greene, *A Sort of Life*

Hinduism

The seer sees not death,
Nor richness, nor any distress.
The seer sees only the All.

Upanishads, Chandogya

Islam

It belongs not to any human being that God should speak to him except by revelation or from behind a veil.

Koran, 42:50

Nonsectarian

The fact of revelation implicitly denied the validity of reason and explicitly demanded an act of faith. . . . Even Aquinas, the most rational of theologians, was to boast that such a mystery as the Trinity mocked man's effort to understand and thus proved the glory of God.

Herschel Baker, *The Image of Man*

RIGHTEOUSNESS

Buddhism

All the teachings of the Buddha can be summed up in one word: . . . *Dharma.* . . . It means truth, that which really is. It also means law, the law which exists in a man's own heart and mind. It is the principle of righteousness.

U Thittila, "The Fundamental Principles of Theravada Buddhism"

Christianity/Judaism

He leadeth me in the paths of righteousness for his name's sake.

Holy Bible, Psalms 23:3

The righteous shall flourish like the palm tree: he shall grow like a cedar in Lebanon.

Holy Bible, Psalms 92:11

The wicked flee when no man pursueth; but the righteous are bold as a lion.

Holy Bible, Proverbs 28:1

Christianity

Blessed are they which are persecuted for righteousness' sake: for theirs is the kingdom of heaven.

Holy Bible, Matthew 5:10

Men are of two kinds only: the righteous who think themselves sinners; the rest, sinners who think themselves righteous.

Blaise Pascal, *Pensées*

Jesus assumes that there are righteous men. . . . He expects those who are gathered round him listening to the Sermon on the Mount to become a shining light of goodness for others.

Albert Schweitzer, *The Kingdom of God and Primitive Christianity*

Confucianism

Confucius said, "A superior man in dealing with the world is not for anything or against anything. He follows righteousness as the standard."

Confucius, *Analects*

Islam

Truly the righteous shall dwell in bliss.

Koran, 83:22

Judaism

Every human being has merits and iniquities. One whose merits exceed his iniquities is righteous. He whose iniquities exceed his merits is wicked.

Maimonides, *Mishneh Torah*

So committed is the Jewish tradition to the equality of the non-Jew who leads a righteous life that it accords to him the coveted title of "Chasid" and assures him salvation just as it is vouchsafed to righteous Jews themselves.

Emanuel Rackman, *One Man's Judaism*

Zoroastrianism

The Persians send their children to school that they may learn righteousness, as we [Greeks] do that they may learn letters.

Xenophon

SACRIFICE

Christianity/Judaism

I desired mercy, and not sacrifice; and the knowledge of God more than burnt offerings.

Holy Bible, Hosea 6:6

Wherewith shall I come before the Lord, and bow myself before the high God? shall I come before him with burnt offerings, with calves of a year old?

Will the Lord be pleased with thousands of rams, or with ten thousands of rivers of oil? shall I give my firstborn for my transgression, the fruit of my body for the sin of my soul?

Holy Bible, Micah 6:6-7

Christianity

It is not possible that the blood of bulls and goats should take away sins.

Holy Bible, Hebrews 10:4

I am God's wheat, and I am ground by the teeth of wild beasts that I may be found pure bread of Christ.

St. Ignatius of Antioch

In the New Testament sacrifice is not meant to be a conciliatory influence, putting an angry demon into a good mood. . . . Unlike the temple priests, Jesus offered not merely external, material gifts (fruits, animals), but himself: a voluntary, personal self-surrender in obedience to God's will and in love for men.

Hans Küng, *On Being a Christian*

Confucianism

Tzu-kung wanted to do away with the sacrificing of a lamb at the ceremony in which the beginning of each month is reported to ancestors. Confucius said, "Tzu! You love the lamb, but I love the ceremony."

Confucius, *Analects*

Hinduism

Verily, the dawn is the head of the sacrificial horse; the sun, his eye; the wind, his breath; universal fire, his open mouth.

Upanishads, Brihadaranyaka

No sacrifice is worth the name unless it is a joy. Sacrifice and a long face go ill together.

Mohandas K. Gandhi

Judaism

All sacrifices, except the offering of thanks, will be abolished in the World to Come.

Talmud, Tanhuma Emor 18

SAINTS

Christianity/Judaism

To which of the saints wilt thou turn?

Holy Bible, Job 5:1

Christianity

Do ye not know that the saints shall judge the world?

Holy Bible, 1 Corinthians 6:2

From somber, serious, sullen saints, deliver us, O Lord, hear our prayer.

St. Teresa of Avila

A saint who is sad is a sad saint.

St. Francis de Sales

God's saints are shining lights. . . .
They are—indeed—our pillar fires
    Seen as we go;
They are that City's shining spires
    We travel to.

Henry Vaughan, "God's Saints"

God hath seen meet that . . . we should, as in a looking glass, see the conditions and experiences of the saints of old; that finding our experience answer to theirs, we might thereby be the more confirmed and comforted, and our hope of obtaining the same end strengthened.

> Robert Barclay, *An Apology for . . . the Principles and Doctrines of the People Called Quakers*

Some reputed saints that have been canonized ought to have been cannonaded.

> Charles Caleb Colton, *Lacon*

I would be the happiest of men if I could become a saint soon and a big one.

> St. Joseph Cafasso

I hope those old water-logged saints that died soaking in damp stone cells were taken to heaven. They had hell enough on earth.

> Henry Ward Beecher, *Royal Truths*

Though the public policy of the Church may seem to display few signs of divine guidance, the lives of the saints do not disappoint us.

> William Ralph Inge, *Wit and Wisdom of Dean Inge*

The veneration in which a Tolstoy, a St. Francis, a crucified Christ, and the saints of all the ages have been held proves that, in the inner sanctuary of their souls, selfish men know that they ought not to be selfish, and venerate what they feel they ought to be and cannot be.

> Reinhold Niebuhr, *Moral Man and Immoral Society*

I knew her [Mother Cabrini] and didn't know she was a saint. She didn't know, either.

> Adela Rogers St. Johns, *Some Are Born Great*

[Note: St. Frances Xavier Cabrini, 1850–1917, was canonized in 1946, the first U.S. citizen to achieve sainthood.]

The wonderful thing about saints is that they were *human*. They lost their tempers, got hungry, scolded God, were egotistical or testy or impatient in their turns, made mistakes and regretted them. Still they went on doggedly blundering toward heaven.

> Phyllis McGinley, *Saint-Watching*

The saints, when they remember their sins, do not remember the sins but the mercy of God, and therefore even past evil is turned by them into a present cause of joy and serves to glorify God.

> Thomas Merton, *The Seven Storey Mountain*

Existentialism

Can one be a saint if God does not exist? That is the only concrete problem I know of today.

Albert Camus, *The Plague*

Hinduism/Islam

Remain in the company of saints, though you get but chaff to eat.

Kabir, *Sakhi*

Judaism

If one avoids haughtiness to the utmost extent and is exceedingly humble, he is termed a saint, and this is the standard of saintliness.

Maimonides, *Mishneh Torah*

SALVATION

Atheism

There is no personal salvation; their is no national salvation except through science.

Luther Burbank

Buddhism

O priests, diligently work out your salvation; for not often occur the appearance of a Buddha in the world . . . and the opportunity to hear the true Doctrine.

Henry Clark Warren, *Buddhism in Translations*

Buddhist salvation is . . . nothing other than an awakening to reality through the death of ego.

Masao Abe, "Man and Nature in Christianity and Buddhism"

The original Buddhist goal of nirvana (or "salvation," if one wishes to use a Western term) was the realization that life's meaning lay in the here-and-now and not in some remote realm or celestial state far beyond one's present existence.

Nancy Wilson Ross, *Buddhism: A Way of Life and Thought*

Christianity/Judaism

Lead me in thy truth, and teach me: for thou are the God of my salvation.

Holy Bible, Psalms 25:5

The harvest is past, the summer is ended, and we are not saved.

Holy Bible, Jeremiah 8:20

Christianity

Strait is the gate, and narrow is the way, which leadeth unto life, and few there be that find it.

Holy Bible, Matthew, 7:14

I am the resurrection and the life: he that believeth in me, though he were dead, yet shall he live.
And whosoever liveth and believeth in me shall never die.

Holy Bible, John 11:25-26

For a little benefit great journeys are undertaken, but for everlasting life people will scarcely lift their feet once from the ground.

Thomas à Kempis, *The Imitation of Christ*

Now St. Luke says plainly that it was not that some were more clever than others, or that there was more inclination to virtue in them than in others, but that God had specially ordained them to salvation.

John Calvin, *Sermons on the Epistle to the Ephesians*

Holy Scripture containeth all things necessary to salvation.

Book of Common Prayer

Rock of Ages, cleft for me,
Let me hide myself in Thee.

Augustus M. Toplady, "Rock of Ages"

There is only one means of salvation . . . take yourself and make yourself responsible for all men's lives.

Fyodor Dostoevsky, *The Brothers Karamazov*

Let the lower lights be burning!
Send a gleam across the wave!
Some poor fainting, struggling seaman
You may rescue, you may save.

Philip P. Bliss, "Let the Lower Lights Be Burning"

What is most contrary to salvation is not sin but habit.

Charles Peguy, *Basic Virtues: Sinners and Saints*

The conditions of salvation . . . are discussed as though they were conditions for membership in some fantastic club like the Red-Headed League. They do not purport to be anything of the kind. Rightly or wrongly, they purport to be necessary conditions based on the facts of human nature.

Dorothy L. Sayers, *The Mind of the Maker*

There is many a young man in the city, bright in the nighttime like day, his pulses racing with the throb of jungle drums and the moan of the saxophone, intoxicated with the lure of the city and in strong temptation, who could be saved were he to hear once again on the heavy night air the lowing of homeward-driven cattle and the calls of the old farmyards.

Peter Marshall, *Mr. Jones, Meet the Master*

Deism

No man has the right to abandon the care of his salvation to another.

Thomas Jefferson, "Notes on Locke and Shaftsbury"

Hinduism

For these two paths, light and dark,
    Are held to be eternal for the world;
By one, man goes to non-return,
    By the other he returns again.

Bhagavad Gita, 8:26

Judaism

Thou must redeem us eventually. Why delay?

Talmud, Midrash Tehillim 87

Man was meant to realize the divine potential within him. He misses the mark when he fails to do so. He has attained salvation when he achieves his full spiritual potential as a human being, created in the image of God.

Roland B. Gittelsohn, *The Meaning of Judaism*

Salvation came once gain to the Jewish people in our time [when the Holocaust ended], just as it did in previous times; this time, however, it came too late, and all that is new and unprecedented in the contemporary Jewish religious situation is due to this circumstance.

Emil L. Fackenheim, *What Is Judaism?*

Secularism

From the very beginning of apostolic Christianity, it was hampered by a dispute as to whether salvation was to be attained by a surgical operation or by a sprinkling of water: mere rites on which Jesus would not have wasted twenty words.

George Bernard Shaw, *Androcles and the Lion*, Preface

Unitarianism

God is my strong salvation:
What have I to fear?
In darkness and temptation,
My light, my help is near.

James Montgomery, "God Is My Strong Salvation"

SCIENCE

Christianity

This fool [Copernicus] wishes to reverse the entire scheme of astronomy; but sacred Scripture tells us that Joshua commanded the sun to stand still, and not the earth.

Martin Luther

The arguments that prove the stability of the sun and the motion of the earth have now rendered it indisputable.

Cotton Mather

An undevout astronomer is mad.

Edward Young, *Night Thoughts*

True science is complete vision; . . . true religion is sense and taste for the Infinite.

Friedrich Schleiermacher, *On Religion*

There will be nothing changed, by any progress of science, which will touch the foundations [of religion].

Henry Ward Beecher, "The Sure Foundations"

The church saves sinners, but science seeks to stop their manufacture.

Elbert Hubbard, *The Roycroft Dictionary and Book of Epigrams*

When science as a descriptive method of knowledge comes face to face with the facts of religious experience it is utterly incapable of dealing with the *essential* features of it. It studies it from the outside as an observable phenomenon, but it misses just the interior attitude of the participant that makes all the difference.

Rufus M. Jones, *A Preface to Christian Faith in a New Age*

Man has needed neither microscope nor electronic analysis in order to suspect that he lives surrounded by and resting on dust. But to count the grains and describe them, all the patient craft of modern science was necessary.

Pierre Teilhard de Chardin, *The Phenomenon of Man*

Scientists, however liberal, are prone, as everyone is, to overvalue the intellectual equipment they have tested in their particular field, and in the handling of which they have full competence.

Jacques Maritain, *On the Use of Philosophy*

The indubitable progress of science in all fields leads particularly in the industrial nations to the rise of many doubts in regard to belief in religion.

Hans Küng, *Eternal Life?*

Christian Science

Jesus of Nazareth was the most scientific man that ever trod the globe. He plunged beneath the material surface of things, and found the spiritual cause.

Mary Baker Eddy, *Science and Health with Key to the Scriptures*

Cosmic

Science without religion is lame; religion without science is blind.

Albert Einstein, *The World as I See It*

Deism

Science spreads and faith vanishes. Everyone wants to teach good behavior, no one wants to learn it. We have all become doctors, and we have ceased to be Christians.

Jean Jacques Rousseau, Reply to the King of Poland

Islam

The Darwinian theory of evolution, which is metaphysically impossible and logically absurd, has been subtly woven in certain quarters into some aspects of Islam to produce a most unfortunate and sometimes dangerous blend.

Seyyed Hossein Nasr, "The Western World and Its Challenges to Islam"

Science knows the qualities of electricity, but not its real essence.

Mahmoud Mohammed Taha, *The Second Message of Islam*

Judaism

To observe and explore the world is the task of science; to judge it and determine our attitudes toward it is the task of religion.

Leo Baeck, *The Essence of Judaism*

Our task is to interpret *all* experience. Science helps us to interpret *some* experiences. But it should not presume to say that what it cannot interpret is not experience at all. That would be substituting a method for the material to which the method is applicable.

Emanuel Rackman, *One Man's Judaism*

Even the physicist does not simply photograph reality, but rather creates a world of constructs that only parallels a concrete, empirical correlative.

Joseph B. Soloveitchik, *Halakhic Man*

Nonsectarian

Historically, religion came first and science grew out of religion. Science has never superseded religion, and it is my expectation that it never will supersede it.

Arnold J. Toynbee, *Surviving the Future*

Unitarianism

The religion that is afraid of science dishonors God and commits suicide.

Ralph Waldo Emerson, *Journals*

The first conclusion we draw from the New Physics is that even the most sophisticated instruments of observation cannot touch the ineffable.

William F. Schulz, "Pour Forth the Angels and See Them Dance"

SELF-CONTROL

Buddhism

Who else but the self can be master of the self? With self well controlled, another master is hard to find.

Dhammapada

Christianity/Judaism

He that is slow to anger is better than the mighty; and he that ruleth his spirit than he that taketh a city.

Holy Bible, Proverbs 16:32

Christianity

Christ . . . suffered for us, leaving us an example, that ye should follow his steps:

Who did no sin, neither was guile found in his mouth:

Who, when he was reviled, reviled not again; when he suffered, he threatened not.

Holy Bible, 1 Peter 2:21-23

There is no higher rule than that over oneself, over one's impulses.

Baltasar Gracian, *The Art of Worldly Wisdom*

Confucianism

He that requires much from himself and little from others will keep himself from being the object of resentment.

Confucius, *Analects*

Hinduism

Sweet are the winds to him who desires for himself moral order; for him the rivers flow sweet.

Rig-Veda

When a man lacks discrimination and his mind is uncontrolled, his senses are unmanageable, like the restive horses of a charioteer. But when a man has discrimination and his mind is controlled, his senses, like the well-broken horses of a charioteer, lightly obey the rein.

Upanishads, Katha

Let the disciplined man ever discipline
    Himself, abiding in a secret place,
Solitary, restraining his thoughts and soul,
    Free from aspirations and without possessions.

Bhagavad Gita, 6:10

Stoicism

Freedom is not procured by a full enjoyment of what is desired, but by controlling the desire.

Epictetus, *Discourses*

Taoism

He who conquers others is strong.
He who conquers himself is mighty.

Lao-tzu, Tao-te ching

SELF-DENIAL

Christianity

If any man will come after me, let him deny himself, and take up his cross, and follow me.

Holy Bible, Matthew 16:24

Renunciation of riches is the origin and preserver of virtues.

St. Ambrose

If self-sacrifice is, as we are told, "glorious madness," then certainly undeviating self-assertion is inglorious madness. Either path leads alike to annihilation. Both end alike "in the dark night where all cows are black."

Rufus M. Jones, *Social Law in the Spiritual World*

I often think the doctrines of fasting in Lent and having meatless days are old-fashioned. It might be better to give up television. That would be a more meaningful self-denial in this day and age.

Arthur Michael Ramsey, Archbishop of Canterbury,
Speech upon enthronement, 1962

Hinduism

Now, what people call "silent asceticism" is really the chaste life of a student of sacred knowledge, for only in finding the soul [does one discover] Brahma's citadel, the golden hall of the Lord.

Upanishads, Chandogya

Judaism

Sanctify thyself in the things that are permitted by denying thyself . . . something of what is allowed.

Talmud, Yebamot 20a

To deny oneself various comforts is . . . easier in thought than in deed.

Golda Meir, Letter, August 24, 1921

SELF-KNOWLEDGE

Buddhism

A monk in China asked an ancient master, "What made Bodhidharma come from the West to our country?"

Surprised, the master countered with a question of his own, "Why do you ask about Bodhidharma instead of about yourself?"

Daisetz Teitaro Suzuki, "Self the Unattainable"

Christianity/Judaism

How many are mine iniquities and sins? make me to know my transgression and my sin.

Holy Bible, Job 13:23

Christianity

A humble knowledge of thyself is a surer way to God than a deep search after learning.

Thomas à Kempis, *The Imitation of Christ*

Know then thyself, presume not God to scan;
The proper study of mankind is man.

Alexander Pope, *An Essay on Man*

Resolve to by thyself; and know that he,
Who finds himself, loses his misery!

Matthew Arnold, "Self-Dependence"

One may understand the cosmos, but never the ego; the self is more distant than any star.

G.K. Chesterton, *Orthodoxy*

The grandeur of man lies in the fact that he is created in the image and likeness of God. . . . If he fails to recognize his dignity he does not know himself; if he insists on it without referring it to a greater than himself, he founders on the rock of vainglory.

Etienne Gilson, *The Spirit of Medieval Philosophy*

Confucianism

The Master said, "In vain have I looked for a single man capable of seeing his own faults and bringing the charge home against himself."

Confucius, *Analects*

Hinduism

Him who is this person in the mirror—him indeed I reverence.

Upanishads, Kaushitaki

Praise shames me, for I secretly beg for it.

Rabindranath Tagore, *Stray Birds*

Judaism

We become what we think of ourselves.

Abraham Joshua Heschel, *Who Is Man?*

Nonsectarian

Unfortunately there is no doubt about the fact that man is, as a whole, less good than he imagines himself or wants to be. Everyone carries a shadow, and the less it is embodied in the individual's conscious life, the blacker and denser it is.

Carl Jung, *Psychology and Religion*

Poetics

Seek not the depths of your knowledge with staff or sounding line.
For self is a sea boundless and measureless.

Kahlil Gibran, *The Prophet*

SIN

Christianity/Judaism

Be sure your sin will find you out.

Holy Bible, Numbers 32:23

Though your sins be as scarlet, they shall be white as snow.

Holy Bible, Isaiah 1:18

Christianity

He that is without sin among you, let him first cast a stone.

Holy Bible, John 8:7

The wages of sin is death.

Holy Bible, Romans 6:23

Those that will turn truly to Christ must flee occasions, words, sights, and deeds exciting to sin.

John Wycliffe, *The Poor Caitiff*

Plate sin with gold,
And the strong lance of justice hurtless breaks;
Arm it in rags, a pigmy's straw does pierce it.

William Shakespeare, *Measure for Measure*, Act 4, Sc. 4

Consider your evil inclinations, and how far you have followed them. By these two points you shall discover that your sins are more numerous than the hairs of your head, yea, than the sands of the sea.

St. Francis de Sales, *Introduction to the Devout Life*

One leak will sink a ship, and one sin will destroy a sinner.

John Bunyan, *The Pilgrim's Progress*

He that once sins, like him that slides on ice,
Goes swiftly down the slippery way of vice.

John Dryden, *Journal*

Adam's guilt our souls hath split,
    His fault is charg'd upon us;
And that alone hath overthrown,
    And utterly undone us.

Michael Wigglesworth, *The Day of Doom*

Sin is a transient matter, but Christ is eternal.

Fyodor Dostoevsky, *Diary of a Writer*

The Greeks always held that sin was "missing the mark"—that is what the Greek word for sin means—failure to arrive at, to reach, the real end toward which life aims. Sin is defeat.

Rufus M. Jones, *Spiritual Energies in Daily Life*

As we read the Bible, we read a bit of human history. We read a good deal of injustice and bloodshed in it. But have you never found it remarkable how little weight is attached to it? We are simply told, man is lost; he is dead in his sins. Few words for a long, long story; but they tell the whole story.

Karl Barth, *God in Action*

Sin is the turning towards ourselves, and making ourselves the center of our world.

Paul Tillich, *The Eternal Now*

The very soil has been smitten with the curse which came because of the sin of man. Thorns, thistles, and deserts are on this globe because they reflect the heart of man.

Donald Grey Barnhouse, *Words Fitly Spoken*

There has never yet been a bomb invented that is half so powerful as one mortal sin—and yet there is no positive power in sin, only negation, only annihilation.

Thomas Merton, *The Seven Storey Mountain*

We only tarnish the shining promises of God if we persist in dwelling on our own sinfulness.

J.B. Phillips, *Good News*

Hinduism

If ever we have any sin committed
Against the gods, or friend, or houses' chieftain,
Of such may now our hymn be expiation.
O heaven and earth, from dreadful darkness save us.

Rig-Veda

Islam

Shall I tell you upon whom the devils descend?
They descend upon every sinful, lying person.

Koran, 26:221-222

Sin begins in thought, which is the intimation of conscience. So, if the conscience holds sin, then its thoughts shall be evil.

Mahmoud Mohammed Taha, *The Second Message of Islam*

Judaism

Rabbi Akiba said: "In the beginning, sin is like a thread of a spider's web; but in the end, it becomes like the cable of a ship."

Talmud, Bereshit Rabbah 22:6

"I have sinned." Thus speaks the soul and abolishes shame. By speaking thus, referring purely back into the past, it purifies the present from the weakness of the past.

Franz Rosenzweig, *The Star of Redemption*

Stoicism

A man does not sin by commission only, but often by omission.

Marcus Aurelius, *Meditations*

SOLITUDE

Buddhism

Twilight whippoorwill—
Whistle on, sweet dreamer
Of dark loneliness.

Basho

Christianity/Judaism

They wandered in the wilderness in a solitary way; they found no city to dwell in.

Hungry and thirsty, their soul fainted in them.

Then they cried unto the Lord in their trouble, and he delivered them out of their distresses.

Holy Bible, Psalms 107:4-6

Christianity

We need no wings to go in search of Him, but have only to find a place where we can be alone—and look upon Him present within us.

St. Teresa of Avila

A man, alone, is either a saint or a devil.

Robert Burton, *The Anatomy of Melancholy*

Alone, alone, all, all alone,
Alone on a wide wide sea!
And never a saint took pity on
My soul in agony.

Samuel Taylor Coleridge, "The Rime of the Ancient Mariner"

'Tis solitude should teach us how to die;
It hath no flatterers; vanity can give
No hollow aid; alone—man with his God must strive.

Lord Byron, Childe Harold's Pilgrimage

Solitude vivifies; isolation kills.

Joseph Roux, Meditations of a Parish Priest

The embrace of it, the silence! I had entered into a solitude [at Notre Dame de Gethsemani] that was an impregnable fortress. And the silence that enfolded me, spoke to me, and spoke to me louder and more eloquently than any voice.

Thomas Merton, The Seven Storey Mountain

Islam

He who is afraid of solitude and wishes to be in the company of man is very far from salvation.

Fudail bin Iyad, A Rosary of Islamic Readings

Judaism

Let each one withdraw into his corner, to the seclusion of his own soul; let him meditate or weep in solitude over the fate of him who has passed, over the fate of all mankind.

Aaron David Gordon, "The Immortality of the Soul"

Solitude is a necessary protest to the incursions and the false alarms of society's hysteria, a period of cure and recovery.

Abraham Joshua Heschel, Who Is Man?

Unitarianism

Why should I feel lonely? is not our planet in the Milky Way?

Henry David Thoreau, Walden

SORROW

Christianity/Judaism

By sorrow of the heart the spirit is broken.

Holy Bible, Proverbs 15:13

Sorrow is better than laughter: for by the sadness of the countenance the heart is made better.

Holy Bible, Ecclesiastes 7:3

They have heard evil tidings: they are fainthearted; there is sorrow on the sea.

Holy Bible, Jeremiah 49:23

Christianity

Godly sorrow worketh repentance to salvation . . . : but the sorrow of the world worketh death.

Holy Bible, 2 Corinthians 7:10

They have erred from the faith, and pierced themselves through with many sorrows.

Holy Bible, 1 Timothy 6:10

Can I see another's woe,
And not be in sorrow too?
Can I see another's grief,
And not seek for kind relief?

William Blake, "On Another's Sorrow"

When sorrow so works as to broaden our life, as to bring down our offending faculties into the proper position, as to make us take anew our bearings and carry ourselves as sons of God destined to immortality should do, then it works toward salvation and toward life.

Henry Ward Beecher, "Sources and Uses of Suffering"

Through the night of doubt and sorrow
Onward goes the pilgrim band,
Singing songs of expectation,
Marching to the promised land.

Sabine Baring-Gould, "Through the Night of Doubt and Sorrow"

Children's griefs are little, certainly; but so is the child . . . . Grief is a matter of relativity.

Francis Thompson, "Shelley"

There is an alchemy in sorrow. It can be transmuted into wisdom.

Pearl S. Buck, *The Child Who Never Grew*

Unitarianism

'Tis sorrow builds the shining ladder up,
Whose golden rounds are our calamities,
Whereon our feet planting, nearer God,
The spirit climbs and hath its eyes unsealed.

James Russell Lowell, "'Tis Sorrow Builds the Shining Ladder Up"

SOUL

Buddhism

Karma—all that total of a soul
Which is the things it did, the thoughts it had,
The "Self" it wove.

Sir Edwin Arnold, *The Light of Asia*

Christianity/Judaism

The Lord God formed man of the dust of the ground, and breathed into
his nostrils the breath of life; and man became a living soul.

Holy Bible, Genesis 2:7

Christianity

What is a man profited, if he shall gain the whole world, and lose his
own soul?

Holy Bible, Matthew 16:26

When God made man, he put into the soul his equal, his active, everlasting
masterpiece.

Meister Eckhart, *Sermons*

God never deserts the soul, but abides there in bliss forever.

St. Julian of Norwich

Every subject's duty is the king's; but every subject's soul is his own.

William Shakespeare, *Henry V*, Act 4, Sc. 1

Souls are God's jewels, every one of which is worth many worlds.

Thomas Traherne, *Centuries of Meditations*

O strong soul, by what shore
Tarriest thou now?

Matthew Arnold, "Rugby Chapel"

The soul is the sense of something higher than ourselves, something that stirs in us thoughts, hopes, and aspirations. . . . The soul is a burning desire to . . . remain children of light.

Albert Schweitzer, *Reverence for Life*

We must not forget that the human soul, however independently created our philosophy represents it as being, is inseparable, in its birth and in its growth, from the universe into which it was born.

Pierre Teilhard de Chardin, *The Divine Milieu*

A single human soul is of more worth than the whole universe of bodies and material goods. There is nothing above the human soul—except God.

Jacques Maritain, *Scholasticism and Politics*

The men and women who, neglecting every effort to improve their souls, assert that they are happy anyway are merely lying to us and to themselves: their despair may be invisible as yet, but it is latent and it is real.

Fulton J. Sheen, *On Being Human*

Hinduism

If the slayer think to slay,
If the slain think himself slain,
Both these understand not.
This one slays not, nor is slain.

Upanishads, Katha

[Note: This stanza about the eternal, indestructible soul is echoed in the first stanza of Ralph Waldo Emerson's poem "Brahma."]

Unborn, eternal, everlasting, this ancient one
    Is not slain when the body is slain.

Bhagavad Gita, 2:20

Islam

Every soul is the hostage of its own deeds.

Koran, 74:38

Judaism

In Rabbinic phrase the human soul is a tiny lamp kindled from the Divine torch; it is the vital spark of heavenly flame.

Talmud, Berekot 10a

The story is told of a blind man who carried a lame man into an orchard where together they stole some fruit. To the question of which was the guilty party, the rabbis answered: both—neither could have carried out the theft without the other. The two men represented the body and soul of man. Together they constitute an indivisible unity.

Roland B. Gittelsohn, *The Meaning of Judaism*

Secularism

O Lord, if there is a Lord, save my soul, if I have a soul.

Ernest Renan, *Priere d'un Sceptique*

Unitarianism

Build thee more stately mansions, O my soul.

Oliver Wendell Holmes, "The Chambered Nautilus"

SUCCESS

Christianity/Judaism

Be thou strong and very courageous, that thou mayest observe . . . all the law, which Moses my servant commanded thee. . . .

For then thou shalt make thy way prosperous, and then thou shalt have good success.

Holy Bible, Joshua 2:7–8

Christianity

And a very great multitude spread their garments in the way; others cut down branches from the trees, and strewed them in the way.

And the multitudes that went before, and that followed, cried, saying, Hosanna to the son of David: blessed is he that cometh in the name of the Lord; Hosanna to the highest.

And when he was come into Jerusalem, all the city was moved, saying, Who is this?

And the multitude said, This is Jesus the prophet of Nazareth and Galilee.

Holy Bible, Matthew 21:8–11

[Note: The preceding verses describe Jesus' triumphant entry into Jerusalem to celebrate Passover. He arrives as "thy King . . . sitting upon an ass," echoing the prophecy in Zechariah 9:9.]

Let us work as if success depends on ourselves alone, but with the heartfelt conviction that we are doing nothing and God everything.

St. Ignatius of Loyola

Here I have lived a quarter of a century and have passed from a young to an old man. Here my children have been born, and one is buried. I now leave, not knowing when or whether ever I may return, with a task before me greater than that which rested upon Washington. Without the assistance of that Divine Being, who ever attended him, I cannot succeed. With that assistance, I cannot fail.

Abraham Lincoln, Speech at Springfield, Illinois, February 11, 1861

Success is full of promise till men get it; and then it is last year's nest from which the birds have flown.

Henry Ward Beecher, *Life Thoughts*

America! America!
     May God thy gold refine,
Till all success be nobleness,
     And every gain divine!

Katharine Lee Bates, "America the Beautiful"

When a successful figure becomes especially prominent and conspicuous, the majority give way to the idolization of success. They become blind to right and wrong, truth and untruth, fair play and foul play. They have eyes only for the deed, for the successful result.

Dietrich Bonhoeffer, *Ethics*

He who tries to use this world's textbooks on success in the things of the Spirit will end up like the man who offered to sell a set of books on "How to Succeed" for a month's room and board.

Vance Havner, *The Vance Havner Quotebook*

Hinduism

The man who seeks success and aid approaches
The son of strength, with feast and newest worship.

Rig-Veda

Judaism

Among the humble and great alike, those who achieve success do so not because fate and circumstance are especially kind to them. Often the reverse is true. They succeed because they do not whine over their fate but take whatever has been given to them and go on to make the most of their best.

Sidney Greenberg, *Say Yes to Life*

SUFFERING

Buddhism

The Four Noble Truths: Suffering, the origin of suffering, the cessation of suffering, and the Noble Eightfold Path which leads to the cessation of suffering.

Dhammapada

It is not easy to accept the premise that one of life's basic conditions is inescapable suffering, true though this proves to be.

Nancy Wilson Ross, *Buddhism: A Way of Life and Thought*

Christianity/Judaism

My flesh is clothed with worms and clods of dust; my skin is broken and become loathsome.
    My days are swifter than a weaver's shuttle, and are spent without hope.

Holy Bible, Job 7:5-6

Christianity

The sufferings of this present time are not worthy to be compared with the glory which shall be revealed in us.

Holy Bible, Romans 8:18

I take pleasure in infirmities, in reproaches, in necessities, in persecutions, in distresses for Christ's sake: for when I am weak, then am I strong.

Holy Bible, 2 Corinthians 12:10

To suffer persecution for righteousness' sake is a singular comfort. For it ought to occur to us how much honor God bestows upon us in thus furnishing us with the special badge of his soldiery.

John Calvin, *Institutes on the Christian Religion*

I would willingly endure all the sufferings of this world to be raised a degree higher in heaven, and to possess the smallest increase of the knowledge of God's greatness.

St. Teresa of Avila

Man's grandeur stems from his knowledge of his own misery. A tree does not know itself to be miserable.

Blaise Pascal, *Pensées*

You must accept your cross; if you carry it courageously it will carry you to heaven.

St. John Vianney

The temple of the spirit is raised through work and suffering; and I would add that suffering counts for more than work.

St. Anthony Mary Claret

If you suffer, thank God—it is a sure sign you are alive.

Elbert Hubbard, *Epigrams*

When the world has caved in; when the last extremity has been reached; when the billows and waterspouts of fortune have done their worst, you hear the calm, heroic voice of the lonely man saying: "God is our refuge and fortress; therefore we will not fear though the earth be removed, though the mountains be carried into the middle of the sea."

Rufus M. Jones, *Spiritual Energies in Daily Life*

On a hill far away stood an old rugged cross,
The emblem of suffering and shame.

George Bennard, "The Old Rugged Cross"

Christianity has been reproached for trying to deceive people about the reality of earthly suffering by comforting them with the prospect of heavenly blessedness awaiting them. Jesus was not thinking of vague future bliss. For he does not say: Blessed eventually will be those who now suffer. Rather he promises: Blessed are you now, right this minute, while you are suffering.

Albert Schweitzer, *Reverence for Life*

Sufferers . . . are not useless and dwarfed. They are simply paying for the forward march and triumph of all. They are casualties, fallen on the field of honor.

Pierre Teilhard de Chardin, *Human Energy*

God whispers to us in our pleasures, speaks in our conscience, but shouts in our pains: it is His megaphone to rouse a deaf world.

C.S. Lewis, *The Problem of Pain*

Not only action but also suffering is a way to freedom. In suffering, the deliverance consists in our being allowed to put the matter out of our own hands into God's hands.

Dietrich Bonhoeffer, *Letters and Papers from Prison*

The more you try to avoid suffering, the more you suffer, because smaller and more insignificant things begin to torture you, in proportion to your fear of being hurt.

Thomas Merton, *The Seven Storey Mountain*

This age is interested in medals, but not in scars.

Billy Graham, *Till Armageddon*

Islam

God has no need for your suffering if you are thankful and believing.

Koran, 4:147

Judaism

Rabbi Akiba said: "A man should rejoice in chastisements more than in good fortune; for if a man lives in good fortune all his life, his sin is not remitted. How is it remitted? Through chastisements."

Talmud, Sifre Deuteronomy 32

To understand the bitter cry of the anguished soul, we must . . . at the very least have felt with those who have suffered.

Leo Baeck, *The Essence of Judaism*

Suffering comes to ennoble man, to purge his thoughts of pride and superficiality, to expand his horizons. In sum, the purpose of suffering is to repair that which is faulty in a man's personality.

Joseph B. Soloveitchik

Unitarianism

A great grief has taught me more than any minister, and when feeling most alone I find refuge in the Almighty Friend.

Louisa May Alcott

TEMPTATION

Buddhism

As the wind throws down a shaky tree, so temptation overthrows him who lives only for pleasure, who is immoderate, idle, and weak.

Dhammapada

Christianity/Judaism

Hast thou eaten of the tree, whereof I commanded thee that thou shouldest not eat?

And the man said, The woman whom thou gavest to be with me, she gave me of the tree, and I did eat.

And the Lord said unto the woman, What is this that thou hast done? And the woman said, The serpent beguiled me, and I did eat.

Holy Bible, Genesis 3:11-13

Christianity

Lead us not into temptation, but deliver us from evil.

Holy Bible, Matthew 6:13

Watch and pray, that ye enter not into temptation: the spirit indeed is willing, but the flesh is weak.

Holy Bible, Matthew 26:41

Give not way to temptation, be it ever so grievous. For the greater the battle the more glorious the victory, and the higher the crown.

John Wycliffe, *The Poor Caitiff*

There is no order so holy nor place so secret where there be not temptations or adversities. There is no man that is altogether safe from temptation whilst he lives; for in ourselves is the root thereof.

Thomas à Kempis, *The Imitation of Christ*

To lose our souls with swearing . . . disobedience . . . drunkenness . . . are instances fit to be put in the stories of fools and madmen. And all vice is a degree of the same unreasonableness; the most splendid temptation being nothing but a pretty, well-weaved fallacy, a mere trick, a solipsism.

Jeremy Taylor, "The Foolish Exchange"

A weak, tempted heart must take refuge in the thought of a future world.

Friedrich Schleiermacher, *On Religion*

No man knows how bad he is until he has tried to be good. There is a silly idea . . . that good people don't know what temptation means.

C.S. Lewis, *The Screwtape Letters*

You can't keep the birds from flying over your head, but you can keep them from building nests in your hair.

John A. Redhead, *Putting Your Faith to Work*

THANKSGIVING

Christianity/Judaism

Enter into his gates with thanksgiving, and into his courts with praise.

Holy Bible, Psalms 100:4

Christianity

Rejoice evermore.
Pray without ceasing.
In every thing give thanks: for this is the will of God.

Holy Bible, 1 Thessalonians 5:16-18

Where is your thanksgiving if you so gorge yourself with banqueting or wine that you either become stupid or are rendered useless for the duties of piety and of your calling?

John Calvin, *Institutes of the Christian Religion*

We gather together to ask the Lord's blessing;
He chastens and hastens his will to make known;
The wicked oppressing now cease from distressing,
Sing praises to his name: He forgets not his own.

"We Gather Together," Netherlands folk hymn

Some people always sigh in thanking God.

Elizabeth Barrett Browning, *Aurora Leigh*

Come, ye thankful people, come,
Raise the song of harvest home;
All is safely gathered in,
Ere the winter storms begin.

Henry Alford, "Come, Ye Thankful People, Come"

The abundance of a grateful heart gives honor to God even if it does not
turn to Him in words. An unbeliever who is filled with thanks for his
very being has ceased to be an unbeliever.

Paul Tillich, *The Eternal Now*

Islam

Your Lord is bountiful to mankind: yet most of them do not give thanks.

Koran, 27:73

Judaism

Rabbi Judah, after recovering from illness, was visited by Rabbi Hanan
of Baghdad and other rabbis.

They said: "Blessed be the Compassionate One, who gave thee to us and
not to the earth."

He said: "Amen." Then he said to them: "My response is sufficient to
fulfill the duty of thanksgiving."

Talmud, Berakot 54

TIME

Buddhism

As neither does the past reach to the present nor does the present reach
to the past, every thing, according to its nature, remains for only one
period of time.

Seng-chao, *Treatises*

The conception of time as an objective blank in which particular events . . .
succeed one after another has completely been discarded. The Buddha . . .
knows no time-continuity; the past and the future are both rolled up in this
present moment of illumination.

Daisetz Teitaro Suzuki, *Essays in Zen Buddhism*

Christianity/Judaism

To every thing there is a season, and a time to every purpose under the
heaven:
　　A time to be born, and a time to die; a time to plant, and a time to pluck
up that which is planted;
　　A time to kill, and a time to heal; a time to break down, and a time to
build up;
　　A time to weep, and a time to laugh; a time to mourn, and a time to
dance. . . .
　　A time to rend, and a time to sew; a time to keep silence, and a time to
speak;
　　A time to love, and a time to hate; a time of war, and a time of peace.

Holy Bible, Ecclesiastes 3:1-4, 7-8

Christianity

It is high time to awake out of sleep: for now our salvation is nearer than
. . . we believed.

Holy Bible, Romans 13:11

Brethren, the time is short.

Holy Bible, 1 Corinthians 7:29

Which beginning of time according to our Chronologie [i.e., Creation] fell
upon the entrance of the night preceding the twenty-third day of October
in the year of the Julian calendar 710 [4004 B.C.].

James Ussher, *Annales Veteris et Novi Testamenti*

Time, like an ever-rolling stream,
　　Bears all its sons away;
They fly, forgotten, as a dream
　　Dies at the opening day.

Isaac Watts, "O God, Our Help in Ages Past"

Time hath a taming hand.

John Henry Newman, "Persecution"

This self began in time. But nothing begins absolutely. Everything which begins existed before itself in a certain way, to wit, in its causes. Insofar as it is material, the thinking self existed before itself in time, namely, in the ancestral cells, physiochemical materials and energies utilized by life all along the line from which the self has sprung. Whatever of it existed before it preexisted in time.

Jacques Maritain, *Approaches to God*

Time is our destiny. Time is our hope. Time is our despair. And time is the mirror in which we see eternity.

Paul Tillich, *The Shaking of the Foundations*

If you picture Time as a straight line along which we have to travel, then you must picture God as the whole page on which the line is drawn.

C.S. Lewis, *Mere Christianity*

Hinduism

From time flow forth created things.
From time, too, they advance in growth.
Likewise in time they disappear.
Time is a form and formless, too.

Upanishads, Maitri

Judaism

One cannot begin a conversation with the end, or a war with a peace treaty (as the pacifists would like), or life with death. Willy-nilly, actively or passively, one must await the given time; one cannot skip a single moment.

Franz Rosenzweig, *The New Thinking*

The peoples of the world . . . foresee a time when their land with its mountains and rivers will lie beneath the sky, even as now, but be inhabited by others, a time when their language will be buried in books and their customs and laws stripped of living force.

Franz Rosenzweig, *The Star of Redemption*

Poetics

The Moving Finger writes; and, having writ,
Moves on: nor all your Piety nor Wit
    Shall lure it back to cancel half a Line,
Nor all your Tears wash out a Word of it.

Edward FitzGerald, *The Rubaiyat of Omar Khayyam*

Let today embrace the past with remembrance and the future with longing.

> Kahlil Gibran, *The Prophet*

Unitarianism

All hail the pageant of the years
That endless come and go,
The brave procession of the spheres
In time's relentless flow.

> John Haynes Holmes, "The Pageant of the Years"

TOLERANCE

Buddhism

Buddhism, . . . recognizing no permanency, no finite stabilities, no distinctions of character or class or race, except as passing phenomena—nay, no difference even between gods and men—has been essentially the religion of tolerance.

> Lafcadio Hearn, "Nirvana"

Christianity/Judaism

Then said the Lord . . .
    Should not I spare Nineveh, that great city, wherein are more than sixscore thousand persons that cannot discern between their right hand and their left hand?

> *Holy Bible*, Jonah 4:10-11

Christianity

If a donkey bray at you, don't bray at him.

> George Herbert, *Jacula Prudentum*

The question, whether the prince may tolerate divers persuasions, is no more than whether he may lawfully persecute any man for not being of his opinion.

> Jeremy Taylor, *The Liberty of Prophesying*

God is the only being in the universe who has a right to be intolerant. In fact, if He were tolerant He would not be God.

> Donald Grey Barnhouse, *Words Fitly Spoken*

Modern sentimentality has reduced God to a tolerant, indulgent, grand-fatherly being who winks at our transgressions.

Vance Havner, *The Vance Havner Quotebook*

Tolerance implies no lack of commitment to one's own beliefs. Rather it condemns the oppression or persecution of others.

John F. Kennedy, Letter to the National Conference of Christians and Jews,
October 10, 1960

Christian Science

I would no more quarrel with a man because of his religion than I would because of his art.

Mary Baker Eddy, "Harvest"

Hinduism

Those who genuinely though erroneously worship other gods are really worshipping the true God [according to Hinduism], though they do not know it; and God accepts their worship, imperfect though it be.

Franklin Edgerton, *The Bhagavad Gita*

Judaism

Religious tolerance is in the main a modern notion advanced by thinkers like Spinoza, John Locke, and John Stuart Mill. . . . we shall look in vain for anything like the modern ideal in the classical sources of Judaism, but no one with a sense of history will expect it to be otherwise.

Louis Jacobs, *What Does Judaism Say About . . . ?*

TROUBLE

Christianity/Judaism

Man is born unto trouble, as the sparks fly upward.

Holy Bible, Job 5:7

Man that is born of a woman is of few days, and full of trouble.

Holy Bible, Job 14:1

If thou faint in the day of adversity, thy strength is small.

Holy Bible, Proverbs 24:10

Christianity

We glory in tribulations . . . knowing that tribulations worketh patience;
And patience, experience; and experience, hope.

Holy Bible, Romans 5:3-4

Many love Jesus as long as no adversity befalls them, and can praise and
bless Him whenever they receive any benefits from him, but if Jesus with-
draws a little from them and forsakes them a bit, they soon fall into some
great grumbling or excessive dejection or into open despair.

Thomas à Kempis, *The Imitation of Christ*

Nobody knows the trouble I've seen,
Nobody knows but Jesus.

"Nobody Knows the Trouble I've Seen," American spiritual, author unknown

We are too little to be always able to rise above difficulties. Well, then,
let us pass beneath them quite simply.

St. Thérèse de Lisieux

When the going gets particularly tough, we know, people do tend to turn
their thoughts to religion. It is this fact that is responsible for the saying,
"Man's extremity is God's opportunity."

Gordon W. Allport, *Waiting for the Lord*

As soon as you matriculate in the university of life you discover that one
of the required courses is called trouble.

John A. Redhead, *Putting Your Faith to Work*

One of the things Christ definitely promised us was trouble.
    "In the world ye shall have tribulation,"
    He said.
But we must never forget that He added:
    "But be of good cheer."

Peter Marshall, *Mr. Jones, Meet the Master*

Troubles will come to you sooner or later. Sometimes, when the south
winds are blowing softly and you have money in the bank; as far as you
know you have perfect health and everything seems to be going your way,
disaster will strike and everything will go wrong. At those times you must
hold fast to the fact that God makes no mistakes; He has not forsaken
you.

Jerry Falwell, *Finding Inner Peace and Strength*

Hinduism

Transport us to the farther shore of trouble
In safety; frustrate all attacks of mischief.

Rig-Veda

Islam

When trouble toucheth a man, he crieth unto us in all postures—lying down, on his side, or sitting, or standing. But when we have solved his trouble, he passeth on his way as if he had never cried to us for a trouble that touched him! Thus do the deeds of transgressors seem fair in their eyes!

Koran, 10:12

If you have no troubles—buy a goat.

Muslim proverb

Judaism

Picture the situation to yourself. Surrounded by armed bandits, I cry out "Help! Help! Danger!" Is not every man bound to hasten to my help? Is it not a fearful, an indelible disgrace, [if] I am forced to prove first of all that my danger affects other people, affects the whole human race?

Ahad Ha-am, "Slavery in Freedom"

Unitarianism

The mass of men lead lives of quiet desperation.

Henry David Thoreau, *Walden*

TRUTH

Christianity/Judaism

He is . . . a God of truth.

Holy Bible, Deuteronomy 32:4

His truth shall be thy shield.

Holy Bible, Psalms 91:4

The truth of the Lord endureth for ever.

Holy Bible, Psalms 117:2

Christianity

The truth shall make you free.

Holy Bible, John 8:32

Jesus answered, Thou [Pilate] sayest that I am a king. To this end was I born, and for this cause came I into the world, that I should bear witness unto the truth. . . .
Pilate saith unto him, What is truth?

Holy Bible, John 18:37-38

Why does truth call forth hatred?

St. Augustine, *The City of God*

What is truth? Truth is something so noble that if God should turn aside from it, I could keep to the truth and let God go.

Meister Eckhart, *Fragments*

We ought . . . to read devout and simple books. . . . Let not the authority of the writer move thee, whether he be of small or great learning: but let the love of pure truth draw thee to read. Search not who said this, but mark what is said.

Thomas à Kempis, *The Imitation of Christ*

All we know of the truth is that the absolute truth, such as it is, is beyond our reach.

Nicholas of Cusa, *De Docta Ignorantia*

A man may be in as just possession of truth as of a city, and yet be forced to surrender.

Sir Thomas Browne, *Religio Medici*

Who ever knew Truth put to the worse in a free and open encounter?

John Milton, *Areopagitica*

Why is truth so woefully
Removed? To depths of secret banned?
None understands in time! If we
But understood betimes, how bland
The truth would be, how fair to see!
How near and ready to our hand!

Goethe, *"Westostlicher Diwan"*

A truth that's told with bad intent
Beats all the lies you can invent.

William Blake, "Auguries of Innocence"

Truth, crushed to earth, shall rise again.

William Cullen Bryant, "The Battlefield"

If anyone could prove to me that Christ is outside the truth, and if the truth really did exclude Christ, I should stay with Christ rather than with the truth.

Fyodor Dostoevsky, Letter to N.A. Fonvizina, February 20, 1854

Truth is not something finished, but something unfolding as life goes forward.

Rufus M. Jones, *Finding the Trail of Life*

Great truths are felt before they are expressed.

Pierre Teilhard de Chardin

What religion believes to be true is not wholly true, but ought to be true, and may become true if its truth is not doubted.

Reinhold Niebuhr, *Moral Man and Immoral Society*

"Telling the truth" . . . is not solely a matter of moral character; it is also a matter of correct appreciation of real situations and of serious reflection upon them.

Dietrich Bonhoeffer, *Ethics*

I cannot explain . . . the truth that darts like a flash of lightning into the soul of man and changes his whole life. Yet here is Paul, and here is Augustine, and here is Francis of Assisi, and here is—well, you can fill in the names you know.

John A. Redhead, *Putting Your Faith to Work*

Confucianism

They who know the truth are not equal to those who love it, and they who love it are not equal to those who delight in it.

Confucius, *Analects*

Absolute truth is indestructible. Being indestructible, it is eternal.

Confucius, *The Doctrine of Mean*

Hinduism

If people should say to him, "You are a superior speaker," he should respond, "I am a superior speaker." He should not deny it.

Upanishads, Chandogya

One should speak truth, and speak what is pleasant; one should not speak unpleasant truth.

Laws of Manu

The special mental attitude which India has in her religion is made clear by the word *yoga*, whose meaning is to effect union. Union has its significance not in the realm of *to have*, but in that of *to be*. To *gain* truth is to admit its separateness, but to *be* true is to become one with truth.

Rabindranath Tagore, *The Religion of Man*

Islam

Speaking the truth to the unjust is the best of holy wars.

Muhammad

Do not veil the truth with falsehood, nor conceal the truth knowingly.

Koran, 2:42

Judaism

The great sickness and the grievous evil consist in this: that all the things that man finds written in books, he presumes to think of as true—and all the more so if the books are old.

Maimonides, Letter on Astrology

Truth is given once and for all, and it is laid down with precision. Fundamentally, truth merely needs to be transmitted.

Gershom Scholem, "Revelation and Tradition as Religious Categories in Judaism"

The world wants to be deceived. The truth is too complex and frightening; the taste for truth is an acquired taste that few acquire.

Walter Kaufmann, "*I and Thou*: A Prologue"

Mormonism

By the power of the Holy Ghost ye may know the truth of all things.

Book of Mormon, Moroni 10:5

Unitarianism

No man thoroughly understands a truth until he has contended against it.

Ralph Waldo Emerson, "Compensation"

Truth never yet fell dead in the streets; it has such affinity with the soul of man, the seed however broadcast will catch somewhere and produce its hundredfold.

Theodore Parker, *A Discourse of Matters Pertaining to Religion*

UNDERSTANDING

Buddhism

Few men reach the other shore. The rest run up and down this side of the torrent.

Dhammapada

Christianity/Judaism

Understanding is a wellspring of life unto him that hath it.

Holy Bible, Proverbs 16:22

Christianity

And Jesus said, Are ye also yet without understanding?

Holy Bible, Matthew 15:16

Understanding is the reward of faith. Therefore seek not to understand that thou mayest believe, but believe that thou mayest understand.

St. Augustine, *On the Gospel of St. John*

Hinduism

Understanding, assuredly, is more than meditation. . . . Reverence understanding.

Upanishads, Chandoyga

Speech is not what one should desire to understand. One should know the speaker.

Upanishads, Kaushitaki

Judaism

He who has understanding has everything.

Talmud, Nedarim 41a

Taoism

My words are easy to understand
    and easy to put into practice.
Yet no one under heaven understands them
    or puts them into practice.

Tao-te ching

Unitarianism

To paraphrase Saint Augustine's admonition to theologians who were driven to write about God, "If you can understand it, then it is not God."

F. Forrester Church, *Entertaining Angels*

VALUES

Christianity/Judaism

Honor thy father and thy mother: that thy days may be long upon the land which the Lord thy God giveth thee.

Thou shalt not kill.

Thou shalt not commit adultery.

Thou shalt not steal.

Thou shalt not bear false witness against thy neighbor.

Thou shalt not covet thy neighbor's house, thou shalt not covet thy neighbor's wife, nor his manservant, nor his ox, nor his ass, nor anything that is thy neighbor's.

Holy Bible, Exodus 20:12-17

[Note: The Ten Commandments appear in a slightly different form in Deuteronomy 5:16-21.]

Christianity

Therefore all things whatsoever ye would that men should do to you, do ye even so to them.

Holy Bible, Matthew 7:12

[Note: The Golden Rule is usually expressed in a more modern way: Do unto others as you would wish them to do unto you; *or*, Do as you would be done by.]

Do not be disturbed by the clamor of the world, which passes like a shadow. Do not let the false delights of a deceptive world deceive you.

St. Clare of Assisi

For us, with the rule of right and wrong given us by Christ, there is nothing for which we have no standard.

Leo Tolstoy, *War and Peace*

To its own impulse every creature stirs;
Live by thy light, and earth will live by hers!

Matthew Arnold, "Religious Isolation"

A civilized nation honors its idealists, and recognizes the immense benefit which they confer on the community by creating or revealing new and inexhaustible values.

William Ralph Inge, "Our Present Discontents"

Confucianism

Hold faithfulness and sincerity as first principles.

Confucius, *Analects*

Hinduism

Play not with dice, but cultivate thy tillage,
Enjoy thy riches, deeming them abundant.

Rig-Veda

Judaism

Man increasingly discovers God within himself, in his correct impulses, even when those inner drives . . . appear on the surface to stray from what is conventionally held to be the true road.

Abraham Isaac Kuk, *The Zionist Idea*

Values are measured in terms of what a person is willing to pay for them. The price may be life itself, as in *kiddush ha-Shem*, the sacrifice of an individual's life for the sake of others, for his country, for liberty, justice, or honor.

Yeshayahu Leibowitz, "Heroism"

Nonsectarian

Spiritual values . . . are not the exclusive possession of organized churches . . . they do not need supernatural concepts to validate them, . . . they are the general responsibility of *all* mankind.

Abraham H. Maslow, *Religions, Values, and Peak-Experiences*

VANITY

Christianity/Judaism

Vanity of vanities; all is vanity.

Holy Bible, Ecclesiastes 1:2

Christianity

Turn from these vanities unto the living God, which made heaven, and earth, and the sea, and all things that are therein.

Holy Bible, Acts 14:15

And the name of that town is Vanity: and at the town there is a fair kept called Vanity Fair.

John Bunyan, *The Pilgrim's Progress*

How many kingdoms remain ignorant of us!

Blaise Pascal, *Pensées*

Deism

Provided a man is not mad, he can be cured of every folly but vanity.

Jean Jacques Rousseau, *Emile*

Islam

Remember, earthly life is comparable with vanities. So do not be deceived by earthly life, and do not be led astray by deception against God.

Take warning from those that passed away before you. And be serious and forget not, for you are not forgotten.

Hazrat Othman, Sermon as Third Caliph of Islam

WAR

Christianity/Judaism

The Lord is a man of war.

Holy Bible, Exodus 15:3

The might of the Gentile, unsmote by the sword,
Hath melted like snow in the glance of the Lord!

Lord Byron, "The Destruction of Sennacherib"

[Note: Byron's poem is based on the events described in 2 Chronicles 32:1-22.]

Christianity

Ye shall hear of wars and rumors of wars: see that ye be not troubled: for all these things must come to pass, but the end is not yet.

Holy Bible, Matthew 24:6

All they that take the sword shall perish with the sword.

Holy Bible, Matthew 26:52

From whence come wars and fightings among you?

Holy Bible, James 4:1

In order for a war to be just, three things are necessary. First, the authority of the sovereign. . . . Secondly, a just cause. . . . Thirdly, a rightful intention.

St. Thomas Aquinas, *Summa Theologica*

Fondly do we hope—fervently do we pray—that this mighty scourge of war may speedily pass away. Yet, if God wills that it continue, until all the wealth piled by the bondman's two hundred and fifty years of unrequited toil shall be sunk, and every drop of blood drawn with the lash shall be paid by another drawn with the sword, as was said three thousand years ago, so still it must be said, "the judgments of the Lord are true and righteous altogether."

> Abraham Lincoln, Second Inaugural Address, March 4, 1865

I have read a fiery gospel writ in burnished rows of steel.

> Julia Ward Howe, "Battle Hymn of the Republic"

The church seeks its own life, and therefore while it is against war, speaking piously about "the Prince of Peace," it always justifies any present war.

> George A. Buttrick, *God, Pain, and Evil*

Deism

It is forbidden to kill; therefore all murderers are punished unless they kill in large numbers and to the sound of trumpets.

> Voltaire, *Philosophical Dictionary*

Islam

Now, when you meet the unbelievers in battle, strike off their heads. At length, when you have thoroughly subdued them, bind your captives firmly. Then be generous to them, or else take ransom from them, until the war lays down its burdens.

> *Koran*, 47:4

War is good if its object is God.

> Muhammad Iqbal, *The Secrets of the Self*

In justifying the use of the sword [in spreading Islam], we may describe it as a surgeon's lancet and not a butcher's knife. When used with sufficient wisdom, mercy, and knowledge, it uplifted the individual and purified society.

> Mahmoud Mohamed Taha, *The Second Message of Islam*

Judaism

King David was not allowed to build the Temple in Jerusalem because he had been a man of war; the privilege of constructing the Temple was reserved for his son, Solomon, whose very name is derived from *shalom* ["peace"].

Roland B. Gittelsohn, The Meaning of Judaism

Platonism

The origin of all wars is the pursuit of wealth, and we are forced to pursue wealth because we live in slavery to the cares of the body.

Plato, Phaedo

Stoicism

We are mad, not only individually, but nationally. We check manslaughter and isolated murders; but what of war and the much vaunted crime of slaughtering whole peoples?

Seneca, Epistles

Taoism

Stretch a bow to the very full,
And you will wish you had stopped in time.

Lao-tzu, Tao-te ching

Unitarianism

War is the antithesis of life. . . . Its one supreme triumph is to turn a busy factory into a pile of wreckage, a fertile field into a desert, a home of joy into an ash-heap of sorrow.

John Haynes Holmes, The Messiah Pulpit

WEALTH

Christianity/Judaism

Wealth maketh many friends.

Holy Bible, Proverbs 19:4

Let not the rich man glory in his riches.

Holy Bible, Jeremiah 9:23

Christianity

It is easier for a camel to go through the eye of a needle, than for a rich man to enter into the kingdom of God.

Holy Bible, Matthew 19:24

Nothing is more fallacious than wealth. It is a hostile comrade, a domestic enemy.

St. John Chrysostom, *Homilies*

Christ utterly rejects the material goods and show of this world, from which it follows that those who amass wealth in His name grossly abuse Him when they make Him a cloak to hide their avarice and arrogance.

Huldrych Zwingli, "Sixty-seven Theses" (No. 23)

Let none admire
That riches grow in Hell; that soil may best
Deserve the precious bane.

John Milton, *Paradise Lost*

I heard it said once by a beggar in a passion that the rich took nothing with them down to death. In the literal acceptation of the text he was wrong, for the rich take down with them to death flattery, folly, illusion, pride and a good many lesser garments which have grown into their skins.

Hilaire Belloc, "On Poverty"

There was nothing of inverted snobbery in the attitude of Jesus to wealth. He did not glorify poverty as such. He had friends in every walk of life. . . . Even if we insist on the dangers of riches, we cannot fly to the other extreme, and make poverty itself a virtue.

William Barclay, *Ethics in a Permissive Society*

Hinduism

Thou, lord of all prosperity,
Best wielder of the golden ax,
Make wealth easy for us to gain.

Rig-Veda

Islam

The material things which ye are given are but the conveniences of this life and the glitter thereof; but that which is with God is better and more enduring: Will ye not then be wise?

Koran, 28:60

He who is kind and helpful to his neighbors, he will find that God will increase his wealth.

Ali Raza, *A Rosary of Islamic Readings*

Mormonism

Because of the steadiness of the church they began to be exceedingly rich, having abundance of all things whatsoever they stood in need. . . .

And thus they did prosper and become far more wealthy than those who did not belong to their church.

Book of Mormon, Alma 1:29,31

Unitarianism

What is the true use of increasing wealth in a city? It is not that more magnificent structures should be reared, but that our dwellings should be inhabited by a more intelligent and virtuous people.

William Ellery Channing, *Works of . . .*

WISDOM

Agnosticism

The only medicine for suffering, crime, and all the other woes of mankind is wisdom.

T.H. Huxley, *Science and Education*

Buddhism

As a solid rock is not shaken by the wind, wise people falter not amidst blame and praise.

Dhammapada

All those who appear as Buddhas . . . awake to . . . right and perfect enlightenment because they have relied on the perfection of wisdom.

The Heart Sutra

Great Master Hui-neng declared, "Good and learned friends, perfect wisdom is inherent in all people. It is only because they are deluded in their minds that they cannot attain enlightenment by themselves. They must seek the help of good and learned friends of high standing to show them the way."

The Platform Scripture

Christianity/Judaism

The price of wisdom is above rubies.

Holy Bible, Job 28:18

The fear of the Lord is the beginning of wisdom: and the knowledge of the holy is understanding.

Holy Bible, Proverbs 9:10

Wisdom excelleth folly, as far as light excelleth darkness.

Holy Bible, Ecclesiastes 2:13

Let not the wise man glory in his wisdom.

Holy Bible, Jeremiah 9:23

The first and wisest of them all confessed
To know this only, that he nothing knew.

John Milton, *Paradise Regained*

Wisdom makes but a slow defense against trouble, though at last a sure one.

Oliver Goldsmith, *The Vicar of Wakefield*

Knowledge is proud that he has learn'd so much;
Wisdom is humble that he knows no more.

William Cowper, "Winter Walk at Noon"

Confucianism

Confucius said, "The man of wisdom . . . is active; the man of humanity is tranquil. The man of wisdom enjoys happiness; the man of humanity enjoys long life."

Confucius, *Analects*

If one extends knowledge to the utmost, one will have wisdom. Having wisdom, one can then make choices.

Ch'eng I, *I-shu*

Hinduism

He whose mind is not troubled in sorrow and has no desire in pleasure, his passion, fear, and anger departed, he is called a steady-minded sage.

Bhagavad Gita, 2:56

There is no purifier in this world equal to wisdom.

Bhagavad Gita, 4:38

Islam

Reflection is an ocean, and wisdom is the pearl you will find in it.

Abu Ghalib Abd al-Hamid, *A Rosary of Islamic Readings*

The wise man is he who does today
What fools will do three days later.

Abdullah ibn Mubarak

Judaism

Excellent is wisdom when associated with an inheritance.

Talmud, Kohelet Rabbah 7:11

Taoism

He who knows others is learned; he who knows himself is wise.

Lao-tzu, *Character of Tao*

Great wisdom is generous; petty wisdom is contentious.

Chuang-tzu, *On Leveling All Things*

Unitarianism

It is a characteristic of wisdom not to do desperate things.

Henry David Thoreau, *Walden*

WOMAN

Christianity/Judaism

It is not good that the man should be alone; I will make him a help meet
for him. . . .
     And the rib, which the Lord God had taken from man, made he a woman,
and brought her unto the man.

Holy Bible, Genesis 2:18,22

As a ring of gold in a swine's snout, so is a beautiful woman who lacks
discretion.

Holy Bible, Proverbs 11:22

Christianity

Let the woman learn in silence with all subjection.

But I suffer not a woman to teach, nor to usurp authority over the man, but to be in silence.

Holy Bible, 1 Timothy 2:11-12

Whatever you say against women, they are better creatures than men, for men were made of clay, but woman was made of man.

Jonathan Swift, *Polite Conversation*

I'm not denyin' that women are foolish; God Almighty made 'em to match the men.

George Eliot, *Adam Bede*

Confucianism

Confucius said, "Women and servants are most difficult to deal with. If you are familiar with them, they cease to be humble. If you keep a distance from them, they resent it."

Confucius, *Analects*

Hinduism

Where women are honored, there the gods delight; where they are not honored, there all acts become fruitless.

Laws of Manu

Islam

Men are the protectors and maintainers of women because Allah has made the one superior to the other. . . . Therefore, righteous women are devoutly obedient.

Koran, 4:34

Those that defame virtuous women and cannot produce four witnesses [to support their allegations] shall be scourged with eighty lashes.

Koran, 24:4

It is commonly and, I believe, accurately said of Pakistan that her women are much more impressive than her men . . . their chains, nevertheless, are no fictions. They exist. And they are getting heavier.

Salmon Rushdie, *Shame*

Judaism

God has endowed women with a special sense of wisdom which man lacks.

Talmud, Niddah 45

Close thine eyes against beholding a charming woman, lest thou be caught in her net.

Talmud, Yebamot 63

Eight hours each, then, for sleep, making a living, and studying Torah. . . . Not [all] the people, however, . . . could be scholars, or even begin to attempt to abide by the rule governing a scholar's day. The first and most obvious exception were women.

Emil L. Fackenheim, *What Is Judaism?*

Unitarianism

To me it has always been a fundamental belief that God transcends the duality of male and female, and represents that unity which binds us together.

Barbara W. Merritt, "Empowerment"

WORK

Christianity/Judaism

In the sweat of thy face thou shalt eat bread.

Holy Bible, Genesis 3:19

Six days thou shalt labor, and do all thy work:
    But the seventh day is the sabbath of the Lord thy God: in it thou shalt not do any work.

Holy Bible, Deuteronomy 5:13-14

Whatsoever thy hand findeth to do, do it with thy might; for there is no work, nor device, nor knowledge, nor wisdom, in the grave, whither thou goest.

Holy Bible, Ecclesiastes 9:10

Christianity

Every man's work shall be made manifest: for the day shall declare it, because it shall be revealed by fire.

Holy Bible, 1 Corinthians 3:13

He who labors as he prays lifts his heart to God with his hands.

> St. Bernard of Clairvaux

In the things of this life, the laborer is most like to God.

> Huldrych Zwingli

God doth not need
Either man's work or his own gifts. Who best
Bear his mild yoke, they serve him best. His state
Is kingly: thousands at his bidding speed
And post o'er land and sea without rest;
They also serve who only stand and wait.

> John Milton, "On His Blindness"

Free men freely work: whoever fears God fears to sit at ease.

> Elizabeth Barrett Browning, *Aurora Leigh*

We will lie down for such a long time after death that it is worthwhile to keep standing while we are alive. Let us work now; one day we shall rest.

> St. Agostina Pietrantoni

The Puritan wanted to work in a calling; we are forced to do so. For when asceticism was carried out of monastic cells into everyday life, and began to dominate world morality, it did its part in building the tremendous cosmos of the modern economic order.

> Max Weber, *The Protestant Ethic and the Spirit of Capitalism*

Woe to them if, in their preoccupation with toil, they forget their soul's need!

> Rudolf Bultmann, *This World and the Beyond*

Physical labor is a certain contact with the reality, the truth, and the beauty of this universe and with the eternal wisdom which is the order in it.

For this reason it is sacrilege to degrade labor in exactly the same sense that it is sacrilege to trample upon the Eucharist.

> Simone Weil, "Human Personality"

Islam

By wishes alone you cannot a livelihood make.
Roll up your sleeves, send your bucket down
With those that others send.
Then behold!
At times, it will come up full,
Full to the brim;
At times, full with mud,
And perhaps a little water.

Abd al-Aswad al-Duwali, A Rosary of Islamic Readings

Judaism

There is no occupation which does not have its usefulness. . . . The world needs both perfumers and tanners, but fortunate is he who works with perfume, while this is not true for those who work in tanneries.

Talmud, Kiddushin 82b

Which work is higher, which work is lower? Who knows! Each one of us is given his own work, and until we have done it, this is the highest for us.

Lionel Blue, To Heaven, with Scribes and Pharisees

It has been argued that rabbinic sermons in praise of work were intended, among other things, to shore up the social status of those rabbis who were workers or artisans.

Abraham Shapira, "Work," Contemporary Jewish Religious Thought

Zoroastrianism

Work is the salt of life. Without work our life is idle and useless.

Modi Catechism

WORSHIP

Christianity/Judaism

Worship the Lord in the beauty of holiness.

Holy Bible, Psalms 29:2

O come, let us worship and bow down: let us kneel before the Lord our maker.

Holy Bible, Psalms 95:6

Christianity

For where two or three are gathered together in my name, there am I in the midst of them.

Holy Bible, Matthew 18:20

Henceforth burn what thou hast worshipped, and worship what thou hast burned.

St. Remy

[Note: These words were spoken at the baptism of Clovis, a Frankish warrior-king, in the year 496.]

In all our thoughts and actions we ought to remember the presence of God, and account all lost in which we think not of Him.

St. Bernard of Clairvaux

Worship is transcendent wonder.

Thomas Carlyle, *Heroes and Hero-Worship*

[Question:] Why does the Church insist that we all worship God in the same way?
[Answer:] It doesn't.

Andrew M. Greeley, *The Catholic WHY? Book*

Hinduism

Verily, this whole world is Brahma. Tranquil, let one worship It as that from which he came forth, as that into which he will be dissolved, as that in which he breathes.

Upanishads, Chandogya

From the rain-god food arises;
From worship comes the rain.

Bhagavad Gita, 3:14

All twice-born Hindus recognize their five daily obligations: the offering to the gods, the offering to the Seers, the offering to the forefathers, the offering to lower animals, and the offering to humanity.

Sivaprasad Bhattacharyya, "Religious Practices of the Hindus"

Islam

Allah is great. Allah is great. Allah is great. Allah is great.
I bear witness that save Allah there is no god.
I bear witness that save Allah there is no god.
I bear witness that Muhammad is the Prophet of God.
I bear witness that Muhammad is the Prophet of God.
Come to the prayers.
Come to the prayers.
Come to the Salvation.
Come to the Salvation.
Allah is great. Allah is great.
Save Allah there is no god.

The Azan (Call to Prayer)

Public worship is seventeen times better than private worship.

Al-Ghazali, *The Beginning of Guidance*

Judaism

A fear of action descends upon the worshipper which deepens into a fear of greatness, an awe of the heavenly majesty; this mood grows in exaltation by degrees, reaching down to the roots of the soul, softening the hard quality of coarse matter and adjusting one's life to the absorption of the gentle sweetness of the light of holiness, in the fulness of its splendor.

Abraham Isaac Kuk, *Banner of Jerusalem*

Everything is in a sense divine service and has its mood and its dignity. . . . Judaism does not lead man out of his everyday world, but relates him to God within it.

Leo Baeck, *Judaism and Christianity*

Stoicism

He worships God who knows Him.

Seneca, *Letters to Lucilius*

Unitarianism

Men are idolators, and want something to look at and kiss and hug, or throw themselves down before; they always did, they always will, and if you don't make it of wood you must make it of words.

Oliver Wendell Holmes, *The Poet at the Breakfast Table*

WRITING

Christianity/Judaism

And Moses turned, and went down from the mount, and the two tables of the testimony were in his hand: the tables were written on both their sides. . . .

And the tables were the work of God, and the writing was the writing of God, graven upon the tables.

Holy Bible, Exodus 32:15-16

Tell it not in Gath, publish it not in the streets of Askelon.

Holy Bible, 2 Samuel 1:20

Christianity

Your names are written in heaven.

Holy Bible, Luke 10:20

Had ye believed Moses, ye would have believed me [Jesus]: for he wrote of me.

But if ye believe not his writings, how shall ye believe my words?

Holy Bible, John 5:46-47

Against the disease of writing one must take special precautions, since it is a dangerous and contagious disease.

Peter Abelard, Letter to Heloise

If the typewriter were abolished tomorrow, a mass of vapid thought that goes on between human beings would be vastly reduced and the danger of war would be vastly decreased.

Geoffrey Fisher, Archbishop of Canterbury, Speech, March 15, 1955

Islam

Reporter: A cat waiting at a mousehole.

Mullah Do-Piaza

Hinduism

How many pens are broken, how many ink bottles are consumed, to write about events that have never occurred?

Talmud, Tanhuma Shofetim 18

Mormonism

Be it known unto all nations, kindreds, tongues, and people, unto whom this work shall come: That Joseph Smith, Jun., the translator of this work, has shown unto us the plates of which hath been spoken [the untranslated Book of Mormon], which have the appearance of gold . . . and we also saw the engravings thereon, all of which has the appearance of ancient work, and of curious workmanship. And . . . we have seen and hefted, and know of a surety that the said Smith has got the plates of which we have spoken.

Book of Mormon, "The Testimony of Eight Witnesses"

Unitarianism

Speaking is free, preaching free, printing free. No administration in America could put down a newspaper or suppress the discussion of an unwelcome theme. The attempt would be folly and madness.

Theodore Parker, "The Position and Duties of the American Scholar"

YOUTH

Aristotelianism

The young think they know everything and are confident in their assertions.

Aristotle, *Rhetoric*

Christianity/Judaism

The glory of young men is their strength.

Holy Bible, Proverbs 20:29

Rejoice, O young man, in thy youth; and let thy heart cheer thee in the days of thy youth.

Holy Bible, Ecclesiastes 11:9

It is good for a man that he bear the yoke in his youth.

Holy Bible, Lamentations 3:27

Christianity

Let no man despise thy youth; but be thou an example . . . in word, in conversation, in charity, in spirit, in faith, in purity.

Holy Bible, 1 Timothy 4:12

Time is the rider that breaks youth.

George Herbert, *Jacula Prudentum*

No young man believes he shall ever die.

William Hazlitt, "On the Feeling of Immortality in Youth"

I felt so young, so strong, so full of God.

> Elizabeth Barrett Browning, *Aurora Leigh*

How beautiful is youth! how bright it gleams
With its illusions, aspirations, dreams!

> Henry Wadsworth Longfellow, "Morituri Salutamus"

Judaism

If you do not bend the twig of a vine when it is young, you cannot bend it when it hardens.

> *Talmud*, Midrash Mishle 22

Youth is the time of total openness. With totally open senses, it absorbs the world's variegated abundance; with a totally open will, it gives itself to life's boundlessness. It has not yet sworn allegiance to any one truth for whose sake it would have to close its eyes to all other perspectives.

> Martin Buber, *On Judaism*

What youth needs is a sense of significant being, a sense of reverence for the society to which we all belong.

> Abraham Joshua Heschel, *The Wisdom of Heschel*

ZEAL

Christianity/Judaism

My zeal hath consumed me.

Holy Bible, Psalms 119:139

He put on the garments of vengeance for clothing, and was clad with zeal as a cloak.

Holy Bible, Isaiah 59:17

Christianity

They have a zeal of God, but not according to knowledge.

Holy Bible, Romans 10:2

Had I but serv'd my God with half the zeal
I serv'd my king, he would not in mine age
Have left me naked to mine enemies.

William Shakespeare, *Henry VIII*, Act. 3, Sc. 2

Zeal without knowledge is fire without light.

Thomas Fuller, *Gnomologia*

I believe it is imperative that we recapture that passion for human equality and justice which inspired the early Christians to create a world of ethical behavior to replace barbarism.

Walter F. White, Secretary of NAACP, 1931-1955

Hinduism

Striving zealously,
    With sins cleansed, the disciplined man,
Perfected through many rebirths,
    Then goes to the highest goal.

Bhagavad Gita, 6:45

Secularism

Zeal's a dreadful termagant,
That teaches saints to tear and rant.

Samuel Butler, *Hudibras*

THUMBNAIL
BIOGRAPHIES

This is a selective group of persons quoted in the Treasury. Literary figures are included only if their words appear frequently or if some of their works are primarily or notably religious. Individual authors of books of the Bible are not included (for example, St. Matthew and St. Paul), nor are other religious or academic figures who are cited only once or twice. Where appropriate, one representative book, essay, or hymn is noted at the end of each sketch.

ADAMS, SARAH FLOWER (1805–1848) English Unitarian (later Baptist) hymn writer. Noted for her hymn, "Nearer, My God, to Thee," 1840.

ALLPORT, GORDON W. (1897–1967) American behavioral psychologist and Christian religious writer. Taught at Harvard University, 1938–1966. *The Individual and His Religion*, 1950.

AMBROSE, SAINT (340–397) German bishop of Milan (under Roman rule). Opposed the Arian heresy in the West. Through his eloquent preaching, helped to convert St. Augustine. *On the Christian Faith.*

ARISTOTLE (384–322 B.C.) Greek philosopher. Studied under Plato, tutored Alexander the Great. Lectured in the Lyceum in Athens. Focused on reason and logic. Believed that the Prime Mover, or God, caused matter to move. *Metaphysics.*

ARNOLD, MATTHEW (1822–1888) English poet and critic. Perhaps best known for his poem, "Dover Beach." Late in life wrote well-regarded books on religion. *Literature and Dogma*, 1873.

ASAD, MUHAMMAD (1900–) Moroccan (born in Austria). A convert to Islam and a noted Islamic scholar. *The Road to Mecca*, 1954.

AUGUSTINE [OF HIPPO], SAINT (354–430) Numidian. Early Christian church advocate and philosopher. Bishop of Hippo (near present-day Annaba, Algeria). Considered the greatest of Latin Fathers of the Church. *Confessions*, c.400. *The City of God*, c.412.

BAECK, LEO (1873–1956) German rabbi and scholar. Served as rabbi in Berlin, 1912–1943. Stressed man's obligations to others. Sent to Theresienstadt concentration camp, 1943. Liberated 1945. *The Essence of Judaism*, 1905, tr. 1936.

BARCLAY, ROBERT (1648–1690) Scottish Quaker theologian. Raised as a Presbyterian, he studied to be a Roman Catholic missionary but turned to Quakerism. *An Apology for . . . the Principles and Doctrines of the People Called Quakers*, 1678.

BARCLAY, WILLIAM (1907–1978) Scottish preacher, scholar, and broadcaster. Professor of Divinity and Biblical Criticism at Glasgow University, from 1963. *The Mind of Jesus*, 1961.

BARING-GOULD, SABINE (1834–1924) English hymn writer. Served as pastor of the Established Church at Horbury-Brig, Yorkshire. Best known for his marching hymn, "Onward, Christian Soldiers," 1865.

BARNHOUSE, DONALD GREY (1895–1960) American pastor of Philadelphia's Tenth Avenue Presbyterian Church for 33 years. *Words Fitly Spoken*, 1969.

BARTH, KARL (1886–1968) Swiss Protestant theologian. Criticized the liberal theology of the 19th century. Reaffirmed the basic principles of the Reformation. *Church Dogmatics*, 1932.

BASHO (1644–1694) Born Matsuo Munefusa. Japanese haiku poet, the greatest master of the form. Imbued his poetry with the spirit of Zen Buddhism. *The Narrow Road to the Deep North.*

BATES, KATHARINE LEE (1859–1929) American author and educator. Taught English at Wellesley College, 1891–1925. *The Congregationalist* magazine of July 4, 1895, published her hymn, "America the Beautiful."

BEDE, THE VENERABLE (673–735) English historian, monk, and Christian saint. Spent his life at the monasteries of Wearmouth and Jarrow. One of the most learned scholars of his day. *Ecclestiastical History of the English People*, 731.

BEECHER, HENRY WARD (1813–1887) American Congregational clergyman and reformer. Preached at the Plymouth Church in Brooklyn, NY. Opposed slavery, favored women's suffrage and the theory of evolution. *Evolution and Religion*, 1885.

BELLOC, HILAIRE (1870–1953) English author (born in France). Liberal member of Parliament (1906–1910). Wrote from the Roman Catholic viewpoint. *A Conversation with an Angel*, 1928.

BERNARD OF CLAIRVAUX, SAINT (1090–1153) French Roman Catholic abbot, regarded as the last of the Fathers of the Church. Entered and expanded the Cistercian order. Influenced kings and popes. Wrote eloquently. *On the Love of God*, c.1127.

BLAKE, WILLIAM (1757–1827) English poet, artist, and mystic. Believed that all reality, including God, centers on human life. Thought it natural to see and talk with angels and Old Testament prophets. *The Marriage of Heaven and Hell*, c.1790.

BLUE, LIONEL (1930–) English Jewish rabbi, broadcaster, and feature writer. Lecturer at Leo Baeck College, London, since 1967. *Kitchen Blues*, 1985.

BONHOEFFER, DIETRICH (1906–1945) German Lutheran clergyman and theologian. Opposed Hitler. Arrested by the Gestapo, 1943, for smuggling Jews into Switzerland; hanged, 1945. *The Cost of Discipleship*, 1937.

BROOKS, PHILLIPS (1835–1893) American Episcopal minister. Served as rector of Philadelphia's Holy Trinity Church. After a visit to the Holy Land wrote a Christmas hymn for his Sunday school: "O Little Town of Bethlehem," 1868.

BROWNE, SIR THOMAS (1605–1682) English author and physician. Best known for his attempts to reconcile science and religion. *Religio Medici*, 1642.

BUBER, MARTIN (1878–1965) Austrian Jewish philosopher. A seminal thinker. Taught philosophy and religion at the University of Frankfurt-am-Main, 1924–1933, and the Hebrew University in Jerusalem, 1938–1951. *I and Thou*, 1923.

BUDDHA (c.563–c.483 B.C.). Born Siddartha. Indian philosopher and religious leader. Founded Buddhism. Renounced great family wealth to become a wandering ascetic. Traveled and taught for 45 years. Set up monastic orders. Preached the "eightfold path."

BULTMANN, RUDOLF (1884–1976) German existentialist theologian. Professor at the University of Marburg, 1921–1950. Best known for his "demythologization" of the New Testament. *Theology of the New Testament*, tr. 1951.

BUNYAN, JOHN (1628–1688) English author and lay Baptist preacher. Bunyan's intense study of the Bible and conflict with George Fox's

Quakers led to his religious writing. Best known for his allegory, *The Pilgrim's Progress*, 1678.

BURTON, ROBERT (1577–1640) English clergyman and scholar. Spent his entire working life as librarian at Christ Church, Oxford. *The Anatomy of Melancholy*, 1621.

BUTTRICK, GEORGE A. (1892–1980) American pastor of New York's Madison Avenue Presbyterian Church for 27 years. Taught at Harvard University, Chicago Theological Seminary, and Garrett Theological Seminary. *God, Pain, and Evil*, 1966.

CALVIN, JOHN (1509–1564) French Protestant theologian of the Reformation. Founder of Calvinism, which promoted a rigid doctrine of predestination. *Institutes of the Christian Religion*, 1536.

CAMUS, ALBERT (1913–1960) French humanist writer and philosopher. Associated with existentialists but denied allegiance to the movement. Wrote mainly about the absurd. *The Plague*, 1948.

CHANNING, WILLIAM ELLERY (1780–1842) American Unitarian minister in Boston. Led a movement away from Calvinism. Called "the apostle of Unitarianism." Influenced many New England authors, including Emerson and Thoreau.

CHESTERTON, G.K. (1874–1936) English author. Converted to Roman Catholicism, 1922, and became its strong advocate. Wrote the Father Brown detective stories. *Orthodoxy*, 1908.

CHUANG-TZU (c.369–c.286 B.C.) Chinese Taoist writer. Said to have lived as a hermit. Stressed the relativity of all ideas. Noted for the satire and paradox in his essays. *Chuang-tzu*.

CHURCH, F. FORRESTER (1948–) American Unitarian-Universalist pastor of the Unitarian Church of All Souls in New York City. Son of Senator Frank Church of Idaho. *The Seven Deadly Virtues*, 1988.

COFFIN, WILLIAM SLOANE [JR.] (1924–) American liberal Protestant clergyman. Chaplain, Yale University, 1958–1975. Active in the Vietnam War peace movement. Served as pastor of Riverside Church, New York City, from 1977. *Once to Every Man*, 1977.

COLTON, CHARLES CALEB (1780–1832) Educated for the English Anglican ministry. Became a sportsman, gambler, and eccentric. Known for his book of aphorisms, *Lacon*, 1820.

CONFUCIUS (c.551–479 B.C.) Chinese sage. Very little is known about him for certain. Most information is based on the *Analects*, brief dialogues and sayings that were collected by Confucius's disciples.

COWPER, WILLIAM (1731–1800) English poet and hymn writer. His poems foreshadowed those of the Romantics. His hymns contain vivid imagery. "God Moves in a Mysterious Way," 1779.

DANTE [ALIGHIERI] (1265–1321) Italian poet. Depicted the progress from damnation to heavenly bliss and the gradual revelation of God to the pilgrim in his masterpiece, the *Divine Comedy*, c.1307–1321.

DONNE, JOHN (1572–1631) English poet and divine. Reared a Roman Catholic, converted to Anglicanism. Dean of St. Paul's Cathedral, 1621–1631. "Hymn to God the Father."

DOSTOYEVSKY, FYODOR (1821–1881) Russian novelist. Staunch believer in Russian Orthodoxy. As a youth he spent four years in a Siberian penal colony. Showed profound insight into the human soul. *The Brothers Karamazov*, 1880.

ECKHART, MEISTER (c.1260–c.1328) German mystical theologian. Studied and taught in the Dominican order. Preached evangelically to the poor and ignorant. Charged with heresy just before his death. *Book of Divine Comfort.*

EDDY, MARY BAKER (1821–1910) American religious leader. Founder of the Christian Science movement, 1866, and the *Christian Science Monitor,* 1908. *Science and Health,* 1875.

EDWARDS, JONATHAN (1703–1758) American colonial theologian of Puritanism. Led the Great Awakening of the 1740s. Wrote and delivered fiery and poetic sermons. *The Freedom of the Will,* 1754.

EINSTEIN, ALBERT (1879–1955) American-Swiss Jewish theoretical physicist (born in Germany). Formulated the theory of relativity. Wrote on religion in his later years, advancing a Cosmic belief in an unknowable God. *Ideas and Opinions,* 1954.

ELIOT, T.S. (1888–1965) English poet, critic, and playwright (born in the United States). Found modern life empty and the individual isolated and alone. Experienced a spiritual rebirth in Anglo-Catholicism, 1927. *Murder in the Cathedral,* 1935.

EMERSON, RALPH WALDO (1803–1882) American essayist, poet, and clergyman. Pastor of the Old North Church in Boston (Second Unitarian), 1829–1832. Noted literary figure of the 19th century; leader of the Transcendentalist movement. *Nature,* 1836.

EPICTETUS (c.50–c.138) Phrygian Stoic philosopher who taught in Rome. Emphasized the good within oneself and the brotherhood of man. *Discourses,* collected by Arrian, his disciple.

ERASMUS, [DESIDERIUS] (1466–1536) Dutch Catholic humanist. Ordained as a Roman Catholic priest. Attacked clerical abuses but remained a Catholic all his life. Defended reason, tolerance, and faith. *The Praise of Folly*, 1509.

FACKENHEIM, EMIL L. (1916–) German Jewish philosopher. Ordained a rabbi after his release from Sachsenhausen concentration camp. Taught philosophy at the University of Toronto until 1983. Moved to Israel. *What Is Judaism?*, 1987.

FALWELL, JERRY (1933–) American Baptist television preacher, active in politics. Founded the Thomas Road Baptist Church, 1956, and Liberty University, 1971. Founded the Moral Majority, Inc., 1979. *Strength for the Journey*, 1987.

FOSDICK, HARRY EMERSON (1878–1969) American liberal Protestant clergyman. Pastor of Riverside Church in New York City, 1926–1946. Preached on nationwide radio, the National Vespers. *On Being a Real Person*, 1943.

FOX, GEORGE (1624–1691) English founder of Society of Friends, commonly called Quakers, 1668. Emphasized a God-given "light within" as the source of authority and revelation. *Journal*, 1694.

FRANCIS DE SALES, SAINT (1567–1622) French Roman Catholic priest, Doctor of the Church. Trained initially for the law. Famed for his preaching and converting of Protestants. Patron saint of Roman Catholic writers. *Introduction to the Devout Life*.

FROMM, ERICH (1900–1980) American psychoanalyst (born in Germany). Explored the individual's sense of isolation and estrangement in modern society. *Psychoanalysis and Religion*, 1950.

FULLER, THOMAS (1608–1661) English clergyman and author. Famous for his preaching and his wit. Served briefly as a royal chaplain. *The Holy State and the Profane State*, 1642.

FULLER, THOMAS (1654–1734) English physician and medical writer. One of the leading medical doctors of his day. Wrote three books on pharmacology, but is best remembered for his collections of adages, especially *Gnomologia*, 1732.

GANDHI, MOHANDAS K. (1869–1948) Indian political and spiritual leader. Called "Mahatma." Lived according to Hindu ideals of asceticism. Used nonviolent means to oppose British rule. *The Story of My Experiments with Truth*, 1927.

GHAZALI-AL (1058–1111) Persian theologian, philosopher, and mystic. Regarded as the greatest theologian of the classical age of Islam. Taught at Baghdad, 1091–1095. Became a wandering mystic. *The Revival of the Religious Sciences.*

GIBRAN, KAHLIL (1883–1931) Lebanese-American poet and artist. Best known for his enduringly popular mystical prose-poem, *The Prophet*, 1923.

GILSON, ETIENNE (1884–1978) French philosopher and historian. Taught medieval philosophy at the Sorbonne, 1921–1932. Helped form the Roman Catholic neo-Thomist movement. *The Spirit of Medieval Philosophy*, 1936.

GITTELSOHN, ROLAND B. (1910–) American Jewish author and spokesman for Reform Judaism. Rabbi of Temple Israel in Boston, 1953–1977. *The Meaning of Judaism*, 1970.

GOETHE, [JOHANN WOLFGANG VON] (1749–1832) German poet, dramatist, novelist, and scientist. His religious and philosophical thought are embodied in his great dramatic poem, *Faust*, the work of a lifetime, 1808, 1832.

GRACIAN, BALTASAR (1601–1658) Spanish Jesuit philosopher and writer. Rector of the Jesuit College at Tarragona, Spain. Witty and worldly, he often came into conflict with clerical authority. *The Art of Worldly Wisdom*, 1647.

GRAHAM, BILLY (1918–) American Southern Baptist clergyman and evangelist. Won national prominence with his evangelistic campaign in Los Angeles, 1949. Built a large organization based in Minneapolis. *Revival in Our Times*, 1950.

GREELEY, ANDREW M. (1928–) Roman Catholic priest, theologian, and author. Professor of sociology at the University of Arizona, Tucson. Mystery novelist. Frequent radio and television appearances. *Life for a Wanderer*, 1969.

GREENBERG, SIDNEY (1917–) American rabbi of Temple Sinai in Dresher, Pennsylvania, from 1941. Visiting Lecturer at the Jewish Theological Seminary of America in New York City. *Say Yes to Life*, 1959.

GREENBERG, SIMON (1901–) American Jewish educator and academic leader (born in Russia). Professor and administrator at the Jewish Theological Seminary in New York City for more than 50 years. *A Jewish Philosophy and Pattern of Life*, 1981.

HEARN, LAFCADIO (1850–1904) American author (born in the Ionian Islands). Spent the last 14 years of his life in Japan, taking the name Yakumo Koizumi in 1895. Wrote extensively on Buddhism. *Glimpses of Unfamiliar Japan*, 1894.

HERBERT, GEORGE (1593–1633) English metaphysical poet and clergyman. Ordained an Anglican priest, served as rector at Bemerton. Known as "holy George Herbert" for his devotional poems and ingenious church imagery. *Jacula Prudentum.*

HESCHEL, ABRAHAM JOSHUA (1907–1972) American Jewish philosopher and theologian (born in Poland). Taught at the Jewish Theological Seminary in New York City. Active in the civil rights movement. *Who Is Man?*, 1951.

HOLMES, JOHN HAYNES (1879–1964) American Unitarian clergyman, hymn writer, and social activist. Minister for over 50 years at The Community Church in New York City. A founder of both the ACLU and NAACP. *I Speak for Myself*, 1958.

HOWE, JULIA WARD (1819–1910) American author and social reformer. Promoted emancipation, women's rights, and world peace. "The Battle Hymn of the Republic," 1861.

HUBBARD, ELBERT (1856–1915) American publisher and inspirational writer. Preached rugged individualism. Best known as the author of "A Message to Garcia," 1899.

IGNATIUS OF LOYOLA, SAINT (1491–1556) Spanish priest and founder of the Jesuit order. Spent his youth soldiering. Became a mystic, imitating the life of Christ, after an intense religious conversion. *Spiritual Exercises.*

INGE, WILLIAM RALPH (1860–1954) English prelate and theologian. Served as dean of St. Paul's [Anglican] Cathedral, London, 1911–1934. Called "the gloomy dean" because of his pessimism. Known for his writings on mysticism. *Mysticism in Religion*, 1948.

INGERSOLL, ROBERT G. (1833–1899) American lawyer and orator. Known as "the great agnostic." His views on religion prevented his advancement in politics. "The Gods," 1872.

IQBAL, MUHAMMAD (1876–1938) Indian Muslim poet, philosopher, and political leader. The foremost Muslim thinker of his era. Advocated a separate state for India's Muslims. *The Reconstruction of Religious Thought in Islam*, tr. 1934.

JACOBS, LOUIS (1920–) English Jewish rabbi and author. Served as rabbi at New London Synagogue, from 1964. *What Does Judaism Say About . . . ?*

JAMES, WILLIAM (1842–1910) American psychologist and philosopher of pragmatism. Son of a Swedenborgian theologian. Taught at Harvard, 1872–1907. Rejected transcendent principles. *The Varieties of Religious Experience*, 1902.

JEROME, SAINT (c.347–420) Slavic Christian scholar and saint. A Father of the Roman Catholic Church. Translated Biblical texts from Hebrew into Latin, creating the Vulgate, the official Latin text in use until 1979.

JOHN OF THE CROSS, SAINT (1542–1591) Spanish monk, mystic, and poet. A Doctor of the Church. Worked with St. Teresa of Avila to reform the Carmelite order. *Spiritual Canticle.*

JOHN PAUL II, POPE (1920–) Born Karol Wojtyla. Polish pope, from 1978. First non-Italian to be elevated to the papacy in 456 years. Previously professor of moral theology, archbishop of Cracow, and cardinal. *Love and Responsiblity,* 1960.

JOHN VIANNEY, SAINT (1786–1859) French parish priest. Renowned far beyond his rural parish, especially as a confessor. Credited with many miracles during his lifetime. Canonized, 1925. Named patron saint of parish priests, 1929.

JONES, RUFUS M. (1863–1948) American professor of philosophy at Haverford College, 1893–1934. Helped found the American Friends Service Committee. *The Faith and Practice of the Quakers,* 1927.

JUNG, CARL GUSTAV (1875–1961) Swiss psychologist and psychiatrist. Founded analytical psychology. Propounded a collective unconscious. Stressed the individual's need for internal harmony. *Psychology and Religion,* 1958.

KABIR (1440–1518) Indian mystic and poet. Born a Muslim. Worked as a weaver in Benares. Early in life became a disciple of the Hindu saint Ramananda. Taught the brotherhood of Hindu and Muslim under one God. *The Poems of Kabir.*

KANT, IMMANUEL (1724–1804) German metaphysician (born in Konigsberg, then in Prussia, now in Russia). One of the greatest figures in philosophy. Held that morality requires a belief in God but that the nature of God is unknowable. *Critique of Practical Reason,* tr. 1790.

KEN, THOMAS (1637–1711) English Anglican bishop and hymn writer. Wrote some of the great masterpieces of English hymnody, including the evening prayer, "All Praise to Thee, My God, This Night," 1693.

KIERKEGAARD, SØREN (1813–1855) Danish philosopher and religious thinker. Criticized official Christianity. Stressed the importance of personal experience and choice. Father of Existentialism. *Training in Christianity,* 1850.

KING, MARTIN LUTHER, JR. (1929–1968) American clergyman and civil rights leader. Baptist minister in Montgomery, Alabama. Organized the

Southern Christian Leadership Conference. Won the Nobel Peace Prize, 1964. *Stride Toward Freedom*, 1958.

KUK, ABRAHAM ISAAC (1865–1935) Palestinian Jewish mystic and Orthodox religious thinker (born in Russia). First Chief Rabbi of Palestine, from 1921. Stressed prayer, progress, and Jewish nationalism. *Banner of Jerusalem*, tr. 1946.

KÜNG, HANS (1928–) Swiss Roman Catholic theologian. Taught Fundamental Theology at Tubingen University in West Germany. Adviser to the Second Vatican Council, 1962–1965. Rejected papal infallibility. *The Christian Challenge*, tr. 1979.

KUSHNER, HAROLD S. (1935–) American rabbi of Temple Israel in Natick, Massachusetts. Known for his bestselling book, *When Bad Things Happen to Good People*, 1981.

LAO-TZU (c.600 B.C.) Chinese philosopher (lit. "old master"). Reputedly founded Taoism. Lao-tzu may be a historical figure or only legendary. Traditionally credited as the author of the influential *Tao-te ching*.

LATIMER, HUGH (c.1485–1555) English bishop and Protestant martyr. Gained great popularity as a preacher against abuses of the Roman Catholic Church and clergy. Burned at the stake.

LEWIS, C.S. (1898–1963) English novelist, literary critic, and Christian "apostle to the skeptics." Fellow of Magdalen College, Oxford. Popular defender of Christian orthodoxy. *The Screwtape Letters*, 1942.

LUTHER, MARTIN (1483–1546) German religious reformer. Led the Protestant Reformation. Opposed the sale of indulgences. Posted his "95 Theses" on the door of the castle church in Wittenberg, 1517. *The Freedom of a Christian Man*, 1520.

MAIMONIDES [MOSES] (1135–1204) Spanish Jewish rabbi, philosopher, and physician. Organized the great mass of Jewish oral law, mishnah, into the *Mishneh Torah*. Tried to explain the esoteric ideas in the Bible. *Guide of the Perplexed*.

MARCUS AURELIUS (121–180) Roman emperor, 161–180, and Stoic philosopher. Made many reforms, but persecuted Christians, whom he regarded as enemies of the empire. *Meditations*.

MARITAIN, JACQUES (1882–1973) French neo-Thomist philosopher. Originally Protestant but converted to Roman Catholicism. Defended the scholastic use of reason. *True Humanism*, 1938.

MARSHALL, PETER (1902–1949) American Presbyterian minister and chaplain of the U.S. Senate. Best known for his book, *Mr. Jones, Meet the Master*, published posthumously, 1949.

MASLOW, ABRAHAM H. (1898–1970) American psychologist and educator. Taught psychology at Brooklyn College, 1935–1951, and at Brandeis University, 1951–1970. *Religions, Values, and Peak-Experiences,* 1964.

MENCIUS (c.371–c.288 B.C.) Chinese Confucian philosopher. Believed that people are by nature good. Provided many guidelines for rulers. Known as the Second Sage. Gained veneration in the late 11th century. *The Book of Mencius.*

MERTON, THOMAS (1915–1968) American religious writer and poet (born in France). Converted to Roman Catholicism in college. Became a Trappist monk, 1941. *The Seven Storey Mountain,* 1948.

MILTON, JOHN (1608–1674) English poet and essayist. Intended to become an Anglican minister but became disenchanted with church ritualism. Supported the Presbyterians in their attempts at reform. *Paradise Lost,* 1667, 1674.

MOODY, DWIGHT L. (1837–1899) American Protestant evangelist and urban revivalist. Abandoned a successful business to pursue missionary work. Worked for the YMCA. In 1889 founded the institution that became the Moody Bible Institute, Chicago.

MUHAMMAD (570–632) Arabian prophet and founder of Islam. A wealthy merchant until the age of 40 when he had a vision and began to preach. Called the Prophet of Allah. His many revelations are set forth in the *Koran* (or *Qur'an*).

NEWMAN, JOHN HENRY, CARDINAL (1801–1890) English clergyman. Cardinal of the Roman Catholic Church, 1879–1890. Began as an Anglican preacher but switched to Catholicism in 1845. Wrote the hymn, "Lead, Kindly Light." *Apologia pro vita sua,* 1864.

NEWTON, JOHN (1725–1807) English clergyman and hymn writer. Spent his early years at sea. After ordination, collaborated with William Cowper on *Olney Hymns,* 1779. Wrote "How Sweet the Name of Jesus Sounds" and "Amazing Grace."

NIEBUHR, REINHOLD (1892–1971) American pastor of Detroit's Bethel Evangelical Church, 1915–1928. Despaired of liberal Protestantism and pursued social activism in the '30s. Taught at Union Theological Seminary, 1928–1960. *Faith and History,* 1949.

PARKER, THEODORE (1810–1860) American Unitarian clergyman, theologian, and social reformer. Spent much of his ministry at the 28th Congregational Church in Boston. Active in the Transcendental movement. *Collected Works,* 1863–1879.

PASCAL, BLAISE (1623–1662) French mathematician, physicist, and religious philosopher. Developed the modern theory of probability. Turned to religion after a brush with death. Emphasized the need for a mystic faith. *Pensées*, 1670.

PENINGTON, ISAAC (1616–1679) English Quaker in the early days of the sect. Imprisoned a number of times in Aylesbury Gaol for practicing his faith. Father-in-law of William Penn.

PENN, WILLIAM (1644–1718) English Quaker and champion of religious toleration. Founded Pennsylvania and lived there briefly. *The Great Case of Liberty of Conscience*, 1670.

PETER, SAINT (?–c.64) Bethsaidan fisherman. Most prominent of the Twelve Disciples. Traditionally the first Bishop of Rome. Originally named Simon, nicknamed Peter ("Rock") by Jesus. Familiarly represented as the gatekeeper of heaven.

PLATO (c.427–347 B.C.) Greek philosopher, a pupil and friend of Socrates. Tried to show the rational relationship between the soul, the state, and the cosmos. Taught that the physical world has only relative reality. *Phaedo.*

QUTB, SYED (d.1966) Egyptian. Prominent Islamic scholar of the 20th century. Leader of the Muslim Brotherhood. Educational adviser to the Egyptian government. Executed under Gamal Abdel Nasser. *Social Justice in Islam*, 1953.

RACKMAN, EMANUEL (1910–) American rabbi of the Fifth Avenue Synagogue in New York City, from 1967. Professor of Political Science and Assistant to the President at Yeshiva University. *One Man's Religion*, 1970.

ROSENZWEIG, FRANZ (1886–1929) German Jewish philosopher and theologian. One of the most significant Jewish thinkers of the 20th century. Had great insight into Christianity, once nearly converting to it. *The Star of Redemption*, 1921.

ROUSSEAU, JEAN JACQUES (1712–1778) Swiss-French deistic philosopher. Propounded a romantic view of "natural man." Influenced modern educational theory. *Emile*, 1762.

SANTAYANA, GEORGE (1863–1952) American philosopher and poet (born in Spain). Taught philosophy at Harvard University, 1889–1912. Thereafter lived in Europe, mainly Italy. Argued that religion, although valuable, is not truth about existence. *The Realms of Being*, 1923–1940.

SCHLEIERMACHER, FRIEDRICH (1768–1834) German Protestant theologian and philosopher. Defined religion as the consciousness of absolute dependence on God. Exerted great influence on Protestant theology. *The Christian Faith*, 1822.

SCHULLER, ROBERT H. (1926–) American Protestant television evangelist: "Hour of Power" since 1970. Founder of the Crystal Cathedral in Garden Grove, California. *Tough Times Never Last, But Tough People Do!*, 1983.

SCHWEITZER, ALBERT (1875–1965) French Protestant theologian, musician, and medical missionary. Spent most of his life after 1913 at Lambarene, Gabon. Advocated "reverence for life." *The Quest of the Historical Jesus*, 1906.

SENECA [the Younger] (c.3 B.C.–65 B.C.) Spanish (moved to Rome). Roman philosopher, dramatist, and statesman. Tutored Nero. Wielded great power for a time. Wrote superbly on Stoic doctrines. Committed suicide at Nero's request. *Epistles*.

SHAH, IDRIES (1924–) Leader of the Sufis (Islamic mystics) since 1969. Known as The Sayed. Traces his descent to the Prophet Muhammad. *The Way of the Sufi*, 1969.

SHAKESPEARE, WILLIAM (1564–1616) English playwright and poet. The most quoted individual writer who ever lived. Explored a moral universe in which evil is inevitable and the triumph of good essential. His plays have been performed almost continuously since their first staging. *Hamlet*, 1600.

SHARIATI, ALI (d. 1977) Iranian teacher and activist. Professor at Mashhad University in Iran. A leader of the Islamic revival in Iran. Imprisoned twice by the Shah. Emigated to England, where he was murdered. *Hajj*, tr. 1977.

SHAW, GEORGE BERNARD (1856–1950) Irish Protestant playwright, critic, and Fabian socialist. Satirized Christianity in *Androcles and the Lion*, 1912, and explored the role of the saint in society in *Saint Joan*, 1923.

SHEEN, FULTON J. (1895–1979) American Roman Catholic bishop. An outstanding speaker, he attracted a large radio audience, beginning in 1930. Attacked communism, Freudianism, and birth control. *The Cross and the Crisis*, 1938.

SHESTOV, LEV (1866–1938) Russian Jewish teacher and philosopher (emigrated to France in 1920). Belonged to the existentialist tradition of Kierkegaard. *All Things Are Possible*, 1905.

SMITH, SAMUEL FRANCIS (1808–1895) American Baptist clergyman and poet. Wrote the hymn "The Morning Light is Breaking" but is most famous for the national hymn, "America," 1831.

SOLOVEITCHIK, JOSEPH B. (1903–) American rabbi, educator, and philosopher (born in Poland). Professor of Jewish philosophy at Yeshiva University, New York City. *Halakhic Man*, 1983.

SPINOZA, [BARUCH] (1632–1677) Dutch pantheistic philosopher and lens grinder. Educated as an orthodox Jew; excommunicated, 1656. Adopted the name Benedict, the Latin form of Baruch. Believed that God and Nature are one. *Ethics*, 1677.

SPURGEON, CHARLES H. (1834–1892) English Baptist preacher. Became a highly popular pastor of the New Park Street Chapel, London, at the age of 20. Huge Metropolitan Tabernacle was built for his use, 1861. *John Ploughman's Talks*, 1869.

STEERE, DOUGLAS V. (1901–) American Quaker. Taught philosophy at Haverford College, 1928–1964. Chairman of the Friends World Committee, 1964–1970. Edited *Quaker Spirituality*, 1984.

STEPHEN, CAROLINE (1834–1909) English author of *Quaker Strongholds*, a classic exposition of Quaker beliefs, 1890.

SUNDAY, BILLY (1863–1935) American urban evangelist and professional baseball player. Drew huge crowds to his energetic revivals. Ordained as a Presbyterian minister in 1903. Supported Prohibition.

SUZUKI, DAISETZ TEITARO (1870–1966) Japanese Buddhist scholar. Taught at Tokyo University and other leading universities in Japan, Europe, and the United States. *Essays in Zen Buddhism*, 1927–1933.

SWEDENBORG, EMANUEL (1688–1772) Swedish scientist, religious teacher and mystic. Claimed that "heaven was opened" to him in 1745. Swedenborgianism resulted in the Church of the New Jerusalem, founded after his death. *The True Christian Religion*.

TAGORE, RABINDRANATH (1861–1941) Indian poet, novelist, dramatist, and guru. Echoed fundamental ideas of Hinduism. Awarded the Nobel Prize in Literature, 1913. Knighted, 1915. *Sadhana: The Realization of Life*, 1913.

TAHA, MAHMOUD MOHAMED (1909–1985) Sudanese Muslim engineer, lecturer, and reformer. Promoted pacifism and women's rights. Imprisoned three times. Executed under President Numeiri of Sudan. *The Second Message of Islam*, tr. 1987.

TAYLOR, JEREMY (1613–1667) English Anglican bishop, theological and devotional writer. Called "the Shakespeare and the Spenser of the pulpit." *Holy Living*, 1650.

TEILHARD DE CHARDIN, PIERRE (1881–1955) French Roman Catholic priest, paleontologist, and philosopher. Argued that evolution and Christianity can be reconciled. Helped discover Peking Man while in China, 1926–1946. *The Phenomenon of Man*, 1955.

TEN BOOM, CORRIE (1892–1983) Dutch lay Christian speaker and writer. Hid Jews in the Netherlands during World War Two. Imprisoned by the Nazis. *The Hiding Place*, 1971.

TERESA OF AVILA, SAINT (1515–1582) Spanish Roman Catholic nun of the Carmelite order. Named first woman Doctor of the Church, 1970. One of the Church's great mystics. Instituted many Carmelite reforms. *The Interior Castle*, 1588.

TERESA OF CALCUTTA, MOTHER (1910–) Albanian-born Roman Catholic nun. Entered a convent in India, 1928. Left the convent to work among the poor in Calcutta, India, 1946. Awarded the Nobel Peace Prize, 1979. *Life in the Spirit*, 1983.

THÉRÈSE DE LISIEUX, SAINT (1873–1897) French Carmelite nun. Beloved "Little Flower of Jesus." Known for her humility, simplicity, and holiness. Died of tuberculosis at the age of 24. *The Story of a Soul*.

THOMAS À KEMPIS (1379–1471) German monk and theologian. Served as a copyist at Mt. St. Agnes, near Zwolle, in the Netherlands. Generally credited with writing *The Imitation of Christ*, c.1425.

THOMAS AQUINAS, SAINT (1225–1274) Italian philosopher and theologian, the greatest figure of Scholasticism, which conjoined faith and reason. One of the principal saints of the Roman Catholic Church. *Summa Theologica*, 1267–1273.

THOMPSON, FRANCIS (1859–1907) English Roman Catholic poet. Educated for the priesthood but not ordained. Wrote religious poetry with striking imagery. Best known for "The Hound of Heaven," 1893.

TILLICH, PAUL (1886–1965) American Protestant theologian and philosopher (born in Germany). Opposed Nazism. Taught at Union Theological Seminary, Harvard, and the University of Chicago. *The Courage to Be*, 1952.

TOPLADY, AUGUSTUS M. (1740–1778) English Anglican minister and hymn writer. Engaged in a bitter theological dispute with John Wesley. Best known for his hymn, "Rock of Ages," 1776.

TRAHERNE, THOMAS (1637–1674) English metaphysical poet. Published little during his lifetime. Anglican chaplain to the Lord Keeper of the Great Seal, 1667–1674. Expressed a childlike love of God. *Centuries of Meditations*, 1908.

VAUGHAN, HENRY (1622–1695) English metaphysical poet and physician. Indebted to George Herbert, but was more inspired by nature than by the church. *Silex Scintillans*, 1650, 1655.

VOLTAIRE (1694–1778) French deistic philosopher and writer. Opposed religious fanaticism. *Philosophical Dictionary*, 1759.

WATTS, ISAAC (1674–1748) English Protestant hymn writer and poet. Wrote most of the 210 hymns in the first true hymnbook in English, 1707. Matthew Arnold called Watts' hymn "When I Survey the Wondrous Cross" the finest in the language.

WEIL, SIMONE (1909–1943) French philosopher and mystic. Jewish by heritage, Catholic by conviction. Sometimes termed a Christian Hellenist. Political and religious nonconformist. Fought in the Spanish Civil War. *Gravity and Grace*, 1952.

WESLEY, CHARLES (1707–1788) English Methodist preacher and hymn writer. Led many great revival meetings with his older brother John and George Whitefield. "Hark! the Herald Angels Sing."

WESLEY, JOHN (1703–1791) English Anglican deacon, evangelist, and theologian. Influenced by Moravian missionaries while on a mission to the U.S., 1835. Founded Methodism. Rejected Calvinist doctrine of election. Preached thousands of sermons.

WEST, JESSAMYN (1902–1984) American Quaker novelist, best known for her novel, *The Friendly Persuasion*, 1945. Compiled *The Quaker Reader*, 1962.

WHITEHEAD, ALFRED NORTH (1861–1947) English mathematician and philosopher. Developed a metaphysical theory he called organism. Rejected the idea of a perfect and omnipotent God. *Religion in the Making*, 1926.

WIGGLESWORTH, MICHAEL (1631–1705) American colonial clergyman and poet (born in England). Preached in Malden, Massachusetts. Wrote the first American bestseller, a Puritan poem, "The Day of Doom," 1662.

WILLIAMS, ROGER (c.1603–1683) American clergyman, founder of Rhode Island (born in England). Took Anglican orders, then embraced Puritanism, but advocated broad religious freedom. *The Bloody Tenet of Persecution*, 1644.

WYCLIFFE, JOHN (c.1328–1384) English theologian and religious reformer. Preached the supreme authority of the Scriptures. Held that the church was not the only path to grace. Noted for an English translation of the Bible which bears his name.

ZANGWILL, ISRAEL (1864–1926) English Jewish novelist, journalist, and Zionist. Held that a homeland for Jews was needed immediately. Favored Britain's 1905 offer of territory in Uganda. *Chosen Peoples*, 1918.

ZWINGLI, HULDRYCH (1484–1531) Swiss Protestant reformer. His lectures on the New Testament marked the beginning of the Reformation in Switzerland. Opposed monasticism and clerical celibacy. *Commentary on True and False Religion*, 1525.

THIRTY
RELIGIONS
AND PHILOSOPHIES
IN MICROCOSM

Applying religious labels to people or their words is a venture fraught with peril. One person's devoted Christian may be another's lost heretic. One person's agnostic may be another's "dirty little atheist" (to quote Theodore Roosevelt on Thomas Paine). Nevertheless, in dealing with 30 religions, philosophies, or ethical viewpoints, as this Treasury does, some system of labeling seems desirable.

For one thing, only a person immersed in comparative religion is likely to be able to match each of the various sacred texts—not to mention each of the theologians, religious writers, or academic and literary voices—with the proper religion, philosophy, or viewpoint. The labeling in the Treasury, arguable as the labels may sometimes be, seems preferable to leaving the user entirely unaided.

For another thing, the labels provide an organizational benefit. A reader interested only in Judeo-Christian quotations, for instance, does not have to weed out for himself or herself all the Buddhist or Hindu or Islamic observations. Beyond that, the inclusion of people under a particular heading—especially in the case of literary figures whose religion may be seldom discussed and not widely known—should prove illuminating.

Here is a synopsis of the labels and their meanings.

AGNOSTICISM T.H. Huxley, an English biologist and educator, coined the word *agnostic* in 1869 to describe himself. An agnostic is a religious skeptic who holds that the existence of God cannot be proved or disproved. Robert G. Ingersoll was a well-known 19th-century American agnostic. The great philosopher Immanuel Kant is often classified as an agnostic, but in this book he receives a separate heading, Kantianism. Agnosticism, which accepts the possibility of God, albeit an unknowable God, should not be confused with atheism.

ARISTOTELIANISM This infrequent heading is applied here only to the Greek philosopher Aristotle. Aristotle's complex views on the Prime Mover and the contemplative life and much else had profound influence on the philosophers who followed him, but no attempt has been made in this book to represent his ethical views through extensive quotation.

ATHEISM An atheist denies the existence of God, indeed of any possible gods or supernatural powers. The advance of science over the centuries brought about a corresponding growth in atheism, although many scientists—and particularly contemporary scientists—hold firm religious convictions. The word atheist has often been used as an all-purpose epithet against opponents of orthodoxy. Still, there are real atheists. Among the ones cited in this book (but not very frequently cited) are Karl Marx, Sigmund Freud, and Joseph Stalin.

BUDDHISM Buddhism was founded about 525 B.C. by Siddhartha Gautama, the Buddha ("the enlightened One"), near Benares, India. Buddhism declined gradually but substantially in its native India, but attracted an increasing number of followers elsewhere, especially in Japan. In the United States today the best known major branch of Buddhism is Zen. A galaxy of sects and practices have made Buddhism as a whole virtually indefinable. In this book no attempt has been made to differentiate one branch or sect from another. Zen is not separately labeled. There is no Buddhist bible per se. The sacred texts, many of them called *sutras*, can seem puzzling to literal-minded readers grounded in Western religion. A central goal of Buddhism is the attaining of Nirvana, a state of absolute blessedness beyond suffering, striving, or desire. One of the leading interpreters of Buddhism to the West was Daisetz Teitaro Suzuki (1870-1966), a Japanese scholar and lecturer who spent many years in the United States.

CHRISTIANITY/JUDAISM That this Treasury is a Christian-centered book will be evident from this label. Judaism precedes Christianity historically, and a case could be made for citing the Hebrew Bible rather than the King James version of the Old Testament. However, most Americans, being Christian, would find the Judaic wording unfamiliar. By contrast, much of the King James translation is a familiar part of every English speaker's idiom. The chronologically reversed "Christianity/Judaism" label is used to preserve alphabetically the Old Testament-New Testament sequence for Biblical quotations.

CHRISTIANITY Christianity is the principal focus of the Treasury. The Christianity label is applied as all-inclusively as ecumenism and common sense will allow. Christ is the adhesive that holds the differing and sometimes antagonistic groups together. Among the host of Christians quoted, Southern Baptists mingle with Roman Catholics; early

Calvinists, pious saints, and fire-and-brimstone evangelists appear cheek by jowl with today's liberal Catholics and Protestants; and some (but not all) of the literary figures of Romanticism speak in unmistakably Christian voices through their troubling personal doubts. Still, the line has to be drawn somewhere, and it is. There are three main exclusions from the large Christian roster, resulting in separate labels: Christian Science, Mormonism, and Unitarianism (plus one entry for Universalism). The isolation of these denominations is explained under their separate headings. Otherwise, most professing or presumptive Christians are labeled as such.

CHRISTIAN SCIENCE Mary Baker Eddy (1821–1910) founded the Church of Christ, Scientist, after being treated successfully for her illnesses by Phineas Parkhurst Quimby, a mesmerist and mental healer. Mrs. Eddy's authorized textbook of Christian Science, *Science and Health* (later . . . *with Key to the Scriptures* added) denies the reality of the material world and asserts that sin and illness are illusions to be overcome by the mind. Christian Science churches have no ministers. The service is conducted by two readers, one of whom reads from the Bible, the other from *Science and Health*.

CONFUCIANISM At its inception Confucianism was entirely a cluster of ethical rules for the conduct of life and society. As set forth in the *Analects*—the collected sayings of Confucius, a Chinese sage (c.551–479 B.C.)—the highest good on earth is *jen*, a kind of human-heartedness. During his lifetime Confucius seems to have been primarily a social reformer. Beginning about the first century A.D., worship of Confucius and the offering of sacrifices to him started to transform Confucianism into a quasi-religion. The neo-Confucianism of the Sung dynasty (960–1279) continued this trend. Still, the faithful never professed a belief in the immortality of the soul, and rejected the otherworldliness of Buddhism. Events in China in the 20th century have greatly weakened the religious and ethical influence of Confucianism, although the aphoristic sayings of the *Analects* remain familiar worldwide.

COSMIC The rare Cosmic label features only one quoted person: Albert Einstein, the German-American physicist (1879–1955) who formulated the theory of relativity. Einstein's heritage was Jewish and his beliefs appear basically deistic, but he himself applied the term Cosmic Religion to his affirmation of God as an "illimitable superior spirit . . . revealed in the incomprehensible universe."

DEISM Not many people today call themselves deists, but quite a few did in the rationalistic 17th and 18th centuries. Foremost among them were the French philosophers Voltaire (1694–1778) and Jean Jacques Rousseau (1712–1778). Deists hold that the existence of God is sufficiently proved by the natural world, that formal religion is unnecessary, and that supernatural happenings are of doubtful authenticity. Deists do not regard themselves as anti-Christian but merely neutral. A number of American statesmen of the Revolutionary period held deistic views, among them Benjamin Franklin, George Washington, and Thomas Jefferson.

EXISTENTIALISM Existentialism is a 20th century philosophical position that can appear, and has appeared, in the thought of dedicated Christian religionists. It stresses the need for individuals, who are inevitably isolated and alone, to confront the unique ethical problems facing them, not with reason but with a sense of subjective, individual responsibility. A number of renowned Christian and Jewish thinkers have been influenced by existentialism, including Martin Buber, Karl Barth, Rudolf Bultmann, Paul Tillich, and Reinhold Niebuhr (although these men appear in this book under their Judeo-Christian labels). At its extreme (as, for instance, in the philosophy of Jean Paul Sartre) existentialism is atheistic. The origins of existentialism are cloudy. The seeds of its present-day thought are generally ascribed to Søren Kierkegaard (1813–1855), a Danish philosopher.

HINDUISM The oldest of the world's contemporary religions, Hinduism began in India sometime around 1500 B.C. The major texts are the *Vedas*, including the *Rig-Veda*, the *Upanishads*, and the *Bhagavad Gita*. Hinduism is essentially an unorganized religion. It is fragmented into a confusing number of sects, most of them concentrated in India. There is no such thing as orthodox Hinduism. The religion began with the worship of many gods, and it remains polytheistic, but all of the Hindu gods are seen as a manifestation of divine unity. The only reality, the supreme unity, is Brahman. Life, to a Hindu, is a continuing cycle of birth and rebirth. One can improve one's *karma*—that is, the force based on past deeds and influencing future incarnations—by means of spiritual discipline and pure actions. As in Buddhism, the progression is toward Nirvana, a reunion with Brahma and the extinction of individual existence. Hinduism has the third largest number of adherents in the world after Christianity and Islam.

HUMANISM Humanism has philosophical and literary roots going back to the Renaissance. It is basically a nonreligion in that it makes humankind rather than a higher power central to life and thought. Erasmus, a lifelong Roman Catholic, is usually classed as a humanist, but that label, if unqualified, stretches the definition of humanism too far, in much the same way that the existentialist label tends to get stretched. Humanism's characteristics—admiration for humanity, love of the classics, and respect for scientific endeavor—are traits common to the adherents of many religions. The Humanist label in this book is applied to the French writer Albert

Camus (1913–1960), who applied it to himself, and to the philosopher John Stuart Mill (1806–1873).

ISLAM Founded by the Prophet Muhammad in 622 A.D., Islam has become the world's second largest religion. There are about half as many Muslims throughout the world as there are Christians of all denominations. Islam began in Medina, on the Arabian peninsula, with the first of God's (Allah's) revelations to Muhammad, revelations that eventually were incorporated into the Koran. The Koran was handed down in Arabic, and many Muslims believe it is sacrilege to translate it. Muslims have five fundamental religious duties, including prayer five times a day and, if possible, one pilgrimage to the sacred city of Mecca in a person's lifetime. Except for the apparently irreparable doctrinal rift between Sunnis and Shiites, which goes back almost to the beginning of Islam, there is remarkably little sectarianism. The Sunnis are greatly in the majority and are considered traditional or orthodox. Sufism, a mystic and literary branch of Islam, has produced some of the greatest of the Muslim poets. Quotations from the Sufis, while included under the Islam label, frequently have a clever, charming tone, quite unlike that of the Koran or most of the commentary on Islam. Theoretically and sometimes factually, the state and the Islamic religion are one. Because interpretation of the Koran is expressly forbidden, theological observations comparable to those about Western religions are largely absent from Islam.

JUDAISM The term *Judaism* is relatively new. In the old days the term was *Torah*. Even today *Torah* carries much the same meaning, although to non-Jews it is often thought of as more restricted, applying just to the divinely revealed sacred teachings. Central to the written Torah are the five Books of Moses, the Pentateuch—the first five books of the Christian Old Testament. Thirty-four other books were added later to form the Hebrew Bible. (In this Treasury, the King James edition of the Old Testament rather than the Hebrew Bible is the source quoted.) The oral Torah is recorded in the Talmud, the Midrash, and other writings. Abraham is regarded as the Jewish patriarch, with Moses the leading prophet. Jews consider themselves the chosen people of God. Judaism encompasses a broad range of belief and practices, from the rigid, law-based discipline of Orthodox Jews to the sometimes striking liberalism of Reform Jews. Each synagogue is run by its congregation and is free to choose its own rabbi. Judaism has been vitally important to Western culture and to the Judeo-Christian ethic, yet Jews comprise only .3 percent of the world's religious population, being outnumbered by Christians nearly 110 to 1 and by Muslims approximately 60 to 1. In this book Jewish quotations appear under two headings: Christianity/Judaism and Judaism.

KANTIANISM One could argue that the great German philosopher Immanuel Kant (1724–1824) was simply an agnostic, and, whatever his tremendous influence on later thought, scarcely deserves his own label. But there is a distinction to be made. Whereas an agnostic accepts the possibility of an unknowable God, the agnostic's interest ends there. Kant, on the other hand, maintains that a belief in the existence of God and immortality (however unprovable) is an absolute necessity—that without it there would be no morality.

LENI-LENAPI The American Indian religions, of which there are many, are scantily represented in this book. One Leni-Lenape (Delaware Indian) quotation from the "The Walam Olum," a creation story, is included.

MORMONISM Members of the Church of Jesus Christ of Latter-day Saints believe the Christian Bible to be revealed truth, as the official name of the Mormon Church indicates. But the Mormons have a second scripture as well, the Book of Mormon, which was handed down on gold tablets to the Prophet Joseph Smith in upstate New York in the early 1800s. The Book of Mormon discloses events that took place in America from roughly 600 B.C. to 400 A.D., involving the Lamanites, ancestors of the American Indians, and the Nephites, their enemies. Joseph Smith's book *Doctrine and Covenants* contains the Prophet's later revelations. *The Pearl of Great Price* presents sayings attributed to Abraham and Moses. The Mormon Church emphasized proselytizing from the very beginning, and its membership has expanded rapidly as a consequence. It claims more than four million members in the United States.

NAVAJO Two quotations from the rich and complex Navajo religion appear in the book.

NONSECTARIAN This label is used for remarks about religion made by scholars and writers who represent no specific religion in the works cited. These people may have a religion, to be sure, but it does not color what they have said or written, at least not obviously. The psychologists William James (1842–1910) and Carl Jung (1875–1961), as well as a few novelists, are classed as nonsectarian. James could have been labeled a Pragmatist and Jung a Jungian, but in the interest of economy in labeling nonreligious viewpoints, they and others have been put in this miscellaneous category. The Nonsectarian label is neutral and infrequent.

PANTHEISM Pantheism has two meanings. One is the worship of all gods indiscriminately. That is not the meaning of the label in this book. Pantheism here means the equating of God with the laws and forces of nature. According to pantheism, God is the universe; the universe is God. Pantheistic speculations almost certainly reach back into prehistory. Later, Greek philosophers discussed the immanence of God in nature. Meister Eckhart, a Christian mystical theologian, pursued it. The Dutch philosopher and lens grinder Spinoza (1632–1677) gave pantheism its most thorough and precise expression.

PLATONISM The teachings of the Greek philosopher Plato (c.427–327 B.C.) emphasize that the things of this world are merely reflections of an absolute and transcendent reality. Plato explored the Idea of Good, which he saw as the supreme principle of order and truth. At his Academy in Athens Plato dealt with almost every issue that has concerned later philosophers. He is quoted, though not extensively, as the sole representative of Platonism.

POETICS This unusual label designates two unusual writers: Edward FitzGerald (1809–1883) and Kahlil Gibran (1883–1931). Their achievements are hard to categorize. FitzGerald is the translator (really the poetic rewriter) of *The Rubaiyat of Omar Khyyam*. The poem, originally Persian and Sufi, could conceivably fall under Islam. But to put FitzGerald's version there requires quite a leap of the imagination. Poetics seems more accurate. Similarly with Kahlil Gibran. *The Prophet* is a mystical prose-poem by this Lebanese-American artist. It is not precisely a religious text, but it contains a wealth of nicely worded quasi-religious advice.

SECULARISM For many conservative Christians the term secularism (or, more commonly, secular humanism) is a swear word. The term denotes, as Webster puts it, "indifference to or rejection or exclusion of religion and religious considerations." In fact, secularism is seldom just the avoidance of religion; typically it is a put-down of religion. A secular writer is aware of religion, may even deal extensively with it, but has little use for the believers or their beliefs. Two of the secularists quoted in this book are the Irish playwright George Bernard Shaw and the Baltimore journalist H.L. Mencken.

STOICISM The Greek philosophy of Stoicism, despite its pantheistic elements, has a certain affinity with Christianity. Its ethical teachings—that one should live virtuously and in harmony with nature, that one should put aside passion and unjust thoughts—are principles most Christians can accept. God, said the Stoics, is the reason and soul in human beings. The Stoics wrote many brilliantly worded epigrams. Partly for that reason, Seneca the Younger, Epictetus, and Marcus Aurelius make more frequent appearances in this book than other Greek philosophers.

SWEDENBORGIANISM In 1745 "heaven was opened" to Emanuel Swedenborg (1688–1772), a Swedish scientist, philosopher, and mystic. Angels and visions helped Swedenborg to present his spiritual teachings, which after his death became "the very Word of the Lord" for members of the Church of the New Jerusalem, or New Church. These members are generally called Swedenborgians. They accept the Christian Bible but reject the doctrines of the Trinity, original sin, and eternal damnation. The sect is small; there are fewer than 3,000 Swedenborgians in the United States.

TAOISM Taoism is, or was until recently, one of the major religions of China, along with Confucianism, Buddhism, and Chinese folk religion. Taoism fell victim to the Communist takeover in 1949. Officially banned in China, it exists today in Taiwan, Singapore, Hong Kong, and other places where traditional Chinese culture survives. Taoism is a philosophy and also, separably, a religion. Both are based on the *Tao-te ching* ("the Way" or "the Path"), a book credited to the possibly legendary Lao-tzu (c.600 B.C.). Taoism teaches a very quiet, accepting way of life, a kind of don't-rock-the-boat approach to the world. Effortless action, unaffected simplicity, and freedom from desire are seen as virtues. The leading Taoist authority after Lao-tzu is Chuang-tzu (c.369–c.286 B.C.), a superb writer and satirist. Taoism's search for an elixir of life led to great interest in and involvement with alchemy. Some Chinese who preferred Taosim to Confucianism found greater spirituality and emotional depth in Lao-tzu's "Way" than in Confucius's more down-to-earth ethical pronouncements.

UNITARIANISM Historically, Unitarianism is a form of Christianity that rejects the doctrine of the Trinity. It began in Transylvania in the 16th century as part of the Protestant Reformation. But Unitarianism in the United States has long-since strayed from its original scriptural focus. Under the leadership of William Ellery Channing (1780–1842) and Ralph Waldo Emerson (1803–1882), Unitarianism became a religion of reason and open-mindedness. As such, it swept though the liberal Congregational assemblies of New England in the early 1800s. Unitarianism was closely tied to literary Transcendentalism, and a remarkable number of famous authors during the "flowering of New England" were Unitarians, among them Longfellow, Whittier, Lowell, and Thoreau. Not all of these are cited here under Unitarianism, however, because in those days the denomination was basically Christian-Congregationalist, and not wholly freethinking. In 1961 the Unitarians combined with the Universalists to form the Unitarian Universalist Association.

UNIVERSALISM Universalism dates from 18th century England and, specifically, John Murray (1741–1815), who emigrated to the United States in 1770. Universalists maintain that salvation is extended to all mankind. The most influential voice in Universalism after Murray was Hosea Ballou (1771–1852), a forceful New England minister and writer. The movement made few converts beyond the United States. From the beginning, Universalists shared many beliefs and concerns with Unitarians. The two groups merged in 1961 to become the Unitarian Universalist Association.

ZOROASTRIANISM   Relatively few people today practice the religion founded by Zoroaster, a prophet and teacher of ancient Persia. Nevertheless, those who do, most of whom live in India and Iran, tend to be well-educated and influential. The Avesta, the sacred book of Zoroastrianism, contains hymns, prayers, and codes of purification, all of which have been greatly edited and revised over time. In early Zoroastrianism the priests were known as magi. The supreme lord of creation is Ahura Mazda, but this preeminent God is opposed by evil spirits of considerable strength. Zoroastrians stress personal honesty and a caring attitude toward the natural world. According to Zoroastrianism belief, when a person dies, his or her soul crosses a bridge. The bridge widens to permit safe passage of the righteous, but narrows to a knife-edge at the approach of the unworthy, forcing them to fall to perdition below.

TWO HUNDRED FIFTY
BASIC SOURCES

This is a list of books consulted in compiling the *Treasury of Religious Quotations*. Only books are included, not magazines, newspapers, or other published or unpublished sources that provided some of the quotations. Users will notice that many more sources are cited in the book than are included in the bibliography. This stems from the fact that the quotations sometimes come from existing compilations, from anthologies, or from textual inclusion in other cited single-author books.

Adels, Jill Haak. *The Wisdom of the Saints: An Anthology.* New York: Oxford University Press, 1987.

Adler, Bill, ed. *The Wit and Wisdom of Bishop Fulton J. Sheen.* Englewood Cliffs, NJ: Prentice Hall, 1968.

Adler, Morris. *The World of the Talmud.* New York: Schocken Books, 1963.

Adler, Mortimer, and Charles Van Doren. *The Great Treasury of Western Thought.* New York: R.R. Bowker, 1977.

Ahmad, Khurshid, ed. *Islam: Its Meaning and Message.* London: Islamic Council of Europe, 1976.

Ali, A. Yusuf, tr. *The Holy Qur'an*, 2nd ed. n.p.: American Trust Publications for The Muslim Students' Association, 1977.

Allana, G., ed. *A Rosary of Islamic Readings: 7th to 20th Century.* Karachi: National Publishing House, 1973.

Allport, Gordon W. *The Individual and His Religion.* New York: The Macmillan Company, 1950.

Allport, Gordon W. *Waiting for the Lord: 33 Meditations on God and Man,* ed. by Peter A. Bertocci. New York: Macmillan Publishing Co., 1978.

Alter, Robert. *The Art of Biblical Narrative.* New York: Basic Books, 1981.

Appleton, George, ed. *The Oxford Book of Prayer.* London: Oxford University Press, 1985.

Aquinas, St. Thomas. *Summa Theologica.* New York: McGraw-Hill Book Company, 1966.

Arberry, A.J. *The Koran Interpreted.* London: George Allen & Unwin, 1955.

Asad, Muhammad. *Islam at the Crossroads.* Lahore: Arafat Publications, 1969 .

Baeck, Leo. *The Essence of Judaism.* New York: Schocken Books, 1948.

Baker, Daniel B., ed. *Political Quotations.* Detroit: Gale Research, 1990.

Baker, Herschel. *The Image of Man: A Study of the Idea of Human Dignity in Classical Antiquity, the Middle Ages, and the Renaissance.* New York: Harper & Brothers, 1947.

Barclay, William. *Ethics in a Permissive Society.* New York: Harper & Row, 1971.

Barclay, William. *The Master's Men.* New York: Abingdon Press, 1959.

Barnhouse, Donald Grey. *Words Fitly Spoken.* Wheaton, IL: Tyndale House Publishers, 1969.

Barth, Karl. *Credo.* New York: Charles Scribner's Sons, 1962.

Barth, Karl. *God Here and Now.* New York: Harper & Row, 1964.

Barth, Karl. *God in Action.* Manhasset, NY: Round Table Press, 1936, 1963.

Bartlett, John. *Familiar Quotations,* 15th ed. Boston: Little, Brown and Company, 1980.

Beecher, Henry Ward. *The Sermons of Henry Ward Beecher,* Vol 4. New York: J.B. Ford and Company, 1875.

Bell, Richard. *The Origin of Islam in Its Christian Environment.* London: Frank Cass & Co., 1968 (reprint of 1926 edition).

Belloc, Hilaire. *A Conversation with an Angel and Other Essays.* Freeport, NY: Books for Libraries, 1968 (reprint of 1928, 1956 editions).

Bertram, Martin H., tr. *Luther's Works, Vol. 23.* St. Louis: Concordia, 1958.

Bettenson, Henry, tr. *The Later Christian Fathers: A Selection of the Writings of the Fathers from St. Cyril of Jerusalem to St. Leo the Great.* New York: Oxford University Press, 1973.

Blue, Lionel. *To Heaven, with Scribes and Pharisees: The Jewish Path to God.* New York: Oxford University Press, 1976.

Bonham, Tal D. *Humor: God's Gift.* Nashville, TN: Broadman Press, 1988.

Bonhoeffer, Dietrich. *Ethics*. New York: The Macmillan Company, 1955.

Bonhoeffer, Dietrich. *The Martyred Christian*, ed. by Joan Winmill Brown. New York: Macmillan Publishing Co., 1983.

Bonhoeffer, Dietrich. *No Rusty Swords*. New York: Harper & Row, 1965.

Bonhoeffer, Dietrich. *The Way to Freedom*. New York: Harper & Row, 1966.

The Book of Mormon. Salt Lake City, UT: The Church of Jesus Christ of Latter-day Saints, 1981.

Bounds, E.M. *Power Through Prayer*. Springdale, PA: Whitaker House, 1982.

Bowden, Henry Sebastian. *The Religion of Shakespeare*. New York: AMS Press, 1974 (reprint of 1899 edition).

Brown, Robert McAfee, ed. *The Essential Reinhold Niebuhr: Selected Essays and Addresses*. New Haven: Yale University Press, 1986.

Buber, Martin. *I and Thou*, tr. by Walter Kaufmann. New York: Charles Scribner's Sons, 1970.

Buber, Martin. *On Judaism*, ed. by Nahum N. Glatzer. New York: Schocken Books, 1967.

Buckley, William F. *God and Man at Yale*. Chicago: Henry Regnery Company, 1951.

Bultmann, Rudolf. *This World and the Beyond*. New York: Charles Scribner's Sons, 1960.

Burtt, E.A., ed. *The Teachings of the Compassionate Buddha*. New York: Mentor, 1955.

Buttrick, George A. *Christ and History*. New York: Abingdon Press, 1963.

Buttrick, George A. *God, Pain, and Evil*. Nashville, TN: Abingdon Press, 1966.

Calvin, John. *The Christian Life*, ed. by John H. Leith. San Francisco: Harper & Row, 1984.

Cardiff, Ira D. *What Great Men Think of Religion*. New York: Arno Press & The New York Times, 1972 (reprint of 1945 edition).

Carmody, Denise L., and John T. Carmody. *Shamans, Prophets, and Sages: An Introduction to World Religions*. Belmont, CA: Wadsworth, 1985.

Carruth, Gorton, and Eugene Ehrlich. *The Harper Book of American Quotations*. New York: Harper & Row, 1988.

Chan, Wing-tsit, *A Source Book in Chinese Philosophy*. Princeton, NJ: Princeton University Press, 1963.

Chesterton, G.K. *All Is Grist: A Book of Essays*. Freeport, NY: Books for Libraries Press, 1967 (reprint of 1932 edition).

Chesterton, G.K. *Orthodoxy*. New York: Dodd Mead & Company, 1908.

Church, F. Forrester. *Entertaining Angels*. New York: Harper & Row, 1987.

Coffin, William Sloane. *Living the Truth in a World of Illusions*. San Francisco: Harper & Row, 1985.

Cohen, Abraham. *Everyman's Talmud*. New York: E.P. Dutton, 1949.

Cohen, Arthur A., and Paul Mendes-Flohr, eds. *Contemporary Jewish Religious Thought: Original Essays on Critical Concepts, Movements, and Beliefs*. New York: Charles Scribner's Sons, 1987.

Collins, Robert E. *Theodore Parker: American Transcendentalist*. Metuchen, NJ: The Scarecrow Press, 1973.

Connelly, Marc. *The Green Pastures*. New York: Farrar & Rinehart, 1930.

Conze, Edward, tr. *Buddhist Scriptures*. Baltimore: Penguin, 1959.

Cragg, Kenneth. *Counsels in Contemporary Islam*. Edinburgh: Edinburgh University Press, 1965.

Crim, Keith, ed. *The Perennial Dictionary of World Religions*. San Francisco: Harper & Row, 1981.

Dawood, N.J., tr. *The Koran*, 4th ed. Harmondsworth, Middlesex: Penguin Books, 1974.

Deng, Ming-Dao. *Seven Bamboo Tablets of the Cloudy Satchel*. San Francisco: Harper & Row, 1978.

Deutsch, Eliot, tr. *The Bhagavad Gita*. New York: Holt, Rinehart and Winston, 1968.

Dimock, E.C., and Denise Leverton, tr. *In Praise of Krishna: Songs from the Bengali*. Garden City, NY: Doubleday, 1964.

Duyvendak, J.J.L., tr. *Tao Te Ching, Lao Tzu*. London: John Murray, 1954.

Edgerton, Franklin. *The Bhagavad Gita*. Cambridge, MA: Harvard University Press, 1972.

Editors of Time. *The World's Great Religions*. New York: Time, Inc., 1957.

Ellwood, Robert S., Jr. *Words of the World's Religions: An Anthology*. Englewood Cliffs, NJ: Prentice Hall, 1977.

Enright, D.J., ed. *The Oxford Book of Death*. New York: Oxford University Press, 1983.

Esposito, John L., ed. *Voices of Resurgent Islam*. New York: Oxford University Press, 1983.

Evans, Bergen, ed. *Dictionary of Quotations*. New York: Delacorte Press, 1968.

Fackenheim, Emil L. *What Is Judaism?* New York: Summit Books, 1987.

Falwell, Jerry. *Finding Inner Peace and Strength*. Garden City, NY: Doubleday & Company, 1982.

Falwell, Jerry. *Strength for the Journey: An Autobiography*. New York: Simon and Schuster, 1987.

Feinsilver, Rabbi Alexander, tr., ed. *The Talmud for Today*. New York: St. Martin's Press, 1980.

FitzGerald, Edward. *Rubaiyat of Omar Khayyam*. New York: Thomas Y. Crowell Company, n.d.

Fosdick, Harry Emerson, ed. *Great Voices of the Reformation*. New York: The Modern Library (Random House), 1952.

Fosdick, Harry Emerson. *Riverside Sermons*. New York: Harper & Brothers, 1958.

Francis de Sales, Saint. *Introduction to the Devout Life*, tr. and ed. by John K. Ryan. New York: Harper & Brothers, 1950.

Franck, Frederick, ed. *The Buddha Eye: An Anthology of the Kyoto School*. New York: Crossroad, 1982.

Fromm, Erich. *The Art of Loving*. New York: Harper & Brothers, 1956.

Fromm, Erich. *You Shall Be As Gods: A Radical Interpretation of the Old Testament and Its Tradition*. New York: New York: Holt, Rinehart and Winston, 1966.

Frost, S.E., Jr., ed. *The Sacred Writings of the World's Great Religions*. New York: McGraw-Hill Book Company, 1972.

Fulghum, Robert. *All I Really Need to Know I Learned in Kindergarten*. New York: Villard Books, 1988.

Fuller, Thomas. *The Holy State and the Profane State*. London: Thomas Tegg, 1841.

Gaster, T.H. *The Dead Sea Scriptures in English Translation*. Garden City, NY: Doubleday, 1956.

Ghazali, al-. *The Just Balance*, tr. by D.P. Brewster. Lahore: Sh. Muhammad Ashraf, 1978.

Gibran, Kahlil. *The Prophet*. New York: Alfred A. Knopf, 1988 (reprint of 1923 edition).

Gibson, A. Boyce. *The Religion of Dostoevsky*. Philadelphia: The Westminster Press, 1973.

Gilson, Etienne. *The Spirit of Medieval Philosophy*. New York: Charles Scribner's Sons, 1936.

Gittelsohn, Roland B. *The Meaning of Judaism*. New York: The World Publishing Company, 1970.

Goddard, Dwight, ed. *A Buddhist Bible*. New York: E.P. Dutton, 1938, 1966.

Goodhill, Ruth Marcus, ed. *The Wisdom of Heschel*. New York: Farrar, Straus and Giroux, 1975.

Gracian, Baltasar, tr. by Joseph Jacobs. *The Art of Worldly Wisdom*. New York: Frederick Ungar Publishing Co., n.d. (reprint of 1892 translation).

Graham, Billy. *The Holy Spirit.* Waco, TX: Word Books, 1978.

Graham, Billy. *Till Armageddon.* Waco, TX: Word Books, 1981.

Greeley, Andrew M. *The Catholic WHY? Book.* Chicago: The Thomas Moore Press, 1983.

Greeley, Andrew M. *Life for a Wanderer.* Garden City, NY: Doubleday & Company, 1969.

Greeley, Andrew M. *The New Agenda.* Garden City, NY: Doubleday & Company, 1973.

Greeley, Roger E., ed. *Ingersoll: Immortal Infidel.* Buffalo, NY: Prometheus Books, 1977.

Greenberg, Sidney. *Say Yes to Life: A Book of Thoughts for Better Living.* New York: Crown Publishers, 1982.

Greenberg, Simon. *A Jewish Philosophy and Pattern of Life.* New York: The Jewish Theological Seminary of America, 1981.

Gross, John, ed. *The Oxford Book of Aphorisms.* New York: Oxford University Press, 1983.

Gullen, Karen, ed. *Billy Sunday Speaks.* New York: Chelsea House, 1970.

Harris, William H., and Judith S. Levey. *The New Columbia Encyclopedia.* New York: Columbia University Press, 1975.

Harrison, G.B. ed. *Major British Writers.* 2 vols. New York: Harcourt, Brace & World, 1954, 1959.

Hearn, Lafcadio. *The Buddhist Writings of Lafcadio Hearn,* intro. by Kenneth Rexroth. Santa Barbara: Ross-Erikson, 1977.

Henry, Carl F.H., ed. *Revelation and the Bible: Contemporary Evangelical Thought.* Grand Rapids, MI: Baker Book House, 1958.

Heschel, Abraham Joshua. *God in Search of Man: A Philosophy of Judaism.* New York: Farrar, Straus and Giroux, 1955.

Heschel, Abraham Joshua. *The Insecurity of Freedom: Essays on Human Existence.* New York: Farrar, Straus and Giroux, 1966.

Heschel, Abraham Joshua. *Man Is Not Alone: A Philosophy of Religion.* New York: Harper & Row, 1951.

Heschel, Abraham Joshua. *Who Is Man?* Stanford, CA: Stanford University Press, 1965.

Hester, Dennis J., ed. *The Vance Havner Quotebook.* Grand Rapids, MI: Baker Book House, 1986.

Hill, Caroline Miles, ed. *The World's Great Religious Poetry.* New York: The Macmillan Company, 1923.

Hinnells, John R. *Persian Mythology,* rev. ed. New York: Peter Bedrick Books, 1985.

Holtz, Barry W., ed. *Back to the Sources: Reading the Classic Jewish Texts.* New York: Summit Books, 1984.

The Holy Bible (King James Version). Cleveland: The World Publishing Company, n.d.

Hourani, George F. *Reason and Tradition in Islamic Ethics.* Cambridge: Cambridge University Press, 1985.

Hume, Robert Ernest, tr. *The Thirteen Principal Upanishads,* 2nd ed. London: Oxford University Press, 1931.

Humphreys, Christmas, ed. *The Wisdom of Buddhism,* 2nd ed. London: Curzon Press, 1979.

Hymns for the Celebration of Life. Boston: The Beacon Press, 1964.

Inge, William Ralph. *Outspoken Essays.* London: Longmans, Green, 1919.

Jacobs, Louis. *What Does Judaism Say About...?* New York: Quadrangle/The New York Times Book Co., 1973.

John, DeWitt. *The Christian Science Way of Life.* Boston: The Christian Science Publishing Society, 1962.

John Paul II. *Pilgrimage of Peace: The Collected Speeches of John Paul II in Ireland and the United States.* New York: Farrar Straus Giroux, 1980.

John Paul II. *The Word Made Flesh: The Meaning of the Christmas Season.* San Francisco: Harper & Row, 1985.

Jung, Carl Gustav. *Psychology and Religion.* New Haven: Yale University Press, 1938.

Kaplan, Mordecai M. *The Purpose and Meaning of Jewish Existence.* Philadelphia: The Jewish Publication Society of America, 1964.

Kauffman, Donald T., ed. *The Treasury of Religious Verse.* Westwood, NJ: Fleming H. Revell Company, 1962.

Kierkegaard, Søren. *The Present Age and Of the Difference Between a Genius and an Apostle,* tr. by Alexander Dru. New York: Harper & Row, 1962.

Koestline, Henry. *What Jesus Said About It.* New York: New American Library, 1970.

The Koran, tr. by N.J. Dawood. Harmondsworth, Middlesex: Penguin Books, 1956.

Küng, Hans. *On Being a Christian,* tr. by Edward Quinn. Garden City, NY: Doubleday & Company, 1976.

Küng, Hans. *The Christian Challenge,* tr. by Edward Quinn. Garden City, NY: Doubleday & Company, 1979.

Küng, Hans. *Eternal Life?,* tr. by Edward Quinn. Garden City, NY: Doubleday & Company, 1984.

Kushner, Harold S. *When Bad Things Happen to Good People.* New York: Schocken Books, 1981.

Lane, Hana Umlauf, ed. *The World Almanac Book of Who.* New York: World Almanac Publications, 1980.

Lawson, James Gilchrist, ed. *The Best-Loved Religious Poems.* Old Tappan, NJ: Fleming H. Revell Company, 1933.

Lewis, C.S. *Mere Christianity.* New York: The Macmillan Company, 1952.

Lewis, C.S. *Present Concerns,* ed. by Walter Hooper. New York: Harcourt Brace Jovanovich, 1986.

Lewis, C.S. *The Screwtape Letters.* New York: The Macmillan Company, 1942, 1961).

Lindstrom, Ralph G. *Lincoln Finds God.* New York: Longmans, Green and Co., 1958.

Lin Yutang. *The Wisdom of China and India.* New York: The Modern Library (Random House), 1942.

Locher, Gottfried W. *Zwingli's Thought: New Perspectives.* Leiden: E.J. Brill, 1981.

LEncyclopediayttle, Charles H., ed. *The Liberal Gospel: As Set Forth in the Writings of William Ellery Channing.* Boston: The Beacon Press, 1925.

MacDonell, A.A. Hymns from the Rigveda. London: Oxford University Press, n.d.

Marchant, Sir James. *Wit and Wisdom of Dean Inge.* Freeport, NY: Books for Libraries, 1968 (reprint of 1927 edition).

Maritain, Jacques. *Challenges and Renewals: Selected Readings,* ed. by Joseph W. Evans and Leo R. Ward. Notre Dame, IN: University of Notre Dame Press, 1966.

Marshall, Catherine. *A Man Called Peter.* New York: McGraw-Hill Book Company, 1951.

Marshall, George N. *Challenge of a Liberal Faith.* Boston: Unitarian Universalist Association, 1970.

Marshall, Peter. *Mr. Jones, Meet the Master.* Westwood, NJ: Fleming H. Revell Company, 1949.

Martin, Bernard, ed. *Great Twentieth Century Jewish Philosophers.* London: The Macmillan Company, 1970.

Maslow, Abraham H. *Religions, Values, and Peak-Experiences,* Columbus: Ohio State University Press, 1964.

Mason, John Hope, ed. *The Indispensable Rousseau.* London: Quartet Books, 1979.

Matsunami, Kodo. *Introducing Buddhism,* rev. ed. Rutland, VT: Charles E. Tuttle Company, 1976.

Mawdudi, Abu'l A'la. *Islamic Law and Constitution,* tr. and ed. by Khurshid Ahmad. Lahore: Islamic Publications, 1960.

McCarrol, Tolbert. *The Tao: The Sacred Way.* New York: Crossroad, 1982.

McNulty, James F. *Words of Power.* Staten Island, NY: Alba House, 1983.

Mead, Frank S., ed. *The Encyclopedia of Religious Quotations.* Westwood, NJ: Fleming H. Revell Company, 1965.

Mencken, H.L. *Prejudices: A Selection,* ed. by James T. Farrell. New York: Alfred A. Knopf, 1958.

Merton, Thomas. *Conjectures of a Guilty Bystander.* New York: Doubleday & Company, 1966.

Merton, Thomas. *Love and Living.* New York: Farrar Straus Giroux, 1979.

Merton, Thomas. *The New Man.* New York: Farrar, Straus & Giroux, 1961.

Merton, Thomas. *The Seven Storey Mountain.* New York: Harcourt Brace and Company, 1948.

The Methodist Hymnal. Nashville, TN: The Methodist Publishing House, 1964, 1966.

Miner, Margaret, and Hugh Rawson, eds. *A Dictionary of Quotations from the Bible.* New York: New American Library, 1988.

Morgan, Kenneth W., ed. *The Religion of the Hindus.* New York: The Ronald Press Company, 1953.

Murphey, Cecil B., ed. *The Dictionary of Biblical Literacy.* Nashville, TN: Oliver-Nelson Books, 1989.

Murrow, Edward R. *This I Believe,* ed. by Raymond Swing. New York: Simon and Schuster, 1954.

Newman, John Henry Cardinal. *The Idea of a University,* ed. by Martin J. Svaglic. New York: Holt, Rinehart and Winston, 1960.

Newman, Louis I., with Samuel Spitz. *The Talmudic Anthology.* New York: Behrman House, 1945.

Niebuhr, Reinhold. *Justice and Mercy,* edited by Ursula M. Niebuhr. New York: Harper & Row, 1974.

Niebuhr, Reinhold. *Moral Man and Immoral Society.* New York: Charles Scribner's Sons, 1932, 1960.

Niebuhr, Reinhold. *The Nature and Destiny of Man.* 2 vols. New York: Charles Scribner's Sons, 1941, 1964.

Noss, John B. *Man's Religions,* 6th ed. New York: The Macmillan Company, 1980.

Noveck, Simon, ed. *Contemporary Jewish Thought.* Washington, D.C.: B'nai B'rith Books, 1985.

Panichas, Gaeoge A., ed. *The Simone Weil Reader.* New York: David McKay Company, 1977.

Parrinder, Geoffrey, ed. *A Dictionary of Religious & Spiritual Quotations.* New York: Simon & Schuster, 1989.

Partnow, Elaine. *The Quotable Woman: 1800–1981.* New York: Facts on File, 1977, 1982.

Pascal, Blaise. *Pascal's Pensees,* tr. and ed. by H.F. Stewart. New York: Pantheon Books, 1950.

Penrice, John. *A Dictionary and Glossary of the Koran.* London: Curzon Press, 1971 (reprint of 1873 edition).

Pepper, Margaret, ed. *The Harper Religious and Inspirational Quotation Companion.* New York: Harper & Row, 1989.

Phillips, J.B. *Good News: Thoughts on God and Man.* New York: The Macmillan Company, 1963.

Phillips, Margaret Mann, tr. *Collected Works of Erasmus.* Toronto: University of Toronto Press, 1982.

Pickthall, Mohammed Marmaduke, tr. *The Meaning of the Glorious Koran.* New York: New American Library, n.d.

Pike, James A. *If This Be Heresy.* New York: Harper & Row, 1967.

Porteous, Alvin C. *Prophetic Voices in Contemporary Theology.* Nashville, TN: Abingdon Press, 1966.

Potter, G.R. *Huldrych Zwingli.* New York: St. Martin's Press, 1978.

Prabhavananda, Swami, and Frederick Manchester, trs. *The Upanishads: Breath of the Eternal.* Hollywood, CA: The Vedanta Society of Southern California, 1948, 1957..

Proctor, F.B. *Treasury of Quotations on Religious Subjects.* Grand Rapids, MI: Kregel Publications, 1976.

Rackman, Emanuel. *One Man's Judaism.* New York: Philosophical Library, 1970.

Redhead, John A. *Putting Your Faith to Work.* New York: Abingdon Press, 1959.

Reps, Paul. *Zen Flesh, Zen Bones.* Garden City, NY: Anchor Books (Doubleday & Company), 1961.

Ridler, Anne, ed. *Thomas Traherne: Poems, Centuries and Three Thanksgivings.* London: Oxford University Press, 1966.

Rosenzweig, Franz. *The Star of Redemption.* Boston: Beacon Press, 1972.

Ross, Nancy Wilson. *Buddhism: A Way of Life and Thought.* New York: Alfred A. Knopf, 1980.

Routley, Erik. *Hymns and the Faith*. Grand Rapids, MI: William B. Eerdmans Publishing Company, 1968.

Ryden, E.E. *The Story of Christian Hymnody*. Rock Island, IL: Augustana Press, 1959.

Samra, Cal. *The Joyful Christ: The Healing Power of Humor*. San Francisco: Harper & Row, 1985.

Sayers, Dorothy L. *The Mind of the Maker*. New York: Harcourt, Brace and Company, 1941.

Schleiermacher, Friedrich. *On Religion: Speeches to Its Cultured Despisers*. New York: Frederick Unger Publishing Co., 1955.

Schuller, Robert H. *Tough Times Never Last, But Tough People Do!* Nashville: Thomas Nelson Publishers, 1983.

Schweitzer, Albert. *The Kingdom of God and Primitive Christianity*. New York: The Seabury Press, 1968.

Schweitzer, Albert. *Reverence for Life*. New York: Harper & Row, 1969.

Seldes, George. *The Great Quotations*. New York: Lyle Stuart, 1960, 1966.

Seldes, George. *The Great Thoughts*. New York: Ballantine Books, 1985.

Shah, Idries. *Caravan of Dreams*. Baltimore: Penguin Books, 1972.

Shah, Idries. *The Way of the Sufi*. New York: E.P. Dutton, 1970.

Shariati, Ali. *Hajj*, tr. by Ali A. Behzadnia and Najla Denny. Houston: Free Islamic Literatures, 1980.

Shaw, [George] Bernard. *Androcles and the Lion*. Baltimore: Penguin Books, 1951 (reprint of 1913, 1941 editions).

Sheen, Fulton J. *On Being Human: Reflections on Life and Living*. Garden City, NY: Doubleday & Company, 1982.

Simpson, James B. *Contemporary Quotations*. New York: Thomas Y. Crowell Company, 1964.

Singh, Trilochan, et al., tr. *The Sacred Writings of the Sikhs*. London: George Allen & Unwin, 1960.

Smart, Ninian, and Richard B. Hecht, eds. *Sacred Texts of the World: A Universal Anthology*. Blauvelt, NY: Freedeeds Library, 1987.

Soloveitchik, Joseph B. *Halakhic Man*. Philadelphia: The Jewish Publication Society of America, 1983.

Spink, Kathryn, ed. *Life in the Spirit: Reflections, Meditations, Prayers— Mother Teresa of Calcutta*. San Francisco: Harper & Row, 1983.

Spinoza, Baruch. *The Book of God*, ed. by Dagobert D. Runes. New York: Philosophical Library, 1958.

Staiger, Emil, ed. *Gedanken ans Griechischen Tragikern*. Berlin/Zurich: Atlantis-Verlag, 1940.

Steere, Douglas V., ed. *Quaker Spirituality: Selected Writings.* New York: Paulist Press, 1984.

Stevenson, Burton, ed. *The Macmillan Book of Proverbs, Maxims, and Famous Phrases.* New York: The Macmillan Company, 1948.

Strack, Hermann L. *Introduction to the Talmud and Midrash.* New York: Harper & Row, 1931.

Stryk, Lucian. *World of the Buddha: A Reader.* Garden City, NY: Doubleday, 1968.

Suzuki, Daisetz Teitaro. *Essays in Zen Buddhism,* 3rd Series. New York: Samuel Weiser, 1970.

Tagore, Rabindranath. *The Religion of Man.* New York: The Macmillan Company, 1931.

Taha, Mahmoud Mohamed. *The Second Message of Islam,* tr. by Abdullahi Ahmed An-Na'im. Syracuse, NY: Syracuse University Press, 1987.

Teilhard de Chardin, Pierre. *The Divine Milieu.* New York: Harper & Row, 1965.

Teilhard de Chardin, Pierre. *On Suffering.* New York: Harper & Row, 1974.

Teilhard de Chardin, Pierre. *The Phenomenon of Man.* New York: Harper & Row, 1959.

Ten Boom, Corrie. *Not I, But Christ.* Nashville: Thomas Nelson Publishers, 1983.

Thomas à Kempis. *The Imitation of Christ.* Garden City, NY: Image Books (Doubleday & Company), 1955.

Tillich, Paul. *The Eternal Now.* New York: Charles Scribner's Sons, 1963.

Tillich, Paul. *My Search for Absolutes.* New York: Simon and Schuster, 1967.

Tillich, Paul. *On the Boundary: An Autobiographical Sketch.* New York: Charles Scribner's Sons, 1966.

Tomlinson, Gerald. *Speaker's Treasury of Political Stories, Anecdotes, and Humor.* Englewood Cliffs, NJ: Prentice Hall, 1990.

Twersky, Isadore, ed. *A Maimonides Reader.* New York: Behrman House, 1972.

Ueda, Makoto. *Modern Japanese Haiku: An Anthology.* Toronto: University of Toronto Press, 1976.

Voss, Carl Hermann, ed. *A Summons unto Men: An Anthology of the Writings of John Haynes Holmes.* New York: Simon and Schuster, 1971.

Waley, Arthur, ed. *The Analects of Confucius.* London: George Allen & Unwin, 1938.

Watt, M. Montgomery. *Islamic Philosophy and Theology: An Extended Survey.* Edinburgh: Edinburgh University Press, 1962, 1985.

Watts, Alan. *Tao: The Watercourse Way*, with Al Chung-liang Huang. New York: Pantheon Books, 1975.

Weber, Max. *The Protestant Ethic and the Spirit of Capitalism*. New York: Charles Scribner's Sons, 1958.

Wells, Albert M., Jr. *Inspiring Quotations: Contemporary and Classical*. Nashville, TN: Thomas Nelson, 1988.

West, Jessamyn. *The Quaker Reader*. New York: The Viking Press, 1962.

Wild, John, et al. *Classics of Religious Devotion*. Boston: The Beacon Press, 1950.

Woods, Ralph L. *The World Treasury of Religious Quotations*. New York: Hawthorn Books, 1966.

Wouk, Herman. *This Is My God*. Garden City, NY: Doubleday & Company, 1959.

Yoo, Young H. *Wisdom of the Far East: A Dictionary of Proverbs, Maxims, and Famous Classical Phrases of the Chinese, Japanese, and Korean*. Washington, DC: Far Eastern Research and Publications Center, 1972.

Zaehner, R.C. *The Teachings of the Magi*. London: George Allen & Unwin, 1956.

INDEX

A

Abe, Masao, 89, 216
Abelard, Peter, 269
Abduh, Muhammad, 130
Achievement, 1–2
Action, 2–4
Adages, 1, 8, 13, 20, 161
Adam Bede, 157, 263
Adams, John, 182, 190
Adams, Sarah Flower, 49, 277
Addison, Joseph, 163
Adelard of Bath, 199
Adels, Jill Haak, 57
Adler, Morris, 20, 28, 67, 134, 143
Adventurous Religion, 53
Advice, 4–5
After Fundamentalism, 124
Against Heresies, 96
Agnosticism (defined), 297
Agostina, Pietrantoni, St., 265
Ahmad, Khurshid, 46, 181, 206
Aids to Reflection, 75
"A l'Auteur du Livre des Trois
    Imposteurs," 98
Alcott, Louisa May, 237
Alford, Henry, 240
Ali, Ameer, 200
Allen, Woody, 124
"All Hail the Power of Jesus' Name,"
    30
*All I Really Need to Know I Learned in
    Kindergarten*, 74, 146, 177
Allport, Gordon W., 10, 121, 139, 156,
    186, 194, 205, 245, 277
All Things Are Possible, 130, 132
Alphonsus Liguori, St., 189
Alter, Robert, 30, 140–141, 202
"Amazing Grace," 106–107
Ambition, 5–6
Ambrose, St., 6, 56, 109, 223, 277
"America," 89

"America the Beautiful," 21, 234
Analects, 3, 24, 26, 44, 51, 59, 63, 66,
    71, 73, 77, 103, 105, 135, 139,
    160, 164, 193, 199, 205, 212, 214,
    222, 224, 248, 254, 261, 263
Anatomy of Faith, 121
Anatomy of Melancholy, The, 155, 228
"Andrea del Sarto," 94
Androcles and the Lion, 19, 32, 182,
    218–219
Angels, 6–7
Anger, 7–8
Annales Veteris et Novi Testamenti, 241
Anselm, St., 209
Anthony Mary Claret, St., 55, 236
Anthony of Egypt, St., 56
"Anticipation, The," 2
Apathy, 9
Apocrypha, The, Ecclesiasticus, 71, 91, 113
Apologia pro vita sui, 159
*Apology for . . . the Principles and
    Doctrines of the People Called
    Quakers, An*, 215
Apotres, Les, 204
Approaches to God, 242
Aquinas (*see* Thomas Aquinas)
Arab proverb, 175
Arcana Coelestia, 7, 42
Areopagitica, 119, 247
Aristotle, 180, 271, 277, 298
Arnold, Matthew, 108, 224, 232, 254,
    277
Arnold, Sir Edwin, 231
Art of Biblical Narrative, The, 30,
    140–141, 202
Art of Loving, The, 4, 137, 150
Art of Worldly Wisdom, The, 20, 65, 68,
    91, 108, 156, 165, 192, 222
Asad, Muhammad, 165, 179, 206, 277
Askari, Hasan, 8
Assistance, 9–10
Atheism (as subject), 10–12

S

X

Y

Z